Sparring with Hemingway

ALSO BY BUDD SCHULBERG

FICTION
What Makes Sammy Run?
The Harder They Fall
The Disenchanted
Waterfront
Some Faces in the Crowd
Sanctuary V
Everything That Moves

NONFICTION
Loser and Still Champion: Muhammad Ali
The Four Seasons of Success
Swan Watch (with Geraldine Brooks)
Moving Pictures: Memories of a Hollywood Prince

PUBLISHED PLAYS AND SCREENPLAYS
A Face in the Crowd (screenplay)
Across the Everglades (screenplay)
The Disenchanted (play, with Harvey Breit)
What Makes Sammy Run? (musical libretto, with Stuart Schulberg)
On the Waterfront

ANTHOLOGY
From the Ashes—Voices of Watts

SPARRING WITH HEMINGWAY

And Other Legends of the Fight Game

Budd Schulberg

Chicago • Ivan R. Dee • 1995

Grateful acknowledgment is made to the following publications for permission to reprint articles they first published: *Boxing Illustrated* for "Foreman-Holyfield" and "The Mystery of the Heavyweight Mystique"; *Esquire* for "The Heavyweight Championship"; the *New York Post* for "Leonard-Duran," "Ali-Holmes," "The Welterweights," "The Gerry Cooney Story," "The Eight-Minute War," "Sugar's Sweet, Marvin's Sour," "Historic Night in the Ring," "They Fall Harder When They're Old," and "Spinks's Magic Act Is Not Enough"; *Newsday* for "Sparring with Hemingway," "In Defense of Boxing," "Journey to Zaire," "The Second Coming of George Foreman," and "Tyson vs. Tyson"; *Playboy* for "The Death of Boxing?"; *Ring* for "The Great Benny Leonard"; *Saturday Review* for "The Chinese Boxes of Muhammad Ali"; *Sports Illustrated* for "Hollywood Hokum," "No Room for the Groom," "Marciano and England's Cockell," "A Champion Proves His Greatness," "The Comeback," and "Boxing's Dirty Business Must Be Cleaned Up Now"; and *TV Guide* for "Where Have You Gone, Holly Mims?"

Library of Congress Cataloging-in-Publication Data:
Schulberg, Budd.
    Sparring with Hemingway : and other legends of the fight game / Budd Schulberg.
        p.   cm.
    Includes index.
    ISBN 1-56663-080-0 (acid-free paper)
    1. Boxing—United States—History.   2. Boxing in literature.
I. Title.
GV1125.S36   1995
796.8'3'0973—dc20

Contents

Preface

WHY ARE WRITERS so drawn to championship prizefights that they will cross continents and fly across oceans to be present at these spectacles?

I was pondering this again some years ago as Norman Mailer and I met at the bar of the Montreal headquarters of Sugar Ray Leonard, counting down the hours to the crucial welterweight title fight with the stone-fisted Panamanian, Roberto Duran. Norman and I traded observations, speculations, breathless predictions as we have been doing ever since a long night in Miami when we dissected until dawn Cassius Clay's curious dethroning of the curiously misnamed Sonny Liston.

Sonny had been the centerpiece of a highly charged gathering in Chicago where he had destroyed the brave rabbit Floyd Patterson in a single round, in a fight scene that could have doubled as a summer writers' conference. In addition to Mailer, who was at his most provocative that week, one could sit in on literary seminars attended by Jimmy Baldwin, Ben Hecht, William Saroyan, and George Plimpton, where Pulitzer Prize judges and ring officials could be denounced with equal intensity.

This marriage of literateurs and hard-core fanciers of the Sweet Science started long before Jack London, Ring Lardner, and Ernest Hemingway. It goes back at least three thousand years, all the way to Homer, who covered the Greek Games where boxing was respected to the point of worship as a liberal art. In 1184 B.C., in the last year of the siege of Troy, Homer was writing a blow-by-blow of the epic battle between Epeus and Euryalus, the Muhammad Ali and Joe Frazier of their day.

> Amid the circle now each champion stands,
> And poises high in air his iron hands:
> With clashing gauntlets now they fiercely close.
> Their crackling jaws reecho to the blows . . .

Three thousand years later poets were still setting down their quills to see and often report a stirring boxing match. In the bareknuckle days of English glory, when prizefights were officially forbidden but stoutly supported by The Fancy, Lord Byron would eagerly push away from an epic poem, hop into a barouche-and-four, and urge his coachman on until they reached the tavern some sixty miles from London where the next great fight for the belt was about to take place. Byron was there, cheering his favorite on, when Gentleman John Jackson relieved Daniel Mendoza of his unprecedented crown by swinging "The Jew Champion" around by his long, thick hair. With Jackson as his boxing instructor and close companion, Byron was at ringside for John Gully's savage sixty-four-round battle with Pierce the Game Chicken. Indeed, Byron hung out at the Horse and Dolphin, the Toots Shor's of its day, where the suave, educated black American fighter Bill Richmond held sway. He was there when the match was made between the British idol Tom Cribb and Richmond's protégé, the formidable ex-slave from Virginia, Tom Molineaux. When the rematch in Leicester drew an unruly crowd of 25,000, Lord Byron was one of the first to reach the grounds. He pasted clippings of the fight on his famous screen.

For a vivid description of a big fight, British nineteenth-century style, there is William Hazlitt's essay on Thomas (the Gasman) Hickman's contest with Bill Neate, "like Ajax, with

Atlantean shoulders fit to bear the pugilistic reputation of all Bristol." The Gasman, in turn, in Hazlitt's celebrated prose, was compared to Diomed, "light, vigorous, elastic, his back glistening in the sun as he moved about like a panther's hide."

From Homer to Hazlitt, Arthur Conan Doyle, and George Bernard Shaw, from London and Lardner to Hemingway, from A. J. Liebling and Nelson Algren to Norman Mailer, Pete Hamill, and Joyce Carol Oates, from Athens to Zaire (where even Dr. Hunter Thompson found his way), we seem irresistibly drawn to these ceremonial combats.

We find ourselves at one with John Milton, that most unexpected of fight fans, who wrote in *Samson Agonistes:*

> I sorrowed at his captive state,
> but minded
> Not to be absent at that
> spectacle.

Let's get it on! the old master seems to be saying if we translate him into twentieth-century vernacular. I'll be looking for him, along with the ghosts of Homer and Lord Byron, at the next writers' conference at Caesar's Palace, or MGM Grand, or wherever the next epic encounter captures the imagination of the writers who see The Fight as a microcosm, an intensification of the life forces we struggle to understand.

Acknowledgments

I AM INDEBTED to Nick Beck, a man of letters who knows his boxing—a dear friend of the late Cus D'Amato and Jimmy Jacobs, Mike Tyson's original mentors—who volunteered to read through some 150 fight pieces and suggested the Contents that gave form to this work.

While Nick provided this service as a labor of love, it was invaluable, unselfish, and thoroughly professional. How can I thank him: a long nostalgic lunch at Musso & Frank's on Hollywood Boulevard for starters, to discuss everything from the Scott Fitzgerald comeback of the century to the impending release of Mike Tyson and his impact on the sorry state of the heavyweight division.

And my thanks to Elizabeth Marlowe, who fused high-tech efficiency to dedication in her paper chase through elusive files and lost folders to bring these pieces to their present form, along with invaluable editorial suggestions that supplemented Nick Beck's expert selections from an overload of material.

Brookside, Quioque, New York
February 1995

Sparring with Hemingway

Sparring with Hemingway

I HAD JUST published my novel on the fight game, *The Harder They Fall*—having managed somehow, after the unforeseen success of *What Makes Sammy Run?,* to hurdle that old second-novel bugaboo. When the new book made the *Times* best-seller list and sold to the movies for Humphrey Bogart, the fact that my two young sons and their mother were suffering from familiar Bucks County winter complaints suggested that a warm-weather vacation was in order. I picked the southernmost spot in the United States: Key West.

Key West had come to mind because my taste in resorts ran to isolated places with deep-sea fishing—the Hemingway kind of place it was. Yes, I had read of Hemingway's connection with Key West, how he had moved there and built there in the early '30s. And of course I had read his Depression novel *To Have and Have Not,* with its haunting, dirgeful opening and its evocation of the violence of wasted lives and the desperation of a tough old salt fighting his losing battle for survival.

There were no poets in Key West then, no overpopulation of literary types, no gay bars and shoppes and quaint tours of local landmarks, including the Hemingway House. The place on Whitehead Street was just a nice, comfortable, sprawling house where the writer had lived before moving on to Cuba with No. 4 wife, Mary—while No. 2, nee Pauline Pfeiffer, still spent her winters in what was simply her house and not "The Hemingway House."

On the one little public beach on the island (the navy seeming to have gobbled up all the rest) we had met what turned out to be the best possible couple to know in Key West, Betty and Toby Bruce, whose children were of an age with ours. Betty was tiny, funny, tomboy-tough, and feisty, and Toby was her perfect running mate, a skinny little beak who looked as if he had just hopped right out of a comic strip. And comic he was, with a twinkle in his eye and a quip on his tongue, bubbling over with ribald innocence. Betty, we discovered, was that rarity, a true Conch, born on the island of Barbados of parents who had pioneered Key West in the 1880s. Toby had met her when he came down from Piggott, Arkansas, with Pauline after she married Ernest. Toby had practically built the Hemingway House, putting up the brick wall with his own small, work-toughened hands, installing the pool and serving as general overseer. In fact, Toby had become indispensable to Hemingway, as his Man Friday running interference against celebrity-seekers, and able to double as boat pilot, hunting and fishing guide, secretary—you name it, and Toby could do it with a flourish. "Hey, mon, what you know bad?" was his trademark greeting. He was such fun to be with while doing everything so neatly nice, including making the best bloodies I ever drank.

I thought of the Bruces as two adorable little people who lived with two adorable little children—right out of a folksy nursery rhyme. It was comical, too, because the Morenos, Betty's mother and father, lived just across the driveway—in a quiet, gracious, and spacious Key West house built in the grand Bahama style. Mrs. Rosina Moreno was a genteel Southern lady, very proper in her ways, while Betty rebelled by dressing and acting like a rough 'n' ready hoyden, her little house as delightful a mess as Mrs. Moreno's was pin-perfect.

One bright morning in old Key West brought ripples of ex-

18

citement. The news was, "Papa's coming to town!" Yes, the Great One, Mr. Key West himself, coming back for a visit to the island outpost he had virtually put on the map. Toby hurried over to our digs, "the southernmost house," the Casa Cayo Jueso, with the announcement: He and Betty and Pauline were throwing an impromptu cocktail party for Papa and Mary in the Bruces' little patio. "Good," I thought, a chance to meet the walking legend. We would talk about the work I had admired from college days and the subjects we had in common: Scott Fitzgerald, tarpon fishing, boxing . . .

Browsing through his marvelous *Fifth Column and the First Forty-nine Stories* to bone up for my adventure, I sipped a little Metusalem, a rum taste I had acquired from "Papa" via Toby, who seemed to enjoy a steady supply from Cuba. Then, high on expectation, I went forth to meet the self-styled and generally acknowledged "champion of American letters."

It was one of those sun-bright late afternoons of Key West winter, when an unblemished canopy of blue sky stretched to the far horizon. But there was one small, totally unexpected dark cloud: As I came into the patio, looking forward to a good time talking and drinking, Toby brought me a no-nonsense Metusalem, saying, "I hope it goes all right. Papa's on the warpath. Been lookin' for you since he got in."

"Me?" I know the Bruces had told him that I was their new friend and that we were planning a cruise through the Keys and the nearby Ten Thousand Islands together. But warpath!

As Toby moved off to his other guests, I leaned back against the back wall of the patio to ponder the mystery. But not for long.

A bull-chested, ruddy-faced man of fifty—barefoot, wearing shorts that looked as if they had been ripped violently from worn bluejeans and a fishing shirt open almost to the navel—shouldered through the crowd and set himself in front of me, feet spread in a fighter's stance, head thrust forward until our faces were not more than a foot apart. He hadn't been stinting on the Metusalem.

The first words out of his mouth were short, sharp jabs. "So you're Schulberg? The book writer?"

"I've written a few books."

Now the hard right: "What do you know about prizefighting—for Christ's sweet sake?"

I retreated to a characteristic I don't admire but often find myself adopting when under attack: apparent humility with a nasty edge. "Maybe I don't know too much about boxing. I've just followed it all my life."

His bare chest pushing against me forced a backward step. Then he looked me in the eye and spat out a name, punctuating it with a little shove. "Billy Papke?"

I stared at him. How do you answer that one? In anger or passivity? Choose the latter. My answer came in robot-monotone:

"Billy Papke was the only middleweight who ever knocked out Stanley Ketchel. That gave him the middleweight championship. Then Ketchel knocked him out. When they fought again, Ketchel won in twenty rounds. After Ketchel was murdered, Papke was champion again. I think he killed himself in California about ten years ago." Monotone, monotone, I cautioned myself. "Papke was famous."

There was absolutely no reaction. Not a flicker. Just "Leo Houck?" and the little shove for punctuation.

"Same weight division. Same period. Fought everybody. Papke, Harry Greb, Gene Tunney. For years he's been the boxing coach at Penn State." That I happened to know because my screenwriting friends, the Epstein twins, had been on his team.

Still no reaction. Nothing. The fistic catechism went on. I could feel my back almost brushing against the wall now. I felt like a fighter bulled into a corner, taking punches. I wondered how long I could take it, or should.

"Pinkey Mitchell?"

Pinkey Mitchell! Did I know Pinkey Mitchell? Now he was moving into *my* generation. "Pinkey Mitchell was the brother of Richie Mitchell, who fought Benny Leonard for the light-weight title. My father took me to the Garden but they wouldn't let me in. I was only seven. Five years later I saw Mushy Callahan, our local favorite in L.A., take the junior welter-weight championship from Pinkey. I saw Pinkey Mitchell. When he came out to fight Mushy, he was a big fighter from the East. He was famous. In fact, when Mushy won he gave me the gloves from the fight. I hung them in a place of honor on the wall above my bed."

No reaction. It had settled into a kind of war of attrition. I wasn't going to lose my temper if I could help it—and "Papa" wasn't about to quit.

"Pete Latzo?" This shove took me right to the wall. I could feel my shoulders against it. I was being bulled out of the patio. The famous bare chest was pressed against mine, push-ing me back.

Pete Latzo? A little like asking Alfred Kazin if he had ever heard of Jack London. But I took a deep breath and began:

"Pete Latzo took the welterweight championship from Mickey Walker. The great Mickey Walker, Ernest [I knew he hated that name but I couldn't get my mouth around "Papa" and so never knew what to call him]. You're asking me famous fighters. Pete Latzo is famous. Anybody who knows anything about boxing knows Pete Latzo." And then, finally, in exasper-ation, I threw a combination of my own:

"Pete Latzo comes from Scranton, Pennsylvania. And, if you'd like to get in touch with him, he's still there. He's an or-ganizer for the Teamsters Union."

And I gave *him* a little shove. I despise physical fighting—"Leave it to the pros," I've always said—but it seemed as if our "moment of truth" had come.

I set my feet, braced for attack or to throw a punch, fantasiz-ing a surprise left hook to the somewhat rum-swollen gut. At the same time, there was ambivalence: a flash replay of Ernest's tangle with radical writer Max Eastman in the office of their editor, Max Perkins, at Scribner's. A messy contribu-

21

tion to the public image of "Papa" that he claimed to resent but too often managed to encourage.

Suddenly, as if reading my mind, he wheeled and lurched back through the gathering to the bar and the kitchen behind it. I leaned back against the wall, seething. I was relieved that we hadn't come to blows, yet I had an impulse to follow him, spin him around, punch the arrogant bully face. Then I thought of getting out, heading for Sloppy Joe's. Or would he corner me there? "Joe is *my* friend. Joe's is *my* place. What do you know about Sloppy Joe's, for Christ's sweet sake?"

I was still leaning against the wall when Toby came back with a refill of the Metusalem.

"Papa's in the kitchen. He says he likes you."

I tried to swallow back the rage and keep my voice steady. Having "Papa" here and a lot of old Key West friends to see him was a big thing for the Bruces, and they didn't deserve a mess.

"Tell 'Papa' I admire him. But from now on I plan to admire him from afar." I took a deep breath. "As far away as I can get."

Toby felt bad. We were both his friends and friendship was Toby's thing.

"Papa's had a bug up his ass all day. A lot of pressure. Pauline being here—and Mary. But he's good people. He wants you to come in and have a drink with him."

"Toby, I'll read 'im. I'll read anything he writes. But he asked me a lot of dumb questions that hurt my feelings. I think it's better if we stay away from each other."

Toby went back to the kitchen to deliver this message. I kept on leaning against the back wall of the patio, still seething and nursing the rum.

A few minutes later Toby was back. "Look, mon, Papa really feels bad. He asked me to tell you again, he *likes* you. He wants to make it up to you. Like to take you fishing in the morning."

But I had heard about "Papa's" fishing expeditions. If someone hooked the first fish, he was teed off. And God help you if you boated the biggest. I liked deep-sea fishing, loved to be out

on the water. But it wasn't life-and-death with me, as everything was with " Papa."

"Tell him thanks but I'd just as soon get my own boat. I c'n
take the family. More relaxing."

"All right, mon." I had never heard Toby argue with anyone.
It wasn't subservience but instinctive respect for other people's
ways of seeing things. Unlike friend "Papa," who was a high-
brow with lowbrow affectations, Toby was a genuine lowbrow
with unspoken and unspoiled sensitivity. As I got to know
them both better, I began to feel that Toby was the man Ernest
truly wanted to be. I could understand why "Papa" liked him
so much. It wasn't simply because Toby hero-worshiped him, although it seemed to me that the need for such worship had already begun to poison the Hemingway well.

A few days later the Hemingways left town, and Key West
settled down again. But Toby and Betty were still convinced
that "Papa" and I were meant to be friends, and that in time
they would bring us together. "You two guys would like one another," they kept insisting, urging me to give him another
chance. I began to feel that maybe I was being the difficult one,
that he had apologized in his own proud way and that perhaps
I should be a little more forgiving.

The following winter I happened to be at the Bruces' when a
phone call came in from "Papa" in Cuba, and when they told him
I was there he asked them to put me on the phone. He was
warm and friendly. He asked me if I was writing and I said yes,
working on another book, and he said he was working on a
book, too, a new novel and he couldn't tell yet whether it was
any good. He didn't ask me what mine was about and I didn't
ask him about his. He said Toby had told him we had been tarpon fishing and that I had caught one large enough to mount
and he urged me to try the waters around Cay Sal, between Key
West and Cuba, one of his favorite fishing grounds. He sounded
the way the Bruces described him. Couldn't have been nicer.

A year later my book was finished—it was called *The Disen-*

chanted—and this time, for the winter respite, we decided to move on from Key West to Cuba. Toby steered us to "Papa's Hotel," the Ambos Mundos, and told us to be sure to call "Papa," who (the Bruces assured me) would like to invite us out to the Finca Vigia for lunch.

At the front desk of the old Spanish-Colonial hotel—the kind I took to immediately, with its faded tiles and worn mahogany—the clerk said there was a message from Don Ernesto. Frankly, I was pleased, in a good mood about the success of my book and more than ready for a truce. But the message from El Papa was: When I arrived, he wanted it clearly understood that I was *not* to call him. The clerk passed this on to me in a world-weary monotone. I had the feeling he was accustomed to handling these negative invitations from El Maestro.

I made some phone calls to learn the nature of my sins. From Arthur Mizener, who had written the first biography of F. Scott Fitzgerald; from Harvey Breit of the *New York Times Book Review,* another friend of Ernest's and mine who had made it his mission to bring us together; finally, from Toby himself, who got it straight from "Papa," I discovered what it was I had done to him this time. *The Disenchanted* drew in good part on my ill-fated cross-country trip from Hollywood to Hanover, New Hampshire, with Scott Fitzgerald to write a movie with him about the Dartmouth Winter Carnival. My central character—the tormented, fading novelist scrambling for movie money so he could shore up his literary reputation— had been based on all the "failed priests" (as Scott had called them) who had worked for my father, the producer B. P. Schulberg. I had known them well—Herman Mankiewicz, Vincent Lawrence, John V. A. Weaver, Edwin Justus Mayer—all of them desperate for that "second chance." Still, I would not argue that Scott Fitzgerald and my Manley Halliday were brothers.

And that, it seemed, was my problem, or was it Ernest's? Scott Fitzgerald was "Papa's" friend. Scott and Zelda belonged to "Papa." "Papa" was outraged that I would dare invade his territory. In his not so humble opinion, both Mizener and I were "gravediggers," disturbing the bones of his old friend, who should be allowed to rest in dignity and peace. "Papa" had already fired off furious letters to Mizener and Breit protesting my invasion of Scott's privacy. Oh yes, I could hear the voice of our literary god bellowing down from his *finca:* "What the hell do you know about Scott Fitzgerald, for Christ's sweet sake?"

And I could see him pushing his hard belly against me and trying to bull me up against the wall. And hear myself trying to hold my temper as I recited my own knowledge of Scott—no, maybe not so deep as Ernest's—but that ordeal at Winter Carnival had brought us together, and when we got back to California we had visited back and forth and had remained friends.

In the autumn of what was to be his last year on this earth, he had volunteered to write what turned out to be a rave notice of *Sammy* for the book jacket and, just a few weeks before the end, in his modest flat off Sunset Boulevard, he had written a touching inscription in my first edition of his *Tender Is the Night* and had shown me the opening chapters of *The Last Tycoon.*

No, "Papa," maybe I didn't know your Scott Fitzgerald from the opening bell, but I had seen him go a couple of rounds, a name fighter from the East who had blown his title, like Pinkey Mitchell. Actually, I had been struck by Scott's generosity, his interest in and sympathy for young writers. Even with his back against the wall, practically pushed through the wall, he had gone out of his way for "Pep" (Nathanael) West, as he had for me and, some twenty years earlier, for Ernest himself. Gratitude was not an easy emotion for "Papa," and so, when I'd had an opportunity to look through Scott's papers at Princeton, I had been surprised to find canceled checks from Scott to Ernest for $100 each, quite a lot of them from the young, hot author of *This Side of Paradise* to the young, still undiscovered Hemingway. Not only that, but an appeal from Ernest to Scott to help him leave his "Jew publishers" (Covici-Friede) for Scott's far more prestigious Scribner's. As the record shows, Scott did intercede for Ernest with Scribner's, which would publish him to the end of his career. "Gratitude" would be expressed only in the reverse English of "Papa's" mean-spirited postmortem on Scott in *A Moveable Feast*.

But that was years later, and this was now at the Ambos Mundos. I was beginning to feel like Charlie Chaplin in *City Lights* with its classic running gag: Whenever the big, rich heavy is drunk, he loves Charlie and insists he come home with him as his guest. But when his fat host wakes up in the morning, now sober, and sees Charlie, he says, "Who is this bum?" and throws him out. It happens all through the picture, and gets funnier every time. But this thing with "Papa" didn't strike me as all that funny.

Toby took it so seriously that he actually flew over from Key West to see if he could patch things up. "Papa's kinda in a bad way right now," he tried to explain. "The new book [*Across the River and Into the Trees*] is taking a beating. The worst of it is critics are trying to tell Papa he's washed up, that this book is gonna finish him. They think he's run out of gas and beginning to repeat himself. So it's a tough time for him. And then, when he saw your book doing so well and on a subject he feels belongs to him—well, I still think he should be big about it and ask you up, but that's the way he gets sometimes. He's feelin' lower'n the belly of a rattlesnake that just slipped off the sidewalk into the gutter. But I still think, if you really got to know him, and he got to know you . . ."

"Toby, thanks, but look, Cuba is a big island. And 'Papa' doesn't own it." Then, half-kidding, I added, "Why doesn't he take everything from Havana up? And I'll take from Havana down, like Veradero. And he doesn't have to ask me up, and I don't have to ask him down."

Toby felt bad, but loyally went up to the *finca* to see "Papa" and then drove down to the house on the beach I had taken for the winter.

"Papa says he's peed off at you about this Fitzgerald thing, but he's having a lot of other trouble. That little Italian princess is there [the one who had sat for her portrait as the aging colonel's *inamorata* in *Across the River*], and Miss Mary ain't too happy about that, even if the girl came over with her Mama as chaperone. It's just Papa worried about his age and needing to feel young again. I still think when things get better for Papa he'll get over his mad on you."

I thought of the Charlie Chaplin running gag. I didn't want to be at the whim of a man who asked me in when he felt good and threw me out when the light turned red. But Toby was still determined to keep working on "Papa."

A few years later—after the opening of *On the Waterfront*—I was back at the Bruces' in Key West when another phone call came in from "Papa." He was back on top again: After striking out with *Across the River,* he had hit one out of the ballpark with *The Old Man and the Sea.* Finally he had come to the perfect story for his knowledge and feeling and enthusiasm. Here was a Hemingway redeemed, at the top of his form, pleasing the critics as much as he had displeased them his last time out, raking in, along with the praise, a lot of money, which was important to him, too, and setting himself up for the Nobel he already felt he deserved.

Once again the Bruces insisted I get on the phone to say hello to "Papa." This time he was in the happy euphoria of Charlie's tormentor in *City Lights*. He had not yet seen *Waterfront*, he said, but he had heard from Harvey Breit that it was "great." Harvey had also told him I was finishing the *Waterfront* novel I had started when it looked as if Hollywood resistance would keep the movie from ever getting made. "You've really done a lot of good work," the benign "Papa" kept pouring it on. Aside from the *City Lights* image, I couldn't help thinking of the cliché or truism about the Germans "who were either at your feet or at your throat."

But I managed to thank Ernest and to congratulate him. "*The Old Man* is really something," I told him. He deserved a lot of points for trying so hard and being so true to the best that was in him when he was good. When the artist in him won the Indian-wrestling match with the bullshit artist, I was tempted to add, but restrained myself.

"Maybe when Toby comes over next time you'll come over with him," "Papa" said. He was back to inviting me in again. Next time. How many fallings-in and fallings-out would there be between now and next time? Anyway, I didn't tell him in this friendly chat that now I had my own chip on the shoulder. Another mutual friend, reporter Sam Boal, had told me the story. He had crossed to Europe with the Hemingways and the Peter Viertels. Mrs. Viertel was my first love, Jigee, and my first wife. When our daughter was only two, Jigee and Peter, a young Hollywood friend of mine, had seduced each other and I had lost her. Probably because I was jealous, I resented Peter's hero-worshiping friendship with "Papa." They all (including Jigee) made a fetish of shooting well and what I call "the Pamplona syndrome," a kind of self-conscious stylish rowdyism that irritated me. On the trip over—according to Sam—"Papa" had made it uncomfortably obvious to everybody that he was drawn to Jigee, and vice versa. He would invite her down to his stateroom and read aloud to her from the work-in-progress, the flawed *Across the River*. Jigee, usually a tough critic, had been awed, flattered, and taken in. On deck, Mary Hemingway had leaned on the railing with Sam Boal and said, "You think he's going to marry her? I don't think the son of a bitch can afford it."

At the Gritti Palace in Venice—so the "in people" gossiped— Jigee had practically moved in with "Papa" for a month. Later, from Ketchum, Idaho, my daughter, then almost twelve, had written me that she had met a very nice man who liked to ski and shoot with Mommy and who read aloud to her and liked cats a lot.

I didn't wish Peter Viertel much good luck, but he *was* my daughter's stepfather now and, according to her, an attentive and helpful one. I resented "Papa" butting in on them, a law unto himself, his own morality. I wished the literary life weren't so ingrown and incestuous. First Peter, my young nov-elist-friend; then "Papa," and then Irwin Shaw, Peter's best friend, cornered by "Papa," not in Sloppy Joe's but in "21." Ticked off by the success of Shaw's *The Young Lions,* "Papa" had asked him what was apparently the standard Hemingway question, "What do you know about war, for Christ's sweet sake?" As Irwin described it to me later, "I told the son of a bitch that I'd be waiting at the bar if he wanted to go outside with me." "Papa" never came back to the bar. I would have bought a ticket for that one.

Anyway, as to incestuous: It seemed that sooner or later every writer messed around with every other writer's wife. In the literary world, everybody knew everybody else, too well. It was what most people thought life in Hollywood was like.

There were a lot of galloping egos in Hollywood, but they would have had to run like John Henry to keep up with an ego like "Papa's." Gary Cooper and Cary Grant and Freddie March and other movie stars I knew would never crowd me with, "What-do-you-know-about . . . ?"

Not that I could fault Ernest that last time on the phone: He couldn't have been nicer. He was actor-nice when he wanted to be and, even when dispensing patronizing crap, still fun to talk to.

I didn't take Ernest up on his invitation. I never did go to the *finca.* The next time I saw him was about two years later in Havana, just after Fidel and his *barbudos* took the city. I was covering the story for a magazine. I was in a dark, narrow restaurant Toby had recommended, and it was fun because a young *Fidelista* captain and a bunch of his young guerrillas were there drinking and singing revolutionary songs. All of a sudden, "Papa" was there, towering over me at the table.

"Did you go to Jigee's funeral?" he asked me. She had died a terrible death, lingering in agony for weeks after her night-gown caught on fire from a cigarette. When I said no—I had been in Mexico and had not heard about it until it was over— "Papa" said, "I hear Peter wasn't there, either. That isn't right.

29

One thing we do, we bury our dead." He didn't exactly salute, but made a small gesture as if about to. I was seething again. I got very quiet, like that time about fifteen years earlier in Key West when he first came at me. Damn it, Jigee had been *my* girl, not "Papa's." We'd had six years together, and a daughter we were both very proud of, and we had managed to stay close through the years. All "Papa" had done was brush against her for a little while. "Bury our dead." The posturing. Why was the *beau geste* so important to him? There was something so . . . *literary* about it. How much was he actually *feeling* for Jigee? I was tempted to ask, "What in hell do you know about Jigee, for Christ's sweet sake?" Instead, I just put my head down.

After a few moments, he asked me how long I planned to be in town, and I said until I got the story and had a chance to interview Fidel. To my relief, he didn't say anything about coming out to the *finca*. I'd had it with Hemingway and his goddam *finca*. I had the feeling he wasn't too crazy about my being over here covering the *Fidelista* victory. I knew he was thinking that, like prizefighting and deep-sea fishing and war, Fidel now belonged to him. I had been in Veradero when Batista took over in 1952, and now I had seen him fall. But Cuba unquestionably belonged to "Papa" until he decided to let it go back into the public domain.

Just the same, there are those marvelous stories and that clean language and the Nobel he deserved. He was true to himself when he was standing there throwing away hours and days of longhand, starting over, and over again, never giving up the quest for *good, better, best.* He deserved to be admired, as I admired him, from afar.

He wrote "The Battler" and "Fifty Grand," high on my own list of favorite fight stories. "The Undefeated" is a beauty on bullfighting. *Death in the Afternoon,* for all its excesses, has a lot to say about the dangers any artist faces, about the need to be brave in the face of danger and adversity. *Green Hills of Africa* is cruel but full of natural wonder. His stock will go up and go down and up and down. He had a curl in the middle of

30

his forehead—or was it his brain?—but when he was good, good and dedicated, he was very, very good. And so, in the end, I had to forgive him all the personal stuff that got in the way.

When Toby Bruce drove out to recover at my place after the funeral in Ketchum, where "Papa" had put a shotgun to his head and put an end to the agony—just like *his* Papa—we talked about all he had done, the books, the long journey and the friends. Toby was badly shaken. "He was really good people. He had a lot of hangups. Hating his Mama and ashamed for his Daddy. Trouble with his brother Leicester, who was always jealous of Papa. It was a pretty good life until it went bad. He got a lot of fun out of life. When he was on vacation, there was nobody more fun to be around. I was always hoping you two would finally hit it off. Until this last year, at the Mayo Clinic, when they told him he couldn't drink, couldn't do this 'n' that, all the things he loved, well, life just wasn't worth going on with anymore."

For Toby's sake, I tried to say only the best things about Ernest. Things that were true, and leaving out the bad, the way he had to puff out his chest like a pouter pigeon, and bait me with bully questions about Lee Houck and Pinkey Mitchell and Pete Latzo.

For through all those years I had been unable to forget the first encounter, when he was bellying me up against the rear wall of the Bruces' patio and asking me what was essentially a literary question: "What do you know about prizefighting, for Christ's sweet sake?"

But if we were to turn the question around—if we were to put it to him, "What do you know about writing, for Christ's sweet sake?"—we'd have to give him the round and raise his hand at the end of the contest.

And so may Ernest or "Papa"—or whatever he felt driven to call himself—rest in peace, a peace he hunted for through sixty-two years of arrogant self-doubt—for Christ's sweet sake.

[September 1985]

White, Black, and Other Hopes

THE NEW YORK TIMES, that bulky, grey journal of moderation, could hardly wait for Joe Frazier's butcher-boy arm to be raised in token of vindication victory over the ghost of Cassius Clay, the mythopoeic Muhammad Ali.

After fifteen rounds more closely contested than any "Fight of the Century" in the history of heavyweights under Queensberry rules, the *Times* had drawn from the phenomenon every possible advantage. A long and crisply reported Sunday Magazine piece. An entire page devoted to pictures of the event. A front-page action-photo and news story. Another full page in the sports section. Then, after all this printable pander, having extracted its last vendable ounce from the most highly publicized fight since Kid Cain flattened Young Abel, the *Times* retreated to nobility.

In a pious postmortem editorial it decried the fight, calling it "a performance that degrades and dehumanizes the state and society that encourage it."

When one pauses to think of all the dehumanizing elements in our society, the Pentagon destruction of Asian hamlets, the defoliation of peasant rice-lands, the brutalization of our soldiery that leads them to slaughter old men, women, and children because, like the good Nazis before them, they thought they were carrying out the order of the day, when the Mafia breaks bread with the mayors and the city councilmen, when the state troopers and the National Guard gun down blacks, students, hippies, peace marchers, when great profits are gouged from ceaseless wars and army intelligence spends your money tailing liberal politicians, when the individual is fed like a helpless Charlie Chaplin into the giant maw of the computer, when the ghettos are allowed to fester while billions are squandered on inhuman devices, when corporate profits soar while rats feast on the toes of Puerto Rican children, when known killers and their patrons enjoy the company of film and nightclub celebrities at Caesar's Palace and the Copa, when the American dream shatters into nightmare, when Tom Jefferson is cruelly transmogrified as George Wallace, and Abe Lincoln as Mayor Daley, when children in a dozen crippled cities stare up at a sky they cannot see and breathe something that once was air, should we not wonder if the good grey *Times* knows what is dehumanizing whom?

Against this cyclorama of social horrors, a boxing match engaging two finely trained athletes respecting rules of restraint that alas do not apply to Indochina, such a contest as was Frazier vs. Ali a.k.a. Clay should not drive us to despair but give us hope that individual skill, spirit, and courage have not been leveled by the glacier of future shock.

Yet the *Times* would have us believe that this Queensberry epic, this drama to rival the best theater New York had to offer last season, signals "the declining days of past civilizations." Having sold its share of newsprint heralding "The Fight," the bloodless *Times* moves on to its annual suggestion that professional boxing be outlawed.

This writer once wrote a novel called *The Harder They Fall,* considered, on what used to be known as Jacobs' Beach (or Cauliflower Alley), the harshest put-down of boxing ever written in America. It exposed the deliberate exploitation of a manufactured champion, the chicanery, the greed, the casual disregard of fighters' sensibilities and economic needs that is pugilism at its worst. But our interest was in the reform of boxing, not its execution. In the film, Bogey's last, liberties were

33

taken in the name of sensationalism posing as poetry: at the curtain Mr. Bogart, actually an odd amalgam of the late fight promoter Hal Conrad and myself, is pounding away at a type-writer that obliges with the conclusion: *Boxing must be destroyed.* I wrote an answer in *Sports Illustrated* attacking my own film for trifling with my convictions. Protect it, I said, don't destroy it. I consider myself a reformer and a muckraker, yes, maybe even of the old school of Tarbell and Steffens and London when he wasn't racisizing. But I know a good thing when I see it. Fistfighting is a good thing. It is like gold in that it is found in a nugget cluster of baser metals often buried in the mud. "The Game," as Jack London called it sixty years ago, is full of baseness and immersed in filth. Every great fight is such a rare nugget, and one can only understand a choice en-counter of champions if he sees it in this context of gold-rock-mud. To see only the mud, like the editorial preacher, is to stumble over and fail to discover the gold. To see only gold is to accept the worst with the best and to excuse the mendacity so commonplace in our society that we bring it home and lay it on and live with it like wallpaper.

But is the hoary *Times* really concerned with the immediate evils termiting the house we live in? Evils that are simply re-flected in the world of boxing as they are in every other repre-sentative walk of American life? It is easy, self-righteous fun to cry, "Outlaw professional boxing!" Just as it was to howl, Out-law booze! No accident that every time boxing has been out-lawed it has persevered in some bootleg form. Like bath tub gin, in a more vicious, disorganized, and dehumanizing form.

If our civilization is indeed declining and if it finally falls, it will not be because Joe Louis clobbered Schmeling or took the measure of Billy Conn. Or because Ali made Bad Sonny Liston quit in his corner. Or because Joe Frazier landed a tremen-dous, humbling left hook on the controversial jaw of gallant braggadocio Muhammad Ali. We have already suggested other seeds of our possible destruction. And it seems to us that the

Times is simplistically wrong in relating boxing to the decline of civilization. It is true, of course, that boxing and civilization—any civilization—stand in delicate balance. But let us first do a bit of roadwork through history and see whose theory, ours or the *New York Times*'s, has the better of the go. Pugilistica as history we might call it, to cop a Mailerism. The *Times* has the tail wagging the dog, but the Manly Art or the Sweet Science or the Game or whatever conceit we invent for the most basic and complex of all our sports has merely been a telltale (if you'll forgive us) appendage to the various dogshapes civilizations have assumed over the past five thousand years.

The art of fisticuffs was celebrated not only when civilizations were declining and falling but when they were rising and flourishing. Will Durant in *The Life of Greece* describes the prosperous Cretans of the middle Minoan period more than four thousand years ago packing the amphitheater to see their favorite heavyweights "coddled with helmets, cheekpieces and long padded gloves, fighting 'til one falls exhausted to the ground and the other stands above him in the conscious grandeur of victory." Cretan predecessors of LeRoy Neiman recorded these contests on vases and bas reliefs. Homer immortalized the victory of Epeus over Euryalus, resorting to verse to describe the blow-by-blow three thousand years before Grantland Rice and Muhammad Ali got into the act.

When boxing came to Rome, it became vulgarized, brutalized, and corrupted like so many Greek arts in tougher Roman hands. There the *Times* would have been closer to the mark in viewing pugilism as a sign of moral breakdown. What had been sport to the Greeks became bloodlust to the Romans who packed the Colosseum in the days of Nero and Caligula. History and progress were moving in opposite directions. The more humane leather gloves of the early Greeks became vicious cesti weighted with iron knobs and pointed thongs. Greek boxers had been freemen and amateurs. Their Roman counterparts were gladitorial slaves forced to bash and rip each other to death for the titillation of a mob debased in an empire that had begun to stink of glut and glory.

There was a long, dark age for boxing, with no recorded history until the seventeenth century when British manhood took to its stout young heart the sport of bareknuckle prizefights to a finish. Two lads would strip to the waist in a twenty-four-foot ring and pummel each other with their naked fists until one of them could no longer come to scratch, a line drawn in the turf to which the bruiser was required to place his toe within thirty seconds after having been knocked or thrown to the ground. In the eighteenth century this cruel and simple sport came into its own, when formal championships were established and belt-holders became national heroes. Not on the down side but on the rise was England then, stretching its imperial muscles and staking out its claims to world supremacy. The prize ring was a natural extension of a vital island people bound for glory. The image of the Britisher—his self-image—was of a tough 'un, scrappy, aggressive, never-say-die. British tars liked to think of themselves as the toughest people on earth. The dandies and the poets of the day, the Marquises of Queensberry and the Byrons, were drawn to the boxing rooms where eminent professors of disciplined savagery instructed them in how to hit out and how to parry.

The Industrial Revolution transforming England may have fathered this revival of the Grecian game. For knights were no longer jousting with their lances. Swords were becoming ceremonial. Daggers were not for Elizabethan nobility but for London cutthroats. No sign of decline was boxing to the British Fancy two hundred years ago. As England moved onward and upward, as the London of Nelson and Wellington sang its power like Caesar's Rome, so did each Anglo-Saxon champion believe himself as invincible as Muhammad Ali before Frazier welcomed him back to the club of nearly mortal men.

"The Fight," be it Frazier-Ali I or III, is only the latest and most electronic of a long and provocative list bridging the reigns of George III and our own Richard the Counter-Revolutionary. It has always been a magnet for all the flying nails, knives, and needles of racial hostility and social tension. We seem to need our knights to go forth and do battle for us. The technological leap that has taken our astronauts (and astrauthor Norman Mailer) to the moon has failed to develop a human psyche to man the inhuman computer.

No matter how enlightened, a Jew still kvells when his gloved *landsman* subdues his Irish rival. And African Americans know in their bones that a new world's a comin' when one of *theirs* smotes one of *ours*. Of course we oversimplify. If Frazier was, as Muhammad needed to believe, "The Great White Hope," still there were thousands of well-heeled honkies at the Garden and millions around the world holding their breath as the human tank called Frazier, peppered with jabs like buckshot, drove the retreating Black Prince into the ropes. At ringside we heard white cries mingled with the black pleas, "Get off the ropes, Ali! Spin 'im and *dance,* Ali. Stick and move, Ali, *move!*"

Yes, the racial and the social lines are never as clear and clean as we moralizers, the eternal simpleminded, would like to have them. Over the centuries there have always been stubborn independents who insist on mucking things up by infiltrating the boundaries of class and race, of culture and nationality. Still, as we shall see, "The Fight" is a convenient shibboleth, a healthy safety valve, and at its best a civilized substitute for war. That is why this timid soul and pacifist finds the spectacle exhilarating rather than debasing, inspiring rather than inhuming. If we cannot exorcise our warlike feelings, our sense of conflict between ins and outs, if man must strike out against the forces from which he feels threatened, then let it be done with fists instead of liquid fire, with educated maulies instead of machine guns. Let our champions go forth and let the innocent look on in closed-circuit television cathedrals instead of from ditches where nearsighted lieutenants can't tell an attacking hostile from a praying peasant.

Boxing as history and The Fight as catharsis: having seen all the heavyweight champions for fifty years, we move back in time to the outdoor ring where Mendoza the Jew, a middleweight marvel from Whitechapel, is stripping for action against Richard Humphries, the champion of Anglo-Saxon prowess in a day when the Corinthians, hurting with the loss of the brash Yankee colonies, and shaken by the chopping off of noble heads in France, wonder if their destiny lies with victorious Clive in India or defeated Cornwallis in savage America. And now, to cap the anxiety, a Jew of Portuguese beginnings dares to come up to scratch in the British manner and, Lord help Merrie England, swears he will be champion of England, which was to all good Britons one and the same as champion of the world.

But look how the Jew maneuvers! He won't stand firm and hold his ground and give as good as he takes like any self-respecting British pug. No, he moves his feet, he dances away from punishment, in and out, side to side—"Stand still, you coward!" brave Humphries cries. "Shame, shame, kill the Jew, Dickie my lad!" call the Fancies. The old print in my den comes to life as I write—the great throng, imagine twenty thousand from all over England, aghast as they wonder what the upstart Jew is up to, against the handsome blond darling of the Bloods.

What Daniel Mendoza was up to was nothing less than a Queensberry revolution, for although it was splendidly British to slug it out toe to toe, the rules said nothing about footwork, about retreating or sidestepping to make your opponent pump his fists foolishly into the air while the man of speed circles and torments him. Teaching the old British bulldog new tricks. In three fierce "Fights of the Century," Mendoza carried the colors. The snobs of London might mimic his East End accent, but eventually they came to his rooms to do their amateur best to imitate his style. Perhaps no heavyweight ever floated like a butterfly in the Olympian manner of Muhammad Ali, but two centuries before Ali's defensive balletics there was a little man of movement who bloodied the nose of an empire on the threshold of world domination. The doors of the clubs and the schools and the companies did not open magically to the benighted people of Whitechapel, but to become a Mendoza was

38

to say, "Yes, I can!" to a closed society. Even if "The Jew Champion," as he was fondly known, was only five feet seven inches in his fighting boots, all the little people of the Jewish Quarter stood a peg taller with his triumphs.

Violence and race, national pride and the undercurrents of history erupted again in 1810 when a new Fight of the Century nearly set jolly England on its ruby red ear. A master of juxtaposition, the God of Boxing knows how to pit overdog against underdog, boxer against slugger, the brute against the bright, the black against the white, the poet against the plodder, the lover against the hater, the warrior against the evader, the philosopher against the rock. Not every championship fight is so neatly cast, but The Fight inevitably levitates itself to the level of allegory. Consider Cribb and Molineaux. Tom Cribb, champion of England, toast of the sporting taverns, houseguest of earls and the stuff of ballads. And in the opposite corner—Tom Molineaux. From where? America! The hated enemy! And if that weren't bad enough, a man of color, a *black,* a slave from the colony of Virginia. Audacious Caliban risen from the mud of rebel wilderness. *Our* Tom will give him what-for! Our Tom will make that black ape wish he had never left the jungle.

As perfectly cast as John Wayne playing fighting colonels winning patriotic wars singlehanded was Tom Cribb, brawny and beefy, hale, hearty, white as the Cliffs of Dover and considered even more durable. And the dark-skinned personification of evil, challenge to Anglo-Saxon pride, was equally well cast for his role—thick-lipped, wirehaired, illiterate, built for heavy work, the British dream or nightmare of the dread savage come to shadow the super race. The mug full of pencils on my desk is decorated with the figures of pink Cribb and dusky Molineaux in knee-breechered fighting stance. Turning the mug we read:

Since boxing is a manly game,
  and Britons recreation.
By boxing we will raise our fame,
  'Bove any other nation

Throw pistols, pomards, swords, aside.
  And all such deadly tools;
Let boxing be the Britons pride,
  The science of their schools.

English hopes were banner high. Like Nelson at Trafalgar five years before, every Briton from country squire to London's growing proletariat knew in his stout British heart that the future was his. Britannia ruled the seas, her fighting men were undeniable, and although the Corsican was still rampaging through Europe, England had the troops and the confidence not only to cut him down but to send a fleet back to the ungrateful colonies and put the muddy capital of Washington to the torch.

It was in this jingo atmosphere that black Tom set to with white Tom—the first Fight of the Century to be reported on both sides of the ocean. Molineaux had won his freedom in the slave fights of Virginia, where plantation owners would pit their champions, betting them in the manner of fighting cocks. There were stories of masters who had lost their entire holdings on the defeat of their black knucklers. A slave's incentive for winning was the offer of freedom, and it was as a recently freed victor that Molineaux went on to Norfolk, gravitating to the docks, engaging British sailors in their favorite sport and proving so formidable that they decided to take him back to England to test the English trial horses. Now a surprising series of victories had brought him to the scratch line with Cribb, the one and only. The Fancy flocked to the match, the first championship fight of international significance. And it was truly a pocket war, for the British press insisted their man must win against this strange import from Africa by way of the slave block. The sporting weeklies, even the staid *Times* of London, were aglow with Saxon fury. Nothing less than the honor of the British Empire was at stake.

But what a battering British honor took that winter day on Copthall Commons! The black proved more than a match for Cribb "the unconquerable." The amazing Molineaux bloodied

40

his mouth and shut his eye. Time after time was Cribb sent reeling to the grass. The confident wagers of the Fancy began to choke in their throats. Ruffians on the fringe of the crowd were pushing closer to the ring. Finally the mighty Cribb was down, and apparently out. As the champion of England lay senseless, a lifeless Union Jack in a dead calm, as bloody black Molineaux waited to be proclaimed the first American and the first of his race to be champion of England, the toughs slashed through the ropes to hurl themselves on the apparent winner. While the exhausted Cribb was dragged to his corner and slowly revived, the thugs saw to it that British honor was avenged. They broke Molineaux's fingers and tightened their own around his bull-like neck. Twenty minutes later, when order was restored, Cribb was refreshed, Molineaux was done in, and the Union Jack was ever so precariously at the top of the flagpole again.

Molineaux won instant celebrity. In the more honest inner lining of their hearts, Englishmen seemed to know he was right and had won. While Molineaux went on an extended exhibition tour disposing of brave plowboys, willing barmaids, and deep tankards of ale, Cribb retired. Having whipped the best the Island had to offer, Black Tom claimed the title. The Pugilistic Club went into shock. And panic seized the Fancy. The press cried to the British heavens (were there any other?) for Cribb to come back and redeem the race. "By boxing we will raise our fame 'bove any other nation . . ."

The first of the Great White Hopes, Cribb tuned himself to his national responsibility. A darling of the blades, he had gone to fat, but now he ran, fasted, and sparred, stripped off the bloat and prepared himself for the next Fight of the Century. It was the talk of England. It was the lightning rod, drawing to it all the crackling pride, prejudice, and passion of a white racist island-society ready to prove its right to rule the world.

And so the allegory was played again, this time before 25,000 mad-dog Englishmen, a crowd as large for its time as the 1.5 million Americans glomming on to Ali reeling from the heavy left-hand hooks of Smokin' Joe Frazier, but rallying with spirit.

41

The Cribb-Molineaux rematch, like so many replays of The Fight that were to follow, was anticlimax, at least for the hapless ex-slave who trained on ale and whole chickens, egged on by accommodating ladies and good-time Tommies who afflict the ignorant and the unprotected in their first shower of success.

Again the American black, an early nineteenth-century version of Frazier in physique if not training habits, hurled his muscular two hundred pounds at the English hero and seemed once more on his way to the victory every good Englishman dreaded. To read the apocalyptic editorials that clouded this classic is to anticipate some of the dire things our officials seemed to think would befall our republic if Muhammad Ali were permitted to retain his title after he refused to step forward and be drafted in 1967. Yes, boxing is not the cause but the lightning rod for all the bolts of destruction ripping up the skies of paranoid nations. Just as Hollywood is a speeded-up and exaggerated version of American profiteering and exhibitionism, so the business of fistfighting makes more vivid the clash of positives and negatives besetting the societies that tolerate or encourage it.

Molineaux was brought down when Cribb's fists collided with his overindulged belly, causing acute stomach disorder. When he fell, the British magnanimously extended the thirty-second rest period so he could be dragged to scratch and felled again. Again and again until his jaw was smashed: when England could see that black was beautiful no longer, the gentry rose to sing "God Save the King" in a paroxysm of patriotic fervor.

For rabble-rousing, for allegory written in blood, there was to be nothing its equal for a hundred years.

Ring the bell for the twentieth century: the world championship belongs to America, which, according to the Schulberg-cum-Toynbee law, was as it should be. It was America that was feeling its muscles now, charging up that hill with Teddy Roosevelt and declaring its manifest destiny. It was the pushy potato eaters from Ireland who produced the Paddy Ryans, the John L. Sullivans, and a brace of James J's—Corbett and Jeffries. First it was "No Irish Allowed," and the Micks were treated hardly better than the Niggers and the Yids. Then they became policemen and politicians, and, of course, pugilists who liked to declaim their ability to "lick any man in the house." The donkey Irish, the harps despised in the hunger days, battled and bribed their way up the ladder until by 1910 they had become a feisty middle-class establishment, looked down on by the white Protestants of the Four Hundred, and in turn looking down on the motley immigrants who came after them and the nonvoluntary migration of blacks that had preceded them.

So the stage is set for the first Fight of the Century of motorcars, movies, and flying machines. It was Cribb and Molineaux in a new land as full of energy and hatred as the old. Even more energy and deeper hatreds because the land was larger and more populated. A pot described as "melting" but that was actually roiled with racial rivalry.

The Fight always invokes a special, rabid, and self-delusive magic. Listen:

So far as the boxing game is concerned the contest next Monday is well named "the fight of the century." These two men, in a class by themselves so far as other fighters go, yet so radically different from each other as to have practically no salient characteristics in common, will fight a battle in a setting like unto nothing the ring has ever displayed. For the first time, two undefeated heavy-weight champions battle, and each goes up against the most dangerous and formidable man he has ever tackled. . . .

From the standpoint of the sporting world, there has never been so amazing a gathering. Almost every champion and ex-champion of every class will be at the ringside. There will be the famous trainers and conditioners of athletes . . . Every figure of sportdom . . . will all be on the ground.

And they will watch these two strangely diverse heavyweights battle, beside whom all other heavies look like middleweights. . . . The fighting boxer will go up against the boxing fighter. Both are cool, both are experienced, both are terrible. It will not be a short fight. It will be a great fight.

And so I say again to all you men who love the game, have the price, and are within striking distance, come. It is the fight of fights, the crowning fight of the whole ring, and perhaps the last great fight that will ever be held.

Are you reading your favorite sports columnist on the eve of Frazier-Ali? Look again: it is Jack London filing for the *New York Herald*—reporting the lull before the storm of Johnson vs. Jeffries. The God of Boxing knew more about casting than Merrick or Zanuck. You who have seen *The Great White Hope* know hardly the half of it. How can you romanticize romance or mythicize myth? For make no mistake about it. Smilin' Jack Johnson, the Ace of Spades as he was revered and denigrated in Reno, vs. grim Jim Jeffries, the King of Hearts to the twenty thousand sporting chauvinists who poured into the desert casino town—did such a black-white match-up really exist? Or was it, as it seemed in London's breathless prose building to the fight, a confrontation of gods, one sired by Homer, the other by Fanon? Tex Rickard was both promoter and referee, but the overall boss of this classic was Packy Prejudice. In our age the wires of prejudice run mostly underground, a potent undercurrent, but eighty years ago they were strung boldly overground from pole to pole from little Old New York to sleepy Hollywood. An Othello had carried off the championship, and the white Iago was determined to wreak vengeance on him for bedding Desdemona. It may be difficult to conjure in these semi-enlightened times the virulence with which white America viewed the blacking of the championship. Jack London, forerunner of Papa Hemingway both in life and literary style, had looked on in dismay as the dark Galveston Giant towered over and toyed with little Tommy Burns. Burns had won his last nine heavyweight title defenses by knockouts while Johnson had been chasing him around the world demanding that the taboo be broken and the black man given his chance. When he finally caught up with Burns in Sydney, Australia (with London egging on his pigmentation pal—"He is a white man and so am I. Naturally I want the white man to win"), Johnson laughingly mouth-fought the mismatched champion all the way, using an exaggerated English accent to taunt him. "Hit me here, Tahmy," exposing his lean right flank. Tommy's punch would land, smack! and Jack would turn on the crowd his superior grin: "Is that the best he can do? Poor little Tahmy!" And so the smiling torture of black cat–white mouse went on until the fourteenth round when the sensibility of the police could bear it no longer. Australian bobbies stormed the ring to save their champion from the final humiliation of being knocked out by a nigger.

At ringside Jack London pounded away on the white keys of his portable: "But one thing remains. Jeffries must emerge from his alfalfa farm and remove that smile from Johnson's face. Jeff, it's up to you!"

But this progenitor of Muhammad Ali, as apt with his mouth as he was with his mitts, wasn't in the least intimidated by fifteen thousand Jack Londons urging on the white champion with "It's up to you!" From the racial rooting section he drew new inspiration just as his descendant Ali had assured his detractors that he thrived on their slurs, and that when the press picked against him or the bigots ranted against him, it was fuel for the inner fire always burning in him, even when he was playing the clown. Ali saw himself as Johnson reincarnated, a bigger, faster, even more controversial Johnson, a world figure where Johnson was merely the world's *bête noire*. In his hideaway cottage in Atlanta on the eve of his comeback fight with Jerry Quarry, Ali was running old Johnson movies, constantly jumping up from the couch to spar in front of the screen, giving cronies and visiting firemen a double image of Johnson as Ali, the black champion deprived of his title by a white ruling class which, if black heavyweight kings were to be thrust on it, insisted that they at least be self-effacing and compliant.

The parallels between Johnson and Ali were far from exact,

not nearly as neat as Ali portrayed them when he saw *The Great White Hope* and cried "That's me! That's the story of Muhammad Ali!" There was nothing overtly political about Johnson's defiance in 1910. He did not, like Ali, challenge the federal government per se, although on a flimsy charge the Feds did challenge *him*. In the Jeffries fight the real encounter was not between glowering Jim and smiling Jack at all. That part of it, the physical part, Johnson easily took care of, giving the slow-moving white champ a boxing lesson that stirred the huge partisan crowd to an eloquent silence. It was not a fight but a primitive dialogue on race relations between all the white champions who had rallied to Jeffries's corner, Corbett and Fitzsimmons, Sullivan and the rest of them versus the black shylock who came to collect his pound of flesh. Johnson parried every racist remark from "Gentleman" Jim Corbett, the cheerleader in this department, with witticisms and running commentary on the ability of Jeffries and his white allies that suggested Ali and Howard Cosell as a single two-headed man doing the fighting and the ringside commentary simultaneously.

Johnson's singular defiance reflected a time when there was no Negro or black movement to relate to, no group of white sympathizers, no national encouragement, no community support. No clenched fist symbolizing black power. No voices calling, "Brother, right on!" All alone, Jack Johnson chose to talk back to Whitey, laughing at him, thumbing his nose, flaunting the high life, fast cars, white women, and imported champagne. Not exactly the saint who grinned and suffered through "The Great White Hope," still he dared to be his own man in a day when Jack London would choose for his lead on the results of The Fight: "Once again has Johnson sent down to defeat *the chosen representative of the white race....*"

We have a theory about the heavyweight championship, that somehow each of the great figures to hold the title manages to sum up the spirit of his time. All the great ones are not merely the best pugs of their day but demigods larger than life. It may all be accidental, but the main currents of their period either shape their personalities or their personalities seem wondrously to reflect their times.

Jeffries was the simple white boilermaker of 1905 and Johnson was the upstart "bad nigger of 1910." Jack Dempsey slugged his way up out of the hobo jungles of the Jack London West, setting up the first million-dollar gate in the postwar boom—his fight with Georges Carpentier: the handsome French war hero against the draft-dodger (they called them slackers then) with the two-day growth. Ladies of the luxury-liner set, grandmothers of the jet-set swingers, the flapper celebrities and premature go-go girls of the early twenties decorated the ringside. Forever onward the Fancy would include a fashion show of lovely ladies from Broadway stars to high society to low society dressed for the ball. Tex Rickard, the architect of the naked race war disguised as an athletic contest (Jeffries-Johnson), introduced ballyhoo to boxing and made a conscious play to the liberated ladies of the Jazz Age. It was no accident that the first Gorgeous George was billed as "The Orchid Man." Flapper hearts went a-flutter when the French war hero rapped the slacker on his granitelike chin. But this was straining the morality play; Carpentier was really little more than a blown-up middleweight, ludicrously mismatched against a lean and still hungry Dempsey.

The war was forgotten, prosperity was on every corner, the market was a game you played for fun and profit, and in this carefree swinging atmosphere, Jack Dempsey came into his own, came to be loved, starring in Hollywood, squiring movie stars, marrying sultry Estelle Taylor, building a great white elephant of a hotel-casino on the sunny shores of Lower California—easy come, easy go. And if Dempsey was the twenties of vigorous flamboyance, his successor Gene Tunney was the perfect face for the other side of the coin. He was the Gatsby who *got* his Daisy behind the orgiastic green light across the sound. The poor, hard-drinking Irish of New York's Lower West Side might never forgive him (longshoremen on the North River mutter about him to this day), but the suave marine was a self-made man who won and *kept* his cool million from the Dempsey rematch of "the long count," married an heiress, went into big business, and became a dignified member of the Affluency, just as his walking companion Bernard Shaw had unconsciously predicted in that granddaddy of boxing novels, *Cashel Byron's Profession.*

If Jack Dempsey (with his piratical rogue manager Jack Kearns) was the ebullient champion of the Harding Days, Gene Tunney boxed with a careful left and a straight right, coolly handling bullish and bearish situations, in and out of the ring. If he was not a champ for all seasons, he was certainly the right man for the right time. It was Coolidge-and-Hoover time, the economy was fundamentally sound, there was a chicken in every pot—two chickens if you put your shoulder to the wheel or had a hot tip in the market.

And when it all came down, when the rich cut back on their servants and the middle class found itself pushed down into the working class and the working class could find no work and started selling apples and muttering about stealing bread before they'd let their loved ones starve, why then we had FDR and the alphabet soup of social revolution. The face of America was forever changed; a society that had reared itself on rugged individualism became a welfare state. Naturally we needed a new breed of heavyweight champion and lo, he materialized like the ancient kings of the Hebrews.

His name was Joe Louis and he was black and he was simply the greatest heavyweight fighter who ever lived. He could defend like Johnson and jab harder than Tunney and punch like Dempsey at Toledo. Maybe the New Deal and hard times had turned our minds around, but all of a sudden it seemed good to have a black champion of the world—what could those know-nothings have been thinking a generation earlier when they had begrudged the great Jack Johnson his hard-earned crown? There had been black fighters before the incomparable Joe L., condescendingly described as "a credit to their race," but

sportswriter Jimmy Cannon said it for all of us when he wrote
of Louis, "He's a credit to his race—the human race."

If there is no God, man needs to invent him, and so it would
seem with our champions and their antagonists. The God of
Boxing is a Machiavelli of social balance. In the thirties, with
radicals chanting, "Black and white, unite and fight!" who
could better champion our hopes and our needs than the
Brown Bomber? Gone was the vicious cheer of Caucasian for
Caucasian. Our Bomber quickly changed all that. We were
there when our white cousins were rooting him on to topple
Primo Carnera and Maxie Baer and Max Schmeling. And what
a blow to our democratic hopes when Schmeling, Adolf's darling and Goebbels's calling card, found the flaw in our young
hero's armor—or call it an Achilles jaw, knocked Louis down in
an early round and down for the count in twelve.

Who in hell pulls these celestial strings? Who decides that
just as Der Führer and his self-styled Supermen are bullying
their way into the Rhineland, a German knight should return
to our shores and smite down our black-white hope?

For the next twelve months our heavyweight championship
moved out of the squared circle into the political arena of
global power. Old Jim Braddock had lifted the title from a
playful Baer. Suddenly Braddock's little manager Joe Gould
found himself playing international chess. As the conqueror of
Louis, Schmeling had credentials as the No. 1 challenger, and
the Garden wanted the match. But crustaceous Mike Jacobs,
who played his chess with ringside tickets, had an exclusive on
Joe Louis and wanted Braddock and that title for his man.
Whoever controlled the heavyweight title controlled the multimillion-dollar business of boxing. But there were even higher
stakes and bigger players. This act of the drama comes from
Joe Gould himself, reliving his glory days. "I'm just sittin'
down t' supper when the phone rings and it's Max Schmeling
callin' from Berlin. He asks me if I signed for Louis yet and I
sez No, but we're gettin' closer. He wants t' know how much
I'm askin' and I say three hunnert t'ousand against 50 percent

of the gross. Max says if we come to Berlin and fight him instead we c'n do even better. I sez for a Jew to bring his champion to Germany and face all them anti-Semites they gotta do a lot better. He sez wait a minute I'm makin' this call from the private residence of Reich Minister Goebbels—I'm goin' to put him on the phone—the German Government is ready to underwrite the fight. Just tell 'im what you want—.

"So there I am, a little Yiddle who didn't have a dime until I got the brainstorm of scraping the washed-up Braddock off the Jersey docks an' bringin' him back from retirement—Joe Gould talkin' long distance to the Number Two Man in Nazi Germany. Goebbels is very polite. He says the Germans are great sports fans and we will be treated like royalty when we come to Germany. He says he would like to bring us to Berchtesgaden to meet Der Führer himself. I can see him and Max all smiles on the other end of that phone. 'Now would you like to tell me your terms,' he sez.

" 'Well for openers I want three hunnert t'ousand in dollars here in the Chase National Bank before we get on the boat,' I sez. 'Ya, you haf it'—sez Goebbels. 'An' another hunnert thou when we get to Berlin.' 'Ya, you haf it,' he sez. 'An' first-class travel and hotel accommodations for six people.' 'Ya, you haf it,' he sez. 'An twenny-five t'ousand trainin' expenses.' 'Ya, ya, you will haf that also. If you come to Berlin right away we will sign the contract.'

"Then I take a big breath," Joe Gould went on, "an' I sez, 'Only one more clause, Mister Goebbels. Before we enter the ring we want every Jew let out of your concentration camps.' "

According to Gould, who gave us this for the book he hoped we'd write, the phone went dead. There was to be no demonstration of Nazi Superman over decadent America in the Sports Palast. The coveted title that would have become the property of the neo-vandals of the Third Reich remained in America. Eventually Gould did sign for a fight with Schmeling, but in New York. Wheeling and dealing, he also signed for his resurrected champion to meet Joe Louis in Chicago. Under the table was a deal for Gould and his fading tiger to enjoy 10 percent of Louis's subsequent winnings. (It was arrangements like this, plus 40 percent tax-free to his first wife, plus shares to his Detroit sponsors, to Mike Jacobs, to his gambling "buddies," and to the Treasury Department, that turned Joe Louis into a million-dollar pauper.) While Max Schmeling showed up for his phantom fight with the sought-after Braddock, Gould's Cinderella Man was gallantly submitting to the quick hard hands of a lithe colored boy, Joe Louis Barrow, born into a large family of hungry mouths in a ramshackle cabin in the cotton country of Alabama.

So the next Fight of the Century was moving into the center ring, clenched fists across the sea. When Max Schmeling returned to America to challenge Joe Louis for the championship of the world, the Wehrmacht was goose-stepping across the Austrian border. Neville Chamberlain was buying time with other people's land and lives. There was a Berlin-Rome-Tokyo Axis. The concentration camps that an eccentric fight manager in his moment of kidding-on-the-level had asked to open were now filling up with victims of bureaucratic madmen tooling for war and drooling for conquest. Nobody on either side of the Atlantic viewed Louis and Schmeling II as anything less than the personification of Good vs. Evil. If Schmeling won, the shadow of the swastika would darken our land. If Louis triumphed, Negroes, Jews, anti-Nazis, pacifists, and everyone who yearned for an order of decency without violence would feel recharged and reassured.

Everyone from That Man in the White House to the Raggedy Anns in the street had a stake in the victory of Joe Louis that long-ago night in Yankee Stadium. The Bomber acknowledged it by leaping from his corner at the bell like War Admiral, another champion of that day, leaving the starting gate. Louis was two hundred pounds of dark and dedicated avenging angel that night, and in the first minute he had hit Goebbels's boy so many terrible lefts and rights that the invader was wishing he had stood in Berchtesgaden. At the end of two minutes

51

Schmeling instinctively turned away to avoid the punishment and Louis, for once uncool, pistoned a left and followed up with the convincer, a bone-crushing right that seemed to turn the German's head around on its socket. Men of the ring are expected to fight like bulls, in stoic silence, but this time Schmeling let out the kind of a scream one hears from the victim of the mugger's knife.

That night we attended a democratic carnival in Harlem. Behind a coffin draped with a Nazi flag, tens of thousands big-appled and cakewalked. It was a spontaneous political demonstration. Joe Louis had gone forth to do battle for all of us and everyone was rejoicing, from Wendell Willkie to the black numbers runner who pulled out a roll and set up drinks for the house at a corner bar we wandered into on Amsterdam Avenue. I told my new friends I had been at ringside and could hear the blow that almost removed the German's head. Everybody laughed and we hugged each other and the closest thing to it I would ever know was V-E night in London. The two victory street operas overlap in my memory—marking the beginning and the end of the long war against gas chambers and Gauleiters. When Herr Schmeling cried out in surrender we were ready psychologically to take on the Luftwaffe and the Waffen-SS. Yes, the God of Boxing and the God of War saw eye to eye that mythological June night in Yankee Stadium. Five years later, at Nuremberg, we learned that Goering had wept when he heard the unnerving news of his champion's humiliation. But at another headquarters, the magnetic Hotel Teresa in Harlem where the Brown Bomber held court, the bright music and the vicarious laughter of the underdog winner mounted into the dawn. Fifteen months after that night of metaphor triumphant there would be blitzkrieg, all of Europe would go under; there would be seven years of blood and death before Der Führer was to turn his head and scream surrender like Max Schmeling after 124 seconds under the bombs of the first black champion of the world to be embraced by white America.

52

The Great Benny Leonard

IN 1920, WHEN my father B.P. was organizing one of the pioneer film companies and setting up shop at the (L. B.) Mayer-Schulberg Studio in downtown Los Angeles, he was a passionate fight fan. An habitue of the old Garden on Madison Square—before our western migration—his favorite fighter had been the Jewish lightweight Benjamin Leiner who fought under the nom-de-boxe of Benny Leonard. On the eve of my seventh birthday, my hero was neither the new cowboy star Tom Mix nor the acrobatic Doug Fairbanks. I didn't trade face cards of the current baseball stars like the other kids on Riverside Drive. Babe Ruth could hit fifty-four homers that year (when no one else had ever hit more than sixteen in the history of the league) and I really didn't care. The legendary Ty Cobb could break a batting record almost every time he came to the plate but no chill came to my skin at the mention of his name. That sensation was reserved for Benny Leonard.

He was doing with his fists what the Adolph Zukors and William Foxes, and soon the L. B. Mayers and the B. P. Schulbergs, were doing in their studios and their theaters, proving the advantage of brain over brawn, fighting the united efforts of the *goyim* establishment to keep them in their ghettos.

Jewish boys on their way to *schule* on the Sabbath had tasted the fists and felt the shoe-leather of the righteous Irish and Italian Christian children who crowded them, shouted

53

"You killed our Christ!" and avenged their gentle Savior with blows and kicks. But sometimes the young victim surprised his enemies by fighting back, like Abe Attell, who won the featherweight championship of the world at the turn of the century, or Abe Goldstein, who beat up a small army of Irish contenders on his way to the bantamweight title. But our superhero was Benny Leonard. "The Great Benny Leonard." That's how he was always referred to in our household. There was The Great Houdini. The Great Caruso. *And* The Great Benny Leonard.

My father gave me a scrapbook, with a picture of Benny in a fighting stance on the cover, and I recognized his face and could spell out his name even before I was able to read. In 1920 he was only twenty-four years old, just four years younger than my hero-worshiping old man, but he had been undefeated lightweight champion of the world ever since he knocked out the former champion, Freddie Welsh, in the Madison Square Garden.

B.P. knew Benny Leonard personally. All up-and-coming young Jews in New York knew Benny Leonard personally. They would take time off from their lunch hour or their afternoon activities to watch him train. They bet hundreds and often thousands of dollars on him in stirring contests against Rocky Kansas, Ever Hammer, Willie Ritchie, Johnny Dundee, Pal Moran, Joe Welling. . . . He was only five-foot-six, and his best fighting weight was a few pounds over 130, but he was one of those picture-book fighters who come along once or twice in a generation, a master boxer with a knockout punch, a poised technician who came into the ring with his hair plastered down and combed back with a part in the middle, in the approved style of the day, and whose boast was that no matter whom he fought, "I never even get my hair mussed!" After his hand was raised in victory, he would run his hand back over his sleek black hair, and my father, and Al Kaufman, and Al Lichtman, and the rest of the triumphant Jewish rooting section would roar in delight, as half a century later Ali's fans would raise the decibel level at the sight of the Ali Shuffle. To share in his invincibility. To see him climb into the ring sporting the six-pointed Jewish star on his fighting trunks was to anticipate sweet revenge for all the bloody noses, split lips, and mocking laughter at pale little Jewish boys who had run the neighborhood gauntlet.

One of my old man's pals practically cornered the market on the early motion-picture insurance business. But all through his life he would be singled out as the unique amateur boxer who not only had sparred with Benny Leonard but had actually knocked Great Benny down! Every time Artie Stebbins came to our house, my father prefaced his arrival by describing that historic event. Artie Stebbins had a slightly flattened nose and looked like a fighter. He would have gone on to a brilliant professional career—B.P. had convinced himself—except for an unfortunate accident in which his opponent had died in the ring. No matter how modestly he dismissed the legendary knockdown of Benny Leonard—"I think Benny slipped . . ." or "I just happened to tag him right"—that knockdown remained with him as a badge of honor. My father would say with a note of awe, "He might have been another Benny Leonard!"

But when I was going on seven, there was only one Benny Leonard; my scrapbook fattened on his victories. In those days fighters fought three or four times in a single month. Benny had been an undernourished fifteen-year-old when he first climbed into the professional ring, getting himself knocked out by one Mickey Finnegan in three rounds. A year later he was knocked out again by the veteran Joe Shugrue. But from the time he reached the seasoned age of eighteen, he had gone on to win more than 150 fights, in an era in which the lightweight division was known for its class. The Great Benny Leonard had gone to the post twenty-six times in 1919 alone, and almost every one of his opponents was a name known to the *cognoscenti*. As for me, I had only one ambition, to become a world champion like The Great Benny Leonard. Or rather, two ambitions, for the second was to see The Great Benny in action.

When I asked my father if he could take me to the Joe Welling fight, he said he thought I was a little young to stay up so late. Instead he promised to tell me all about it when he came home. That night I waited for Father to bring news of the victory. In what round had our Star of the Ghetto vanquished the dangerous Joe Welling? How I wished I were in Madison Square Garden—old enough to smoke big cigars and go to the fights like my father!

I have no idea what time Daddy got home that night. Probably three or four in the morning. Where had he gone with his pals after the fight? The Screen Club? The Astor? "21"? A dozen other speaks? The apartment of a friendly young extra girl who hoped to become a Preferred feature player? When my father finally gave me the blow-by-blow next evening, he admitted that our hero had underestimated Welling's appetite for punishment. B.P. and the rest of the young Jewish fancy had bet that Welling would fall in ten, as Leonard had predicted. But Welling was nobody's pushover, and he had even fought the referee who finally stopped the fight. B.P. was out five hundred smackers. He and his pals had gone back to the dressing room to see the triumphant Benny, and the fistic Star of David, still proud of his hair-comb, apologized for leading his rooters astray. B.P. told Benny about my scrapbook, and the Great B.L. promised to autograph it for me. Then the boys went out on the town to celebrate Jewish power.

When Father told me about the Joe Welling fight and helped me paste the clippings into my bulging scrapbook, I begged him to take me with him to the next Great Benny Leonard fight. "When you're a little older," he promised.

In the early weeks of 1921, he brought me the news. Great Benny had just signed to defend his title against Richie Mitchell in the Garden! Now Richie Mitchell was no ordinary contender. He was a better boxer than Joe Welling, and a harder puncher. He was three inches taller than Benny Leonard, in the prime of his youth, strength, and ability at twenty-five, and had more than held his own against all the good ones and some of the great ones: Wolgast, Kilbane, Tendler, Dundee, Charlie White, Joe Rivers. . . . Only once in his impressive nine-year career had Richie Mitchell been knocked out. The Great Benny Leonard had turned the trick when I was three years old. My old man had taken the train to Milwaukee to see it, and had come back flushed with victory and victory's rewards.

Now it was time for the rematch, and Richie Mitchell had come to New York confident of reversing the only loss on his record. The day of the fight I boasted to my classmates, "I'm g-g-going to M-M-Madison Square Garden tonight t-to s-see the G-G-Great B-B-Benny Leonard!" Even if they had been able to understand me, I don't think the other kids would have known what I was talking about. When it came to boxing they were illiterates. They simply had no idea that the Rematch between the Great Benny Leonard and the Number One Contender Richie Mitchell was more of an earth-shaker than the election of a new president, the arrival of Prohibition, or the publication of *This Side of Paradise*.

When the moment arrived, Mother helped me dress for my mid-January adventure. I was wearing long white stockings and a blue velvet suit with fur-lined coat and hat. All that was lacking was one of my father's big Cuban cigars. But it didn't matter. I would smoke it vicariously as I sat beside him in the front ringside seats near our idol's corner that B.P. always got from the Great Benny Leonard.

"Well, Buddy," my father said as we got out of the cab near the crowded entrance to the Garden, "I kept my promise. Your mother thought you were still too young. I wanted you to see the Great Benny Leonard in his prime. It's something you'll remember the rest of your life."

There were thousands and thousands of big people, a lot of them wearing derbies, a lot of them puffing on big cigars, a lot of them red-faced from winter wind and the forbidden but ever plentiful alcohol, bellying and elbowing their way toward the entrance to the Garden.

57

As we reached the turnstile, my father urged me ahead of him and held out a pair of tickets. A giant of a guard in uniform glanced at him, then looked in vain for the holder of the other ticket. When he saw where Father was pointing, his voice came down to me in a terrible pronouncement: "What are ya, nuts or somethin'? You can't take that little kid in here; ya gotta be sixteen years old!"

My father argued. He bargained and bribed. But in a city known for its Jimmy Walker–like corruption, we had come upon that rare bird, an honest guardian of the law.

By this time Father was telling me to For Christ sake, stop crying! He was frantic. The preliminaries had already started, and in those days before television and radio, there were no extra bouts standing by to hold the audience until the pre-announced time for the star bout. If there were early knock-outs in the prelims, B.P. ran the risk of missing The Great Benny. And we were all the way down on East 23rd Street, miles from home on Riverside Drive near 100th Street. If traffic was heavy he might miss the event of a lifetime. But there was nothing for it but to hail a cab, tell the cabbie to speed across town and up the West Side, wait for him to dispose of his sobbing and expendable baggage, and race back to the Garden. Delivered to my mother, awash with tears, I stammered out my tale of injustice. I would have to wait ten long years to be admitted to the Garden, and by that time our champion would be retired from the ring. Now I would never see him, I cried, never in my whole life!

Mother tried everything in her repertoire of child psychology to console me. But it was too late. For me life simply had come to an end at that turnstile into Madison Square Garden.

To ease the tragedy, I was allowed to wait up until Father came home. And this time, sensitive to the crisis, he did not linger with his cronies over highballs at a friendly speakeasy. He came directly from the Garden, his fine white skin flushed with the excitement of what had happened.

B.P. had given the taxi driver an extra five-spot to disregard the speed limits and get him back to the Garden on a magic carpet. As he rushed through the turnstile and looked for the aisle to his seat, he heard a roar from the crowd that was like the howl of a jungle full of wild beasts. Everybody was standing up and screaming, blocking his view. A frantic glance at the second clock told him it was the middle of round three. When he got closer to his seat and was able to see the ring, the spectacle that presented itself was the Unthinkable. There on the canvas was The Great Benny Leonard. And not only was his hair mussed, his eyes were dimmed as he tried to shake his head back to consciousness. The count went on, "Six . . . seven . . . eight . . ." Thousands of young Jews like my father were shouting "Get up! Get up, Benny! Get up!" And another multitude of Irish and anti-Semitic rooters for Mitchell, "You got 'im, Richie! You got that little mockie sonuvabitch!" But just before the count of 10 The Great Benny Leonard managed to stagger to his feet.

No, I wasn't there, but my father had caught the lightning in a bottle and had brought it home for me. I sat there watching the fight as clearly as if home television had been installed thirty years ahead of time. Our Benny was on his feet but the quick brain that usually directed the series of rapid jabs and classic right crosses was full of cobwebs. Billy Mitchell was leaning through the ropes and cupping his old fighter's hands to urge his son to "move in, move in Richie, finish 'im!" And Richie was trying, oh how he was trying, only a split second from being Lightweight Champion of the World, one more left hook, one more punishing right hand. . . . But Benny covered up, rolled with punches, slipped a haymaker by an instinctive fraction of an inch, and managed to survive until the bell brought Leonard's handlers into the ring with smelling salts, ice, and the other traditional restoratives.

In the next round Richie Mitchell sprang from his corner full of fight, running across the ring to keep the pressure on Leonard and land his bruising combinations while he still held the upper hand. Everybody in the Garden was on his feet.

Everybody was screaming. There had never been such a fight in all of Father's ringside nights, all the way back to 1912 when he had first started going to the fights with Adolph Zukor and the Famous Players crowd. Benny was retreating, boxing cautiously, gradually beginning to focus on Mitchell's combative eyes. "On his bicycle," they called it, dodging and running and slipping off the ropes, using all the defensive tactics he had learned in his street fights on the Lower East Side and in those 150 battles inside the ropes. And as he retreated he was talking to Mitchell (shades of Ali half a century later!), "Is that the best you can do? I thought you hit harder than that? Look, I'll put my hands down, what do you wanna bet you can't hit me? Come on, if you think you've got me hurt, why don't you fight? You look awful slow to me, Richie, looks like you're getting tired. . . ."

That round had been more of a debate than a boxing match, with Benny winning the verbal battle and Richie swinging wildly and futilely as he tried to chop Benny down. At the end of the round the ferocious Richie Mitchell did look tired and a little discouraged. The drumfire of backtalk from Leonard had disconcerted him. He had let Benny get his goat, exactly what the champion wanted. Some remorseless clock in his head was telling him that he was blowing the chance of a lifetime. In the next round Benny was The Great Benny again. His head clearing, his body weathering the storm, he was ready to take charge. Back on his toes, he was beginning to move around the slower Mitchell, keeping him off balance with jabs and rocking his head back with that straight right hand. Near the end of the round Mitchell went to his knees.

How many times Father refought Round 6 for me over the years. Benny Leonard's hair was combed straight back again. There was no more talking to distract the near-victorious opponent. Benny was all business. Lefts and rights found Mitchell's now unprotected face. Both eyes were cut and blood dripped from his nose. Caught in a buzzsaw of fast hard punches that seemed to tear his face apart, the brave Irish brawler went down. But he took his count and rose again to face more of the same. Now it was not boxing but slaughter-house seven and the more humane among the crowd, including the Benny Leonard fans who had bet a bundle it would be over in eight, were imploring the referee to "Stop it! Stop it!" For Mitchell was down again, and he seemed to be looking directly into his own corner, but there was so much blood running down into his eyes that he was unseeing.

"I was watching his father, Billy Mitchell," my father told me. "I could see the whole thing being fought out in Billy Mitchell's face. He was holding a bloody towel, the towel with which he had just wiped the face of his son. His own blood was on that towel. His son Richie got up again. God almighty he was game. He would look at Benny as if to say, 'You're going to have to kill me to stop me.' And Benny, he told us this a lot of times, he loved to win but he doesn't like to punish them once he knows he has them licked. He was hoping the referee would stop the fight. But the ref waved him on. Maybe he was betting on Mitchell. Maybe he figured anyone with the punch of a Richie Mitchell deserved that one extra round to see if he could land a lucky or a desperate punch. Now it seemed as if the en-tire Garden was chanting together 'Stop it! Stop it! For God's sake, STOP IT!' And then as the slaughter went on, as The Great Benny Leonard went on ripping Richie Mitchell's face to bloody shreds, finally Billy Mitchell, that tough Mick, couldn't stand it any longer. He raised the bloody towel and tossed it over the top rope into the ring. And then, while Richie's kid brother Pinkey and another handler climbed into the ring to revive their battered contender, Pop Mitchell lowered his head into his arms on the apron of the ring and cried like a baby."

In the early twenties, Benny Leonard was enjoying the sweet fruits of summer, his harvest season of success. On the New Year's Eve of bountiful 1925 he had saved enough money to announce his retirement as undefeated lightweight cham-pion of the world. Still only twenty-nine, he could look forward to a life of ease as a coupon clipper who could keep one eye on his investments and the other on his physical fitness as he played golf and handball and traveled south for the winter. He was enjoying the autumn of his life, but winter set in prematurely with the Crash of 1929. Leonard saw his ring savings shrink, dwindle, and finally disappear.

In 1931, at the age of thirty-five, he announced his comeback to the ring. After beating a string of nobodies he was matched with Jimmy McLarnin. Back home in Los Angeles I had watched "Baby Face" Jimmy fight his way to the top of his profession, from bantamweight to welter, against top fighters like Fidel LaBarba, Bud Taylor, and Joey Sangor. He seemed to specialize in destroying illustrious Jewish lightweights: Jackie Fields, Sid Terris, Al Singer, Ruby Goldstein. . . .

From Dartmouth College, where I was then a freshman, I phoned my father in Hollywood for an extra fifty dollars to go to New York to see The Great Benny Leonard, at last, against our hometown sensation, the still baby-faced twenty-four-year-old hailed by Western sportswriters as a coming champion. With excitement building in me as on the day of the Leonard-Mitchell debacle, I promised to phone B.P. at the studio after the fight.

But when I got back to my hotel from that chill October fight night I didn't have the heart to place the call. I felt like getting in my Chevy and driving the long winding miles back to New Hampshire. The Great Benny Leonard, when I finally caught up with him ten years too late, was a rather paunchy over-the-hill lightweight with thinning hair, a tentative jab, and uncertain footwork, no match for the fast, young and lethal Jimmy McLarnin who toyed with him before knocking him out in six of the saddest rounds I ever saw.

Our Great Benny Leonard never should have been in there with a gifted young champion like Jimmy McLarnin. In the fall of '32 old Benny was the Ghost of Chanukah Past. Fifteen years later, after serving as a lieutenant commander supervising boxing in the navy, Benny Leonard would be in the ring refereeing a fight in the wonderfully decrepit St. Nicholas

Arena when he received a knockout blow more deadly than anything Richie Mitchell or Jimmy McLarnin could inflict. Felled by a heart attack, he died there in the ring he had dominated throughout my childhood. To this day I can still hear that guardian of the turnstiles who stopped me from seeing The Great Benny Leonard in his glory years.

[May 1980]

Stillman's Gym

Stillman's gym, now defunct, was once the important hangout for fight promoters, managers, trainers, seconds, and—oh, yes—the fighters themselves. A grubby, seedy place, it seemed an aberration of the society at large. But was it? This recall suggests otherwise.

AMERICANS ARE STILL an independent and rebellious people—at least in their reaction to signs. Stillman's gym, up the street from the Garden, offers no exception to our national habit of shrugging off small prohibitions. Hung prominently on the grey, nondescript walls facing the two training rings a poster reads: "No rubbish or spitting on the floor, under penalty of the law." If you want to see how the boys handle this one, stick around until everybody has left the joint and see what's left for the janitor to do. The floor is strewn with cigarettes smoked down to their stained ends, cigar butts chewed to soggy pulp, dried spittle, empty match cases, thumbed and trampled copies of the *News, Mirror,* and *Journal,* open to the latest crime of passion or the race results, wadded gum, stubs of last night's fight at St. Nick's (manager's comps), a torn-off cover of an Eighth Avenue restaurant menu with the name of a new matchmaker in Cleveland scrawled next to a girl's phone number. Here on the dirty grey floor of Stillman's is the telltale debris of a world as sufficient unto itself as a walled city of the Middle Ages.

You enter this walled city by means of a dark, grimy stairway that carries you straight up off Eighth Avenue into a large, stuffy, smoke-filled, hopeful, cynical, glistening-bodied world. The smells of this world are sour and pungent, a stale gamy odor blended of sweat and liniment, worn fight gear, cheap cigars, and too many bodies, clothed and unclothed, packed into a room with no noticeable means of ventilation. The sounds of this world are multiple and varied, but the longer you listen, the more definitely they work themselves into a pattern, a rhythm that begins to play in your head like a musical score: The trap-drum beating of the light bag, counterpointing other light bags; the slow thud of punches into heavy bags, the tap-dance tempo of the rope-skippers; the three-minute bell; the footwork of the boys working in the ring, slow, open-gloved, taking it easy; the muffled sound of the flat, high-laced shoes on the canvas as the big name in next week's show at the Garden takes a sign from his manager and goes to work, crowding his sparring partner into a corner and shaking him up with body punches; the hard breathing of the boxers, the rush of air through the fighter's fractured nose, in a staccato timed to his movements; the confidential tones the managers use on the matchmakers from the smaller clubs spotting new talent, *Irving, let me assure you my boy loves to fight. He wants none of them easy ones. Sure, he looked lousy Thursday night. It's a question of styles. You know that Ferrara's style was all wrong for him. Put 'em in with a boy who likes to mix it an' see the difference;* the deals, the arguments, the angles, the appraisals, the muted Greek chorus, muttering out of the corner of its mouth with a nervous cigar between its teeth; the noise from the telephones; the booths "For Outgoing Calls Only," *Listen, Joe, I just been talking to Sam and he says okay for two hundred for the semifinal at . . .* the endless ringing of the "Incoming Calls Only"; a guy in dirty slacks and a cheap yellow sport shirt, cupping his hairy hands together and lifting his voice above the incessant sounds of the place: *Whitey Bimstein, call for Whitey Bimstein, anybody seen Whitey . . . ;* the garbage-disposal voice of Stillman himself, a big, authoritative, angry-looking man, growling out the names of the next pair of fighters to enter the ring, loudly but always unrecognizably, like a fierce, adult baby talk; then the bell again, the footwork sounds, the thudding of gloves against hard bodies, the routine fury.

The atmosphere of this world is intense, determined, dedicated. The place swarms with athletes, young men with hard, lithe, quick bodies under white, yellow, brown, and blackish skins and serious, concentrated faces, for this is serious business, not just for blood but for money.

I was sitting in the third row of the spectators' seats, waiting for Toro to come out. Danny McKeogh was going to have him work a couple of rounds with George Blount, the old Harlem trial horse. George spent most of his career in the ring as one of those fellows who's good enough to be worth beating, but just not good enough to be up with the contenders. Tough but not too tough, soft but not too soft—that's a trial horse. Old George wasn't a trial horse anymore, just a sparring partner, putting his big, shiny-black porpoise body and his battered, good-natured face up there to be battered some more for five dollars a round. There were sparring partners you could get for less, but George was what Danny called an honest workman; he could take a good stiff belt without quitting. To the best of his ring-wise but limited ability he obliged the managers with whatever style of fighting they asked for. He went in; he lay back; he boxed from an orthodox stand-up stance, keeping his man at a distance with his left; he fought from out of a crouch and shuffled into a clinch, tying his man up with his clublike arms and giving him a busy time with the infighting. Good Old George, with the gold teeth, the easy smile, and the old-time politeness, calling everybody mister, black and white alike, humming his slow blues as he climbed through the ropes, letting himself get beaten to his knees, climbing out through the ropes again and picking up the song right where he had left it on the apron of the ring. That was George, a kind of Old Man River of the ring, a John Henry with scar tissue, a human punching bag, who accepted his role with philosophical detachment.

In front of me, sparr ig in the rings and behind the rings, limbering up, were the fighters, and behind me, the nonbelligerent echelons, the managers, trainers, matchmakers, gamblers, minor mobsters, kibitzers, with here and there a sportswriter or a shameless tub-thumper like myself. Some of us fall into the trap of generalizing about races: the Jews are this, the Negroes are that, the Irish something else again. But in this place the only true division seemed to be between the flat-bellied, slender-waisted, lively muscled young men and the men with the paunches, bad postures, fleshy faces, and knavish dispositions who fed on the young men, promoted them, matched them, bought and sold them, used them, and discarded them. The boxers were of all races, all nationalities, all faiths, though predominantly Negro, Italian, Jewish, Latin-American, Irish. So were the managers. Only those with a bigot's astigmatism would claim that it was typical for the Irish to fight and Jews to run the business, or vice versa, for each fighting group had its parasitic counterpart. Boxers and managers—those are the two predominant races of Stillman's world.

I have an old-fashioned theory about fighters. I think they should get paid enough to hang up their gloves before they begin talking to themselves. I wouldn't even give the managers the 33⅓ percent allowed by the New York Boxing Commission. A fighter has only about six good years and one career. A manager, in terms of the boys he can handle in a lifetime, has several hundred careers. Very few fighters get the consideration of racehorses, which are put out to pasture when they haven't got it anymore, to grow old in dignity and comfort like Man o' War. Managers, in the words of my favorite sportswriter, "have been known to cheat blinded fighters at cards, robbing them out of the money they lost their eyesight to get."

I still remember what a jolt it was to walk into a foul-smelling men's room in a crummy little late spot back in Los Angeles and slowly recognize the blind attendant who handed me the towel as Speedy Sencio, the little Filipino who fought his way to the top of the bantamweights in the late twenties. Speedy Sencio, with the beautiful footwork, who went fifteen rounds without slowing down, an artist who could make a fight look like a ballet, dancing in and out, side to side, weaving, feinting, drawing opponents out of position, and shooting short, fast punches that never looked hard, but suddenly stretched them on the canvas, surprised and pale and beyond power to rise. Little Speedy in those beautiful double-breasted suits and the cocky, jaunty, but dignified way he skipped from one corner to the other to shake hands with the participants in a fight to decide his next victim.

Speedy had Danny McKeogh in his corner in those days. Danny looked after his boys. He knew when Speedy's timing was beginning to falter, when he began running out of gas around the eighth, and when the legs began to go, especially the legs. He was almost thirty, time to go home for a fighting man. One night the best he could get was a draw with a tough young slugger who had no business in the ring with him when Speedy was right. Speedy got back to his corner, just, and oozed down on his stool. Danny had to give him smelling salts to get him out of the ring. Speedy was the only real money-maker in Danny's stable, but Danny said no to all offers. As far as he was concerned, Speedy had had it. Speedy was on Danny all the time, pressing for a fight. Speedy even promised to give up the white girl he was so proud of if Danny would take him back. With Danny it was strike three, you're out, no arguments. Danny really loved Speedy. As a term of endearment, he called him "that little yellow son-of-a-bitch." Danny had an old fighter's respect for a good boy, and although it would make him a little nauseous to use a word like "dignity," I think that is what he had on his mind when he told Speedy to quit. There are not many things as undignified as seeing an old master chased around the ring, easy to hit, caught flatfooted, old wounds opened, finally belted out. The terrible plunge from dignity is what happened to Speedy Sencio when Danny McKeogh tore up the contract and the jackals and hyenas nosed in to feed on the still-warm corpse.

Strangely enough, it was Vince Vanneman who managed Speedy out of the top ten into the men's can. Vince had him fighting three and four times a month around the small clubs from San Diego to Bangor, anyplace where "former bantamweight champion" still sold tickets. Vince chased a dollar with implacable single-mindedness. I caught up with him and Speedy one night several years ago in Newark, when Speedy was fighting a fast little southpaw who knew how to use both hands. He had Speedy's left eye by the third round and an egg over his right that opened in the fifth. The southpaw was a sharpshooter, and he went for those eyes. He knocked Speedy's mouthpiece out in the seventh and cut the inside of his mouth with a hard right before he could get it back in place. When the bell ended the round, Speedy was going down, and Vince and a second had to drag him back to his corner. I was sitting near Speedy's corner, and though I knew what to expect from Vince, I felt I had to make a pitch in the right direction. So I leaned over and said, "For Christ's sake, Vince, what do you want to have, a murder? Throw in the towel and stop the slaughter, for Christ's sweet sake."

Vince looked down from the ring where he was trying to help the trainer close the cuts over the eyes. "Siddown and min' your own friggin' business," he said while working frantically over Speedy to get him ready to answer the bell.

In the next round Speedy couldn't see because of the blood, and he caught an overhand right on the temple and went down and rolled over, reaching desperately for the lowest strand of the rope. Slowly he pulled himself up at 8, standing with his feet wide apart and shaking his head to clear the blood out of his eyes and his brain. All the southpaw had to do was measure him and he was down again, flat on his back, but making a convulsive struggle to rise to his feet. That's when Vince cupped his beefy hands to his big mouth and shouted through the ropes, "Get up. Get up, you son-of-a-bitch." And he didn't mean it like Danny McKeogh. For some reason known only to men with hearts like Speedy Sencio's, he did get up. He got up and clinched and held on and drew on every memory of defense and trickery he had learned in more than three hundred fights. Somehow, four knockdowns and six interminable minutes later, he was still on his feet at the final bell, making a grotesque effort to smile through his broken mouth as he slumped into the arms of his victorious opponent in the traditional embrace.

Half an hour later I was having a hamburger across the street when Vince came in and squeezed his broad buttocks into the opposite booth. He ordered a steak sandwich and a bottle of beer. He was with another guy, and they were both feeling all right. From what Vince said, I gathered he had put up five hundred to win two-fifty that Speedy would stay the limit.

When I paid my check, I turned to Vince's booth because I felt I had to protest against the violation of the dignity of Speedy Sencio. I said, "Vince, in my book you are a chintzy, turd-eating butcher!"

That's a terrible way to talk, and I apologize to anybody who might have been in that short-order house and overheard me. The only thing I can say in my defense is that if you are talking to an Eskimo it is no good to speak Arabic. But what I said didn't even make Vince lose a beat in the rhythmical chewing of his steak.

"Aaah, don't be an old lady," Vince said. "Speedy's never been kayoed, so why should I spoil his record?"

"Sure," I said, "don't spoil his record. Just spoil his face, spoil his head, spoil his life for good."

"Go away," Vince said, laughing. "You'll break my frigging heart."

Hollywood Hokum

WHEN I PROMISED to fill my old space with a critique (or call it a blast) of *The Harder They Fall,* I didn't quite realize what I was letting myself in for. A fairly faithful and certainly forceful motion picture has been adapted by Mark Robson, the director, from my novel, and the film has won kudos from New York to Cannes.

But there is simply no pleasing some people. Take this columnist emeritus of *Sports Illustrated;* him there is no pleasing. As taut and fierce and well acted and vivid in detail as the picture is, it is guilty on at least half a dozen counts of presenting an inaccurate and overstated picture of boxing evils as they exist today.

Let's start with the ads. The picture promised to expose "the swindle that is big-time boxing."

Now I hardly qualify as an apologist for big-time boxing, but to suggest that every fight is fixed, every manager venal, and every fighter a victim is to do a large injustice to hundreds of fine fighters and reliable trainers and managers whose careers ride on the unknown outcome of every big fight. If Sugar Ray wins, the Robinson myth sails on. If Olson loses, he's out of the big time for good and all. The big fights of recent years have all—or nearly all—been on the level. There is no moment of greater drama and uncertainty in the whole world of sports than the tingling few seconds when the antagonists dance in their corners waiting for the bell to send them out to do or be undone.

Yes, there have been barneys in boxing—Fox-LaMotta, Graziano-Davey, Paddy Young–Gene Hairston, Art Aragon–Tommy Campbell, Gavilan-Saxton—to name a few. But boxing is not yet a vaudeville. It is a professional sport which too often hides its face from scandal—a sport infected with Carbos and Palermos and their complacent piecemen. And yet—and here *The Harder They Fall* fell down for me—it's a sport that has served well and been well served by such heroes as Rocky Marciano, Archie Moore, Ray Robinson, Carmen Basilio, and a dozen other stalwarts.

Actually, my book was first outlined in 1940–41 as a follow-up to *What Makes Sammy Run?* It was put aside after Pearl Harbor when the fight world no longer seemed to demand attention. The cobwebs were wiped away in 1946—but the story remained essentially a portrait of the fight game at its base worst in the early 1930s.

If I had been making the picture, I would have 1) frankly planned it as a period piece or 2) updated it to a time when rogues still infest the fight biz but when they no longer operate with the crudity of a waterfront mob.

The opening fix in the movie would never get by today. A second who blinds a fighter he is handling as treated in the film would be caught in the act by any capable referee. And no longer is a handler permitted to throw a towel into the ring to signal the defection of his man. This was outlawed in most places years ago for the precise reason that it led too easily to corruption.

While I have heard aroused fight crowds cry "yellow" at a fighter who is doing his honest but poor best, I was unable to believe the scene in which Gus Dundee, the damaged ex-champion (truly played by Pat Comiskey) crumples to the canvas and is carried out on a stretcher while the crowd reviles him as a quitter and a coward. It is an immensely theatrical scene but, alas, it rings like a nine-dollar bell. It has been my misfortune to see a number of fighters carried out of the ring on stretchers. I was sitting in Willie Pep's dressing room last fall in Tampa when Ferman King was thus removed. There was a typical rowdy fight crowd. But nobody threw nothing, nobody said nothing. There was a hush. Death (two days later) was in the air. When a fighter goes down and fails to get up, when he's down so long as to need a stretcher (Bogey and Mark, listen this time: this is true), even the crassest and cruelest of fans knows something most terrible is wrong. When (in the picture) a fat woman curses the dying ex-champ on his way up the aisle, nobody will ever say that isn't dramatic. But no one who knows the fight game will say it is true.

The Harder They Fall is being advertised as a picture that pulls no punches. I agree. But some of the punches are illegal because the gloves are loaded. In the book, for instance, it was enough that the tame giant was being thrown into the ring with the champion sans handcuffs—somewhat as a built-up Davey was thrown to Gavilan, who needed no dramatic gimmick for wanting to demolish him. The Keed was just so much the superior professional fighter that he could not help destroying Davey—even with his inability to hit the long ball. But what do we have in the film *The Harder They Fall*? A Maxie Baer overplaying Max Baer saying he wants revenge on Toro (my giant) Moreno because Toro's press agent is taking the credit for killing Old Gus in the ring. It was his, Maxie's, punches what really put Gus under the daisies, argues Max. And he wants the glory as the true minister of death.

Birdseed. I have known boxers pretty well over a thirty-year span. I have put in some hours with Fidel LaBarba, Mickey Walker, George Godfrey, Billy Soose, Jackie Fields, Roger Donoghue, Willie Pep, Lee Oma, Abe Simon, Rocky Marciano—all kinds: intelligent, limited, cagey, generous; fighting fools, careful fencers, brilliant, pedestrian—all kinds. Some of them have figured in fatalities or near fatalities. Not one ever voiced any other sentiment but anguish for any permanent damage inflicted on an opponent. Indeed, the men I have known who have suffered the death of an opponent in the ring are obsessed with the tragedy, haunted by the specter of the dead man's face.

So in the name of the boxing fraternity that has no idea I am scribbling these words, I accuse *The Harder They Fall* film-makers of sensationalism above and beyond the call of dramatic art when they twist a heavyweight champion of the world into a leering psychopath. Maxie Baer, who queens through this incredible part, may have been a tamed tiger but he wasn't a monster.

Another point: the unrehearsed candid-camera scene of one Joe Greb, the broken-faced wino, on Skid Row is capsule sociology and lightning theater. A nice touch. But anyone who draws from the frightful scene the conclusion that all old fighters are toothless, penniless punchies should attend the next session of the Veteran Boxers Association. I respect old fighters and I long to see a home for the needy ones, based on the Motion Picture Relief Fund idea. But I know that some of the chief contributors will be veteran boxers themselves who are thriving in a score of enterprises from acting to banking.

Another fundamental difference between the novel and the film: the book opens with a loving account of classic encounters between Frank Slavin and Peter Jackson, Corbett and Choyn-ski. Toro Moreno's benighted career is backlighted with tales of fistic courage, of Charlie Goldmanlike devotion. The book is sprinkled with affectionate vignettes from the liniment world of Eighth Avenue. You can only hate truly the things you love. I accuse my talented friend Mark Robson of making his film out of hating for the sake of hating, without taking the trouble, the artistic trouble, the Dostoevskian trouble of first learning to love that which he would destroy.

It's a helluva picture, Mark—taut, tense, terse, tough, tenacious, terrifying. I think people ought to see it. As long as they know enough not to confuse truculence with truth.

One final nip of the fingers that feed me: in the original film ending, the press agent braved the vengeance of the mob by writing an exposé which began with the flaming phrase: "Boxing must be abolished in America." I filed a protest, partly because this line was typed under the manuscript title of *The Harder They Fall,* smudging this writer's identity with that of Bogart's press agent. My own belief, not new to these columns, is that boxing can no more be abolished than booze, sex, religion, and other hungers, for good or evil, in the soul and tissue of man. Boxing has been abolished, repeatedly, and each time has sprung up in rampant, bootleg form. The accommodating producers revised the line to read: "The boxing business must rid itself of . . . evil influence—even if it takes an act of Congress to do so." It would be churlish even to cite this act of graciousness on the part of Columbia Pictures if so many critics had not based their reviews on press showings before the offending peroration was brought a little closer to my original intention. The result has been a stream of letters asking how I reconcile "abolishment of boxing" with my qualified support for the game in my boxing columns.

Boxing needs no act of Congress. It simply needs what baseball needed thirty-five years ago—a Landis, a Helfand-type commission in authority to bring boxing into line throughout the land. Plus a front office wise enough to cooperate in the rehabilitation of the juvenile delinquent of American professional sport.

If *The Harder They Fall,* with its exaggerated but undeniable dramatic power, calls attention to this need, it may have served its purpose as a haymaking narrative of the worst that can happen.

[June 1956]

The Heavyweight
Championship

THE INTENSE WHITE LIGHTS focused straight down upon the stage: a ring twenty-four feet square set upon a raised platform for all the sporting world to see. The pressure of sixty thousand fans leaning, leering forward in the darkness. The millions of second-degree fans pretending their closed-circuit TV-theater seats are really in the infield of the great stadium. The two fortunate fistfighters facing each other with trepidation and courage while their handlers tenderly massage the backs of their entries and the self-important managers mutter their anxious, last-minute strategies. The jaunty announcer coming to the center of the ring and reaching up for the microphone. The hush of the crowd, and then those measured and immortal words: "Ladies and gentlemen . . . for the heavyweight championship of the world . . ."

How many times have I flown across the country so as not to miss that moment! Let me confess it now. I'm a sucker for heavyweight championships.

I've done my share of muckraking the fight game and agree with Jimmy Cannon and other ambivalent followers of the sweet but sometimes rancid science who have called professional boxing the slum of sports. But a contest for the heavy weight championship is more than a fight, it is a celebration, a ceremony, a profound rite, as truly a blood ritual as the sacrifice of the fighting bulls. Of course there have been ill-equipped, outclassed, farcical, even pathetic challengers for the heavyweight championship, sacrificial lambs cruelly chopped down in the interest of greed and indifference to human pain. I think of feeding frightened Johnny Paychek to Joe Louis, or the hapless flesh of Brian London and Rademacher, the amateur, into the maw of Floyd Patterson and his medieval archbishop, Cus D'Amato. Such as those disgrace the rite and are a sign of boxing's decadence. But when the world champion meets his natural challenger, when it's Dempsey-Tunney, Louis-Schmeling, Louis-Conn, Walcott-Marciano, Marciano vs. Ez Charles or Archie Moore, or even the more recent Patterson-Johansson series, then these primitive two-man wars have magic for me, recalling the myth of man as a simple, indomitable fighting animal, the most ferocious and capable of all such animals on earth, in there alone with only the speed and force of his fisted hands, the durability of his jaw and ribs, belly and skin, the speed and endurance of his legs, plus the decisive intangibles, character, intelligence, spirit, pride—only these for weapons.

When I leap from my seat to cheer Joe Louis as he storms back against the clever, cocky Billy Conn to save his title in the thirteenth round, when I watch my friend Rocky Marciano force himself up off the floor with his eyes still crossed like funny-paper xxxx's, to wear down that old man river who rolls on as Archie Moore, or watch the stylish Ezzard Charles, ahead on points until the closing rounds, stagger from corner to corner like a Bowery drunk but somehow accept the brutal punching of Marciano without surrendering, I do not—as squeamish friends suggest I ought to—feel debased, a sadistic spectator to an inhuman, outmoded spectacle. Instead I feel exhilarated, even inspired. I don't ask: How can you stand the sight of one human being bashing in the head of another? I am reminded, oddly, of Faulkner's intonation from Stockholm: *I decline to accept the end of man. . . . Man is immortal . . . and will . . . endure. . . .*

Nonsense, you say, if man is to endure, it will be with brain, not brawn. I wonder. Take away the Norris–Carbo–Blinky Palermo axis, take away the fix guys, the wise guys, the undercover guys, and you have contest and conflict in its purest and most basic form. Even in this day of electronic miracles, of H. G. Wellsian mechanical brains, artificial moons, and the specter of genocidal push-button wars, the brute effort of the fight of the heavyweight championship of the planet Earth reminds me that man is still man and needs not only atom smashers and radio telescopes but human guts, quick reflexes, inner-directed defenses, and the ability to think and act alone under terrible pressure; in short, the virtues of the genuine champion.

To call those battles Homeric is this side of bombast, for Homer was not only the father of poetry but the progenitor of Red Smith, Jimmy Cannon, and Jesse Abramson, the first reporter of the prizefight. Our Greek scholar may quote us a blow-by-blow description of the championship bout between Epeus and Euryalus:

At length Epeus dealt a weighty blow
Full on the cheek of his unwary foe;
Beneath the ponderous arm's resistless sway,
Down dropped he nerveless and extended lay.

In other words, not exactly Homer's but equally to the point, "Epeus wins it by one-round KO." Write Marciano for Epeus and Walcott for Euryalus, and you have a Grantland Ricelike verse-report of Rocky's brief second encounter with Jersey Joe.

Whether or not the venerable pugilist Archie Moore is truly a god, as he likes to claim, or merely a fine play actor who has a way with Homeric material, I know that the bards of ancient Greece and Rome would have been delighted with him on the night of his ordeal with Marciano. He entered the ring in a flowing regal robe of gold-colored silk, under which he affected another silken robe of saintly white. Aeneas himself could not have borne himself more proudly. His punching and timing in the opening minutes of the battle were worthy of his Olympian forebears, and only Marciano's rare powers of dedication saved him from a demise as sudden and humiliating as Euryalus's and Walcott's. In the later rounds the golden-robed god of the fistic wars was getting the hell beat out of him. The cestuslike fists of Marciano were punishing the old man terribly. In the end he did not fall like a tree but melted down into the canvas like a Winter Carnival ice statue in the spoiling sunshine. Bloodied and bowed, he sat there in great sadness as the referee administered the fight game's numeric version of the last rites. Archie, in his forties, with a couple of decades of combat behind him, was the oldest fighter in the game; for most of those years he had been deprived of his rightful place where the money and the glory are. Too late, his chance had come. There was tragedy in the way he sprawled there with the fight and the will beaten out of him, a very old man of forty-two, who, some thirty minutes earlier, had been such an astonishing young man of forty-two.

Before I lead you into a vale of tears, let us hasten to the epilogue. I am a dressing-room man, long ago discovering that the experience of the fight is not yet total when victor and vanquished leave the ring. This night I followed the robe of silken gold across the infield of the great ball park to the dressing room of the sorely battered loser. For one reason, the dressing room of the triumphant champion would be insufferably crowded. For another, not only the devil but also the drama takes the hindmost. How would you expect to find this man whose hopes as well as his features had been cruelly pounded into submission? Sitting on his rubbing table sobbing into his hands? Lying on his back staring blindly at the ceiling? Cursing his handlers and himself in frustrated rage? Insulting or threatening to attack photographers whose job it was to record his public humiliation? Or hiding in a shower? I have seen all these and more. But I had never seen *this*: Archie Moore, whose robe and triangle of cropped beard under his lower lip gave him the appearance of a swarthy member of the Old Vic done up for Othello, climbed up upon a table, made it his stage, and, smilingly disregarding his wounds and the blows that had beaten him nearly senseless only a few minutes before, stretched out his arms to his small audience and delivered this speech in his finest Elizabethan manner:

"Welcome, gentlemen. I found this evening most enjoyable. I trust you did likewise. Now if you have any questions, I shall be happy to answer them."

You see, Moore, the unlettered but instinctive scholar, knew this was not a mere fight between two retrogressed homo sapiens. It had been as ritualistic as a Japanese No play. One cynical fight reporter that evening cynicked out loud that it was an enjoyable evening for old Arch because his purse of more than $240,000 was the biggest pay night of his long, long trail. But I insist on a dash of romance in my heavyweight championships. Three thousand years ago the prizes for which the champions fought were laurel wreaths and oxen with gilded horns; now they are hundreds of millions of dollars which the Treasury Department is happy to share, and magnificent plaques from the Boxing Writers' Association and a dozen other benevolent societies. So long as the fight is the real thing, the difference is negligible. It is not the money prize but the myth and the mystery that draws those sixty thousand people to the ball park while millions more worshipfully attend theater-TV screens.

On the day of the Marciano-Moore fight I happened to be working with Elia Kazan on a motion picture. Preparing a picture is all-day, all-night work with E.K., and when we met in the morning he said, Let's see, I guess we'll have to knock off at six to have time for dinner and the drive up for the fight. No, I said, the way to experience a big fight is to start seeing it from the moment you get up. First we read all the sports pages at breakfast. The wit of Red Smith. The soundness of Jesse Abramson. The tragic muse of Jimmy Cannon. The acerbic

Dan Parker. Warmhearted Frank Graham. Marciano by KO in three. Marciano by KO in twelve. Moore by upset decision. And all those conflicting opinions backed up by erudition, emotion, firsthand experience, and Ouija-board intuition. We discuss these analyses. We make our own. Then we go over to the Hampshire House to late breakfast with Jimmy "Tomatoes" Cerniglia, the larger-than-life, self-made tomato tycoon from South Florida who backed Rocky with heart and soul and God-sized wagers when his soft-spoken New England champion was still fighting indoors and knocking out the likes of Rex Layne, Lee Savold, and Harry Matthews. Jimmy Tomatoes, a tough spirit encased in monogrammed silk, Georgia affability, and a flair for the high life, was spreading his money around the country. Betting it big. His faith in the Rock was no less passionate than St. Joan's in her voices.

It was D-day and Jimmy was ready with his generous twelve-year-old-scotch highballs. We had enjoyed all-night drinking bouts when Rocky was up there for Ezzard Charles. At 6:30 one morning Rocky had come eagerly down the stairs of his unadorned farmhouse, ready for the road before breakfast, to find us scrambling eggs and fight stories in his kitchen. Oh, you fellers are a big help, Rocky had chided gently and opened the front door to inhale the dawn. There are only a few of us left, Jimmy Tomatoes had boasted, meaning the morning drinkers who can stand up through the night, into the next day, and still make a little sense. Now, in the Hampshire suite, we toasted Rocky. We discussed his condition, his attitude, his feelings about Archie Moore. Rocky, a singularly uncombative man when not engaged in his ring duties, had a genuine liking for Ezzard Charles, almost a reverence for Joe Louis, but had bridled (a rare violence for him) at some of the psychological banderillas the King of Con as well as of Light-Heavyweights had planted in Rocky's sturdy and yet oddly thin-skinned back. Jimmy said the Rock was more worked up than usual and ready to get it over with early.

I wasn't so sure. I went with Moore all the way back to the

California days when he was in there with names unknown to the East but very rugged characters: Jack Chase, Shorty Hogue, Eddie Booker. And then that murderer's row of Negro middleweights carefully avoided by the titleholders—Charley Burley, Bert Lytell, Lloyd Marshall, Holman Williams—and Curtis "Hatchet Man" Sheppard who guided old Arch to his M.A., his degree in Manly Art. He had won from Jimmy Bivins four out of five—three by knockouts—and those of you who saw Bivins will appreciate that statistic. I remember my friend Billy Soose remembering a Bivins hook to the midsection in the early forties. "I could feel that punch inside of me day after day," Billy had told me. "For two weeks I had trouble getting out of bed." Like the great dark champions before World War I, Sam Langford, Joe Jeanette, Sam McVey, who had to keep fighting each other because of the color line, Archie Moore had put in almost twenty years fighting the tough ones nobody wanted, from San Diego to Tasmania. He had been jobbed out of a title shot until he was ten years older than the average retirement age. He hadn't even appeared in Madison Square Garden, the Metropolitan Opera of this art form, until he was in his late thirties, an age when most fighters are tending bar and pointing proudly, if a little sadly, to noble fistic stances when they were twenty-five to fifty pounds better shaped. In other words, Archie was a crafty, hungry, ring-wise veteran of the wars.

Rocky's career was a neat contrast. Where Archie had been the eternal outsider, Rocky, after a few hungry years hitchhiking to New York with his pal Allie Columbo, had become the darling of Al Weill, the Garden matchmaker for James D. (Dependent on Carbo) Norris. Al had brought Rocky along with the tender loving care that belied his gravel-voiced, Eighth Avenue impact. He had inched him by Roland LaStarza and then fed him the ghost of Louis Past and the oversold light-heavy Harry Matthews. So the way was cleared for the title shot with Jersey Joe Walcott. Rocky had become a true champion, perhaps another Jim Jeffries, but with his power, his courage, his pride, he was still—in what was to be his forty-ninth and last fight—still relatively green. Behind Archie Moore were more than three times as many fights and nearly three times as many fighting years. I thought Rocky's strength and the religious regard for his own body would slowly wear down Archie's high IQ and craftsmanship. Thus, in the Hampshire House, as the gold Swiss watches ticked toward noon, we talked fight, drank fight, and prepared to go down to the weigh-in. We were immersed in the mood of the fight, like Method actors living inside their characterizations à la Stanislavsky and Strasberg, long before they take the stage.

The weigh-in is a semiclimactic phase of the ritual. I have attended them for decades, in the offices of the boxing commissioners, in the ring of Madison Square Garden, in the ballrooms of fashionable hotels. Whether it be Louis-Conn, Marciano-Moore, or Patterson-Johansson, the social pattern seems as set as for a blue-book coming-out party. The ceremony has been called for twelve noon and the newspapermen and photographers—great clouds of them—gather and begin to grumble, for the stars of the show are invariably late. Those with nervous dispositions consult their watches every forty-five seconds and begin to grumble that once, *just once,* a Big Fight weigh-in could be run off on time. The philosophical old pros like Frank Graham and Red Smith just smile and shrug and use the time for socializing with the weigh-in acquaintances they see only at these events. I feel that way about it too. I enjoy the chats with Frank and Red and Jesse Abramson and Nat Fleischer, the venerable historian and keeper of the records, and I look around for out-of-town reporters, columnists, sports editors, ex-fighters whom I think of as friends even though we rarely have a chance to meet away from these ceremonies: Shirley Povich from the *Washington Post*, Vince Flaherty from the *Los Angeles Examiner*, Al Abrams, the *Pittsburgh Post-Gazette* . . . Barney Ross, the marvelous welterweight of my youth who came through at least three kinds of wars, Billy Soose who has filled out and prospered as an innkeeper in the

Poconos of Pennsylvania, the gallant little Tony Canzoneri before he died, Gentleman Billy Graham, nimble master of self-defense. We exchange notes and reminiscences—have I seen Fidel LaBarba lately? What's Fritzie Zivic doing? Whatever happened to tough Tommy Bell? We relive the great moments of the great fights—when the inspired light-heavyweight Billy Conn gave away twenty-five pounds to our latter-day nonpareil, Joe Louis, and had Joe outboxed, out-foxed, and trailing on points into the thirteenth round—and how Billy arrogantly or valorously (depending on how you see these things) disregarded cogent corner advice to stick and run and coast into the championship and chose instead to carry the fight to Louis, something you didn't do with this champion if you were interested in survival. Louis caught bumptious Billy in a flurry as dazzling as a lightweight dandy's and as lethal as Jack the Ripper's.

On the eve of that first Louis-Conn I happened to have been sitting in Shor's with Jimmy Cannon and Jackie Conn, Billy's fat-boy, tough, kid brother from the fighting town of Pittsburgh. Every five minutes Jackie was getting up to take the phone and cover another bet on Billy. "You know Billy really feels bad about what he's going to do to Joe tonight," Jackie confided with enough confidence to match his girth and his appetite. "Joe is the one fighter in the world Billy really likes and respects. But I've never seen Billy in such shape before. I know him when he gets that look in his eye. I swear to God he's liable to kill Joe tonight."

Those are some of the stories we pass around as the time drags on to 12:30 and still no-show from the pair who will decide the championship this evening. And while we wait—let's say for Rocky Marciano and Ezzard Charles in one of their two great meets in '54—I tell another tale of the Conn tribe. The Louis-Conn rematch was the Big Fight held over from 1941 to 1946 by World War II. Near the end of that unpleasantness I bumped into Jackie Conn in Paris where, as a most unlikely GI, he was riding a big KO streak over the French gendarmes.

His brother's thirteenth-round caveroo had not discouraged Jackie. He had the next fight all figured out. Joe would be thirty-two and over the hill when they met again. He had been taking on weight. Billy would come in stronger, having grown into a legitimate heavyweight. Joe and Billy were still friends, but, Jackie stoutly averred, next time Billy was going to murder him.

When the Nazis finally went down for the count, champion and challenger were relieved of their patriotic responsibilities and free to pursue their private war. It was 1946, a June night in Yankee Stadium, a hundred dollars a throw for the ringside, and the biggest gate (shading $2 million) since the second Tunney-Dempsey made Gene a millionaire. Potentially this was the most provocative title defense since the night Joe made Max Schmeling scream like a frightened girl or a stuck pig before breaking Herr Goebbels's heart by knocking him out of his senses.

Like that second Louis-Schmeling, or the second Jeffries-Corbett, or, to go back to 1811 and the bareknuckle days of England, the second Tom Cribb–Tom (ex-American slave) Molineaux, the Louis-Conn encore was in the great tradition of natural rematches that turn out to be pale carbons of the originals. Billy Conn never left the dock for his second voyage with the Bomber. He fought as if he had spent those five intervening years in deep freeze. Like an actor who anticipates his cue, he seemed merely to be awaiting the inevitable. It fell as decisively and uncontestedly as a guillotine blade, in the eighth round.

With my leaning toward losers, I had headed for the Conn headquarters at the Edison after the fight. Four hours earlier it had been a teeming fight-hotel-lobby version of Sodom, Gomorrah, Pittsburgh, and Bedlam. A special train of fanatic Conn-men had come to town with its pungent and motley crew, everybody from the mayor and the city politicos to the mob and their fleshy flashy girls, the fighting Zivic family, a full house in themselves, even a blind, down-and-out pug carried along

85

for reasons of sentiment. Now their champion had come back to the hotel on his shield and was stretched out in one of the rooms upstairs too humiliated to show his face. I went to the bar where a few loyal Pittsburghers were staring into their highballs.

"See the fight?" the bartender asked meaninglessly to break the gloom.

"Yeah. Hard to believe it was the same Billy Conn," I muttered bravely.

Next to me sat two brooding figures, a lean young man and a lean, formidable older man.

"But he wasn't yeller, you're not saying he's yeller," they challenged me, straining forward on their stools. "You saw the fight. You say Billy was yeller?"

It was a difficult question and I had to consider it. "No, I wouldn't say yellow. Seems to me he just had too long to think about it. One right move and he'd be the champion of the world. One wrong move and he'd be just another challenger, just another fella Louis took out quicker the second time. All that pressure on him was like a straitjacket he could not fight his way out of."

The two men thought about this. "Okay. Just as long as you don't say he's yeller." They paid their bill and took their leave.

"Brother, you had a close call," the bartender confided. "That was Billy's old man and his kid brother. I was afraid you were going to say *yella*, and they would have belted you."

Looking back, I think the Conns were itching to have some innocent come along and charge their Billy with the most unforgivable adjective in the lexicon of pugilistica. They had a load of pent-up frustration to work off that night.

Remember, we are still at the weigh-in, waiting for the appearance of Marciano and Charles, or Patterson and Johansson. The fighters have finally arrived and are undressing. In the pre-TV days they would strip naked and take their turns on the commission scales, some studiously avoiding each other, some genuinely friendly, some employing do-it-yourself psychology, subtly insulting or belittling the opponent, or training on him a smoldering evil eye. Now a big weigh-in is a dressier affair. The contestants affect trunks in deference to the battery of cameras and to the womenfolk who have begun to decorate these affairs. Marciano-Charles-Patterson-Johansson have finally entered the improvised ring and a hundred sweaty, quick-tempered photogs desperately jockey for position, amidst shouts, curses, and desperate pleas. It is something like a Rugby scrum with every player holding a Graflex in his hand. A little war goes on between the cameramen and the reporters who are being driven back from their vantage points near the ropes. Hangers-on invariably position themselves between the lenses and the fighters. The most unprintable oaths are called down upon them. The fighters bear it all with grim, put-upon stoicism. They assume a make-believe fighter's stance, facing each other with bare hands, while all sorts of visiting firemen, politicians, commissioners, promoters, etc., horn into the act. At the Marciano-Charles weigh-in I noticed Joe Louis hanging back, somehow lost in the pushing crowd, the only man not trying to get into the picture, and the only man in the uncomfortably crowded room who had the right.

Watching the old poker-faced king watching his successors, I was reminded of another night at the Edison Hotel. This was a few years back when Ezzard Charles, who had won half-hearted title recognition with a lackluster win over Jersey Joe Walcott, consolidated his claim to the world's championship by handing a blubbery, sadly overweight Joe Louis a painful licking. Charles hadn't knocked the old Bomber out, because he wasn't a take-'em-out puncher like Rocky, but giving away almost thirty-five pounds to our god of the thirties and forties, he had tormented and humiliated the old champion, who staggered and floundered gallantly on to the end of the fifteenth round.

Back at the Edison, Charles's headquarters, his managers, Jake Mintz and Tom Tannas, were throwing a victory party. I came in on a scene that might have been a George Bellows version of New Year's Eve. Again it was strictly guys and dolls à la Pittsburgh, the home of Ez's oddly contrasted managers. It was Free Loaders' Night, with hangers-on, relatives, gamblers, happy hoods, and a smattering of sportsminded gentry pouring the free scotch and telling each other what a great fighter and prince among men was Ezzard Charles. "I always knew that Joe Louis was a bum," quoth lionhearted and overjoyed Jake ("The Mouth") Mintz. "I tell you, Ez is going to be one of the great heavyweight champions of all time."

"Incidentally, where is Ez?" I asked Jake when I could insert a word or two.

"Upstairs, gowan up if ya wanna," said the late Jake, a language-fracturer in a class with Joe Jacobs and Mushky Jackson.

Upstairs I found a tableau of the fight game. Ezzard, who had looked from ringside an easy winner, was stretched out on a bed and Ray Arcel was attending his swellings and lacerations. This was without question the high night of his career, but instead of smiles and festivity the place had a sick-room atmosphere. "He may be five years over the hill and at least fifteen pounds over his best fighting weight, but that Louis jab can still take your head off," Ray Arcel, the trainer, an old friend of mine, said as he tended the wounds of the victorious fighter. Ez, the new undisputed champion of the world, nodded soberly, as Ray went on tenderly massaging with ice the angry swelling over the new champion's left eye.

When I returned to the ballroom, to the drunks and the coarse laughter and the cigar smoke and the blondine consorts of the victory mob, I felt as if I had descended several layers into the Fighters' Inferno. The room upstairs belonged to Homer and Vergil. But the Ezzard Charles Victory Ball was better adapted to the jaundiced style of Hogarth and Swift.

Now—years later—Marciano and Charles were approaching the weigh-in scales and the unruly crowd cautioned itself to quiet down. The weights were precious figures that would make screaming late-afternoon headlines. "Marciano—187½, Charles—185½." Boxing writers looked at each other in meaningful surprise. An excited murmur ran through this inside audience. Rocky had come in several pounds over his expected fighting weight. Charles, two years earlier when he had failed narrowly to regain his title from Jersey Joe, had scaled 191½. So now these statistics were charged with significance. What did this mean? Would Marciano be stronger or merely a little slower? Was Ezzard down too fine, possibly even through fear of the bruising Marciano, or was he trying to get back to the speed and sharpness (and actual weight) he had brought to the Louis win four years earlier? Sportswriters debated, ran for telephones, dictated learned analyses. On these few ciphers of avoirdupois, gamblers made their shrewd adjustments and the odds trembled.

After the weigh-in there was a long wet lunch at Shor's, a kind of half-public, half-private party with everybody circulating and giving opinions, naturally including that old-style boniface Toots himself, that great tub of sentimentality, affability, generosity, and whiskey-sated, sports-crazed aficionado who has been to the boxing world of the last twenty or twenty-five years what the favorite Publick Houses were to the London prize ring of the early nineteenth century. Then back to Jimmy Tomatoes's suite at the Hampshire House (Kazan, I think you're still with us) to put in a ceremonial call to Rocky himself. Rocky (hiding out at a secret hotel near the site of the impending battle) was just fine. He felt just great. He was just lying down taking it easy. And what were we drunken so-and-so's doing? He'd see us after the fight. The phone call completed, we repeated to each other Rocky's exact words. His simplest statement seemed to us an indication of his attitude, his state of mind, that intangible on which all sportsmen lay great store. State of mind is important for a team player, adding to or subtracting from the general team morale. But the prizefighter—especially when the prize is the heavyweight championship of the world—can beat himself with his mind, tightening up under pressure like Conn in the second Louis, or gathering himself through pain and punishment like Marciano when he refused to let Walcott knock him out the night Rocky took his title, using his own suffering as a source of inspiration for a final, terrible effort that, almost miraculously, put Walcott down and out of the boxing business.

Marciano combined a fanatical devotion to physical condition with the ideal state of mind for a big-fight competitor. There was a serenity about him that could never be mistaken either for overconfidence or complacency. "I've worked nine months to get my body in the best possible shape; if he knocks me down I'm determined to get up; sooner or later I insist on winning." That's what his casual "I feel good—look for you after the fight," always communicated.

The spirit of festivity, of holiday expectancy of the close fans waiting for the fight almost always provides dramatic contrast with the spartan life of the fighter as he withdraws from worldly pleasures and prepares his mind and body with a monklike asceticism.

Most of the heavyweight champions—with the exception of the lethal playboy Maxie Baer—have followed rigid training procedures. Marciano, for example, would sweat out as much as nine months in a crude farmhouse above Grossinger's, often expressing his loneliness for his wife and daughter, but resigned to the hard fact that with the money and the glory went the ordeal. Floyd Patterson, in the same tradition, had slept for months in a room that would hardly satisfy a hired farmhand, hanging his clothes on nails, locked in around the clock with his sparring partners and trainers. It has been an accepted theory through the years that the rough celibate life hardens and toughens a fighter and brings him to the sharp, mean edge necessary to his trial in the ring.

Only Ingemar Johansson has dared to challenge this rugged and lonely way. Spurning Rocky's unadorned farmhouse, he chose a millionaire's ranchhouse closer to the high life of Grossinger's. Where Patterson's personal life had been reduced to a weekly long-distance call to his wife, Ingo had his fetching Swedish dumpling by his side almost constantly. His household had the atmosphere of a happy Swedish weekend party, with friend Birgit, mama and papa, brother Rolf and his pinup-type fiancée, and assorted friends from Garboland. Occasionally he showed up on the dance floor at Grossinger's, and as late as midnight he was seen to wander Liberty's lox-laden main street in search of delicatessen goodies with his Birgit. Meanwhile Champion Floyd had been safely tucked into his cell since ten o'clock. Ingo not only insisted on leading a normal social life but added another mysterious wrinkle when he refused to practice his one big punch, his right, which he regarded with as much awe as the Aztecs attending their God of War. Despite these aberrations he knocked out Floyd Patterson in Version No. 1, and old fighters were going around telling themselves that their world had fallen apart. "My God, all those years I put in living like a damned convict—my wife was ready to divorce me, my youngest kid didn't even know me—and you mean all that time I was torturing myself for nothing!"

Or as a more sophisticated scribe said, "Ingo's victory has done more for sex than anything since Mae West and Sigmund Freud."

But celibacy and self-denial came back into their own in the second Patterson-Johansson when Floyd, who had trained in a drab, abandoned roadhouse in the Connecticut bush for almost a year, knocked out a self-confident Golden Goy from Göteborg in less than five rounds. Ingo lay unconscious for ten minutes while his womenfolk sobbed into their hands, and the many ladies among the paying customers—who responded to Ingo as perhaps to no other pugilist since Gorgeous Georges Carpentier—dripped lovely tears onto their minks.

I had dropped in on both training camps with Archie McBride, the heavyweight who had begun his career on my farm in Pennsylvania. The local New Hope postmaster and I had nurtured him until he was fighting Bob Satterfield, Nino Valdes, Hurricane Jackson, Alex Miteff, and a lot of others in the top ten. Oddly enough, "our Archie," as we called him to differentiate from "The Archie" Moore, was the only man in the world who had been in there with both Patterson and Johansson. So we felt we had an inside morning line. Floyd had knocked out *our* Archie after seven well-fought rounds in the Garden. Archie had gone the distance with Ingo in Göteborg and blew a hometown decision that had even the Göteborgers hooting their hometown boy. Floyd looked hard and crisp in his workouts and he enjoyed some vicious sessions with the big Cuban work horse Julio Mederos. Ingo, the erstwhile champion of the world, pawed through harmless rounds with his little brother, with a nimble Negro middleweight, and with a half-baked light-heavy he had imported from Sweden. The flacks were whipping up a "new look" for Johansson, who was said to be a greatly improved boxer and hitting well with his left as well as the right.

"That ain't no new look," said our Archie. "He just the same as when I box him in Göteborg. He hurt you with the right hand, but he got to throw it from away back. That's all he has. He jab like a girl. And he don't like it at all when you're fightin' inside. I fought a lot better fighters than him. I think I could beat 'im, here in the States. So Floyd, who's got too many hands for me, has got to beat 'im four out of five."

In his training camp interview Ingo was as personable as if he were doing another turn on the Dinah Shore show. Floyd was edgy and testy, as becomes the gladiator on the eve of his going forth to battle.

Press: "Had Ingo hurt you in the first fight?"

Floyd: "Well he knocked me out, didn't he?"

Press: "Have you worked out any new strategy for this next fight?"

Floyd: "If I told you, how long would it be new?"

Press: "What punch was it that you just hurt Mederos with?"

Floyd: "You're the boxing reporter. You were right there. Why don't you tell me?"

Back at the press bar an out-of-town sportswriter was complaining, over his free old-fashioned, about Floyd's lack of the social graces. But I rather liked Floyd's answers. They were smart and ready, if not quite as mellowed as Joe Louis's characteristic retort when asked how he would cope with Billy Conn's speed and boxing ability: "Well, he c'n run, but he can't hide."

Incidentally, I liked Joe's answer when I asked him at lunch at the Patterson camp how he would have rated himself with Ingo. Never one for boasting, Louis had said quietly: "If I fight Johansson, I don't think he even bother to get off the boat."

Part III of the Patterson-Johansson trilogy, mimed in Miami Beach earlier this year, established veteran Archie McBride as a perceptive critic. "Ingo hurt you with the right hand": the talented but tender-chinned Patterson was down twice in one round. "Ingo don't like to get hurt": pain is one of the occupational hazards of this crude profession and once again Johansson proved himself "mune" to punishment, philosophically accepting the "ten-and-out" count near the end of round six.

Are Floyd Patterson and Ingo Johansson in a class with Louis and Conn, Dempsey and Tunney, Jeffries and Corbett? Surely not Ingo, who happened to be the right color at the right time. Tough Sonny Liston and Olympic champion Cassius Clay [soon to become the world-famous Muhammad Ali] are the real thing. Meanwhile Patterson, a dragon-killer with a taste for tame or inexperienced dragons, dallies with young Tom McNeeley of Boston, green in more ways than one.

But when the rightful challenger is in there with the champion, wherever and whenever it happens, I hope to be among those present. As I said when I came in, despite the Carbos, the Blinky Palermos, the Eddie Cocos who have darkened cauliflower alley, the struggle for the heavyweight championship of the world is still epic in form and mythic in content. I minded not to be absent at that spectacle.

[January 1962]

Where Have You Gone, Holly Mims?

ON A RECENT Saturday afternoon, I settled in front of my television set to watch a fight that happily reminded me of the sudsy old days of twenty years ago when the "Friday Night Fights"—followed by Monday nights and Wednesday nights— were a weekly ritual.

If you are a reader under thirty years of age, you may think that the sun of puglism rose—and is now beginning to set—on Muhammad Ali. When you think of television as a medium for boxing, you envision heavyweight extravaganzas staged in far-away places like Africa, the Caribbean, or the Philippines, and brought to you on large screens at your neighborhood theaters.

But the fights I've been watching on the home tube lately— Irish Mike Quarry vs. Jewish Mike Rossman, "White Hope" Duane Bobick vs. Ken Norton's stylish sparring partner Young Sanford—are a throwback to the fifties. They're not multimillion-dollar epics but modest entertainments, the sort of weekly fare that used to rival Uncle Miltie, the early "Lucy" shows, and the "Honeymooners" in those less sophisticated days when television was such a novelty that you invited neighbors in to see the new ten-inch set or went down to the corner saloon where "We've got TV!" was advertised in the window.

Uncle Mike Jacobs, who controlled the fight world from his

power base at Madison Square Garden, was a most unlikely Cupid, but the marriage of boxing and television over which he presided was a union made in the Nielsen heavens. The pioneer showmen of television were casting about wildly for suitable material and there, in his Friday-night Garden fights, Uncle Mike had a natural—two men in a confined space trying to knock each other out. Cameras, still too primitive and few in number to follow complicated games like baseball, basketball, or football, were ideally suited for tracking our gloved gladiators in the squared circle.

It was a case of the right sport at the right time in the right space. For those early television brawls, the high-handed, tightfisted, redoubtable Uncle Mike allowed his "main-go" boys an extra $186.50 for the right to project their contentious shadows on the little screens. And the television fighters enjoyed instant celebrity. People who had never seen a live fight in their lives became overnight aficionados and self-assured experts.

Fortunately for this new audience of parlor or barroom fight fans, there was a wealth of talent in every division: featherweights like Sandy Saddler and Willie Pep; hard-punching lightweights like Jimmy Carter, Bud Smith, and Joe Brown; flashy welterweights like Johnny Bratton, Kid Gavilan, and the uncrowned champion, Billy Graham; tough ones like Tony DeMarco and the undisputed toughest, Carmen Basilio.

For free, you had the privilege of seeing Sugar Ray Robinson, probably the greatest fighter in any division ever, overcoming brave bulls like Jake LaMotta and Gene Fullmer, and the ring-wise Bobo Olson and Randy Turpin.

There was great drama on television in the 1950s, but for sheer suspense, unforgettable character, unexpected setbacks, and superhuman determination to turn a debacle upside down and score a triumph, none of the plays I admired on the tube could compare with the contest in which the forty-five-year-old Archie Moore defended his light-heavyweight crown against the rugged French Canadian Yvon Durelle. I wanted to go to

Montreal because I had followed the Old Mongoose since his California fights twenty years earlier. But I had a conflict. A play of mine was opening on Broadway, and I was still rewriting the ending. So I couldn't jump aboard the Montrealer as I had hoped. If television had not come along, and improved to a point where live events could be telecast from coast to coast and country to country, I think I might have urged postponing our play until the next episode in the Archie Moore story could be revealed. But thanks to the greatest invention since the horseless carriage, I was able to watch the fight from the bar next door to our theater.

In Round 1 of Archie Moore–Yvon Durelle, the aging pride of San Diego was knocked cold. "There goes the old man," said the bartender. By the late fifties, bartenders had been watching as many as five fights a week and could out-commentate Don Dunphy. It *did* look as if the ancient king of the light-heavies had been dethroned. At the count of 5 there was not the slightest sign of life. At 7 the eyes twitched, but the body lay there like a toppled god of stone. At 8 the stone shuddered, and began to move. Just before the stroke of 10, somehow he managed to pull himself to a standing position. How he weathered that round, and the next ten, couldn't help but make me wonder how the most powerful of TV dramas could compete with this primordial struggle. And when Archie finally triumphed by a knockout in the eleventh, I remember staring at the face of the grizzled old warrior and wondering how the climax of my play—or any theatrical climax in proscenium or magic box—could top the impact of this morality play. I would have given Mr. Archibald Lee (as his Mama called him) the Emmy of Emmys for outstanding performance in a dramatic role.

Such championship fights were the frosting on our weekly television boxing cake. The weekly fare built up a kind of stock company of dependable performers—like actors fated never to become stars but always to be counted on to give it their professional best. What was important was not to collapse prema-

turely, because you had to sustain those all-important commercials—fight on for Gillette and Pabst Blue Ribbon—keep
moving in and throwing punches, win or lose. One thinks of
Ernie Durando and Tough Tony Pellone, Paddy Young, Tiger
Jones, Joe Miceli, Gaspar "Indian" Ortega, Chico Vejar, and
the Flanagan brothers. They, and a score of other brave ones
like them, came to fight, picking up the 4Gs in television
money every month or two, happy to spill a little blood to sell a
little beer.

Instead of the handful we have today, there were scores of
welters and middleweights who were a delight to watch because
they knew their trade. There were some great might-have-beens
denied title shots because they weren't drawing cards.

My favorite was the late Holly Mims, the dark, artful dodger
from Washington, D.C., who could hold his own with the
best—Robinson, Dick Tiger, Jimmy Ellis, Emile Griffith. He
would take a fight on an hour's notice. "You think you've got
'im, but he's only giving pieces of himself," an opponent said,
after a battling forty-five minutes with the slippery Holly.
When the pickings got tough, he'd even fight under a nom-de-
combat, picking up half a C-note in the tank towns. Holly
Mims will never follow Sugar Ray into the Hall of Fame, but
whether it's acting, writing, or fighting, it's always a joy to
watch someone up there who knows what he's doing and turns
tough knocks into an art form.

The golden boy of the television circuit was Chuck Davey,
the amateur welterweight champion from Michigan State who
turned pro just as television was beginning to take over the
American living room in the early fifties. Davey was the first
matinee idol of the new wave of fight fans once removed—a
clean-cut college graduate, as American as apple pie, a southpaw with the quick right jab and nimble feet of a talented amateur. His autobiography might have been titled "Somebody
Down Here Likes Me Too," because the word came down
through Cauliflower Alley that Chuck Davey was the "house

97

fighter" of the International Boxing Club and its president Jim Norris.

It made sense to build a television star of this personable Midwestern kid with fresh appeal for the wives and mothers and sisters, who could share with their men an admiration for this well-mannered boxer—the kind of boy you would bring home for supper. The Rocky Grazianos were perfect for the live fight crowds and the barrooms, but here was God's and Norris's gift to the family boxing hour.

For four straight years the impeccable wonder boy went undefeated, with lots of early-round knockouts, even though there were Eighth Avenue cynics who insisted that "the collitch bum can't punch his way out of a paper bag."

It was known that Jim Norris, despite his family fortune, had a predilection for godfather types, and that he was like family with Frankie Carbo, who was the Mob's minister without portfolio to the fight game. Fight managers would tell you—if you promised to protect their anonymity—that Frankie Carbo had a very nice relationship with a long string of Davey's opponents. (Davey knew nothing of the backroom seances that turned tigers into lambs.)

Fighters I knew couldn't believe their eyes when Chuck blithely outpointed Rocky Graziano. "Take the handcuffs off an' Rocky runs 'im outa the ring."

And then, still undefeated after forty celebrated fights, the seemingly invincible college boy climbed into the ring against Kid Gavilan for the welterweight championship of the world.

It was enough to make Davey's army of true believers cry into their milk. From the opening bell, the message was clear. The national television audience was watching a fight between a man and a boy. Gavilan beat on their hero for ten one-sided rounds and finally delivered the *coup de grace* at the end of Round 10. For Chuck Davey it was the end of the rainbow. He's now a respectable boxing commissioner back in Michigan. But for five years, Chuck Davey, as the boxing darling of the TV box, brought a new look to the old fight game, and women who had shunned boxing as a cruel and bloody business took the college champion and his clever, sporty style to their hearts.

"Television and Chuck Davey brought us a much higher type of clientele," says Harry Markson, the literate, pipe-smoking promoter-emeritus of the Garden. "In the old days, if we had a questionable decision, we'd get mail calling us 'lousy thieves' and 'dirty rats.' But with the Davey era, it was more like 'incorrigible reprobates.'"

By the middle sixties, the home television fight game was on the ropes. The reasons came in bunches. Sophisticated techniques could cover the major sports from every angle, and the armchair fans now had their pick of baseball, basketball, football around the clock. In this new world of slo-mo-and-instant-replay sportsmania, even tennis found a mass audience. And our grand old sponsor, Gillette, followed the crowds. The occasional Ali-Fraziers and Ali-Foremans were too big for our living rooms.

Now boxing is on the road back to home television. Not even the inevitable scandals seem to discourage a new generation of living-room fans. On ABC, ex-numbers boss and supposedly rehabilitated jailbird Don King's so-called "United States Boxing Championships" consisted of "house fighters" meeting "opponents" with tricked-up records. A U.S. congressional committee is still looking into it.

High ratings (with Ali-Shavers a recent record-breaker) will keep the networks in the ring. ABC has signed the Olympic gold-medal winner, flashy Sugar Ray Leonard, to a long-term contract. So far he's been knocking over stiffs in what could be an update of the Jim Norris–Chuck Davey saga. To paraphrase McLuhan, the media becomes the manager. CBS is enriching another Montreal golden boy, Howard Davis, $80,000 per fight, with Davis paying his own opponents as little as he can get them for. Not even Norris made it that obvious.

Picking up the chips dropped by Don King and Hank Schwartz, Top Rank's Bob Arum is busy signing European champions, promising to match them against America's best.

Hal Conrad, setting up a Muhammad Ali tournament to establish national championships, is promising "no fixes, no rigging, no house fighters."

So it should be an interesting season, with all three networks ever deeper into the game we've called "show business with blood." And who knows, maybe these new fights in our living rooms will produce another Sugar Ray Robinson, Bronx Bull LaMotta, or Willie Pep. But the new era also needs bread-and-butter fighters, solid citizens of pugilistica like Tiger Jones and Indian Ortega.

Holly Mims, where are you now that we need you?

[April 1977]

No Room for the Groom

TWO OF MY HEROES are Joe Louis and Joe E. Lewis, a couple of champions who know how to set you up and move in and murder you, the former with quicker-than-the-eye combination punches, the latter with smart, jabbing lines, satirical songs, and a mischievous elegance that earns him my vote on the first ballot in the comedians' hall of fame.

This may seem a roundabout way of getting to the main item on our agenda, the forthcoming Saxton-DeMarco welterweight title fight. But bear with us, for both Joes cast their shadows over the Palermo–Sam Silverman thing that is coming up in Boston, April 1. April 1 is, of course, April Fool's Day, which just goes to show that Philadelphia's Blinky and Boston's Sam have a sense of humor. In this case the joke is on Carmen Basilio, the perennial No. 1 welterweight challenger who lost an eyelash title fight decision to Kid Gavilan a year and a half ago and has been doing a lot of road work ever since, chasing first Gavilan and then his successor, the crowned unchampion, Johnny Saxton. Saxton, you may remember, won the title from Gavilan in Blinky's hometown last fall in the smelliest fight since a couple of grapplers wrestled in the mud in *You Asked for It*.

Joe Louis, unlike Blinky and his eight-armed—forgive the word—champion, never walked away from a challenger. Unlike Johnny and practically every heavyweight champion including John L. Sullivan, the Bomber took on the best heavy-weights alive between 1934 and 1951. Call him a champion and you have to find another word for Saxton. This is some indication of what hoods like Palermo are doing to our cruel and noble sport. A Palermo champion leads you out of the world of sport and into the hair-splitting netherworld of semantics.

As for Joe E. Lewis's right to a paragraph or two in a boxing column, I submit that he described the Gavilan-to-Saxton-to-DeMarco runaround of Basilio with all the humor of a Red Smith and all the eloquence of a Jimmy Cannon in a certain ballad with which he used to regale the late-show customers at the Copacabana. It concerns the unhappy lot of a prospective husband whose efforts to wed the lady of his choice are hopelessly thwarted by the crowding in of all sorts of visitors from the butcher to the baker to his uncle who plays the horses at Jamaica.

The butcher, in this case, would be Gavilan, on the basis of what he does to the King's English rather than the King's men. Saxton will do nicely for the baker, a fellow who kneads the dough so desperately that Referee Abe Simon can't pry him loose from the stuff. The uncle who plays the horses at Jamaica could be Blinky, although booking the numbers might put him a little more in character.

Boxing fans from San Ysidro, California, to Fort Kent, Maine, will fill in the name of the groom, Carmen Basilio, who to my mind hasn't lost a fight since the one to Billy Graham nearly three years ago. In 1953 he was uncouth enough to knock Kid Gavilan off his feet and nearly off his throne. The commissioners, whose word is as good as their word, decreed that Gavilan should meet the upstate (New York) left-hooker within six months—another six months—and another. Dissolve through, as we say in the movies, and who's in the ring with the fading mambo dancer? The fifth-ranking Saxton, clearly entitled to the honor by virtue of a draw with Johnny Lombardo, who himself had qualified for Saxton by losing six of his last nine. Before Lombardo, Saxton had gone into the record books as a winner over Johnny Bratton, in another Donnytrickle that gave off a heady perfume of dead fish.

But don't go away, fight fans, your interests were being protected. The commissioners were going to see to it that Saxton defended against Basilio within six months or forfeit his title.

So what could be more logical (for this business) than that Johnny Saxton, inspired by his nontitle defeat at the hands of Ronnie Delaney, meet fourth-ranking Tony DeMarco in Chowder Town this April Fool's Day?

Basilio celebrates his twenty-eighth birthday the following day and is beginning to look a little old for a groom after being left waiting at the church since September 18, 1953. As usual he has been promised a title bout with the Saxton-DeMarco winner on his home ground, Syracuse, on April 29. Norman Rothschild, the youthful, personable and trusting promoter up there, says, "We have contracts on file with the New York State Athletic Commission calling for Basilio to meet whoever is the welterweight champion on that date."

Meanwhile the Massachusetts Boxing Commission has its own contracts on the record, calling for a return Saxton-DeMarco match within ninety days.

Harry (short for harried) Markson, the book-reading Union College graduate who is the managing director of the IBC, really had his heart set on a Saxton-Basilio match. It used to be protocol to stab you in the back in the boxing business. There seems to be a new trend toward the frontal assault. Quoth Markson, "As Joseph Welch, the Boston attorney has said, 'I can stand one stab in the heart a day.' Lamar [Massachusetts boxing commissioner] has stabbed me in the heart this day. From a Harvard man yet."

As Joe E. Lewis's parable would put it, the church is just too crowded. The brother-in-law from Toledo got in, a guy with a misfit tuxedo got in—but the groom . . .

Tony DeMarco is a pretty fair fighter, but Basilio has been all dressed up and no place to go for a long time. April Fool's night in Bean Town, Tony and his soft-shoe partner will be a couple of guys in misfit tuxedos.

P.S. APPPFF (Association for the Protection of the Poor Put-upon Fight Fan) arise! You have nothing to lose but your patience.

[March 1955]

Marciano and England's Cockell

Prefight

AN ENGLISH HEAVYWEIGHT has come over to the States
for a visit. While he's here he hopes to win the championship of
the world. He has a better chance of accomplishing that than
Archie Moore, Nino Valdes, Bob Baker, or any of the other
challengers, because the latest importation from the far shore
is being allowed to meet our champion, Rocky Marciano, in
San Francisco on May 16.

This may signal a victory for modesty over brashness, for
while Archie Moore, the light heavyweight champion, has gone
around the country beating a big bass drum for Archie Moore,
Cockell has remained quietly on his English farm, raising pigs,
growing fat, and waiting for the gods and the IBC (two separate
organizations though sometimes confused) to wave their magic
wand over this stoutish figure and wisp him off to San Francisco for his night of glory. On the other hand, there is a school
of thought which contends that even if Archie Moore outsi-
lenced and outhumbled Don Cockell, the pig farmer with the
soft Battersea accent would still have gotten the shot, because
Al Weill, the last of the Medici, has a soft spot in his heart for
Englishmen who can't hit too hard and who are unable to do

any better against Roland LaStarza than to squeeze through a hometown London decision. That is what Cockell-and-muscles did a year ago, slap through to a decision that turned Roland LaStarza against the United Kingdom.

The champion of England hasn't much of a record. He had outpointed Elizabethan heavyweights like Johnny Williams and Johnny Arthur for the high-sounding but fistically plebeian Empire championship. In three fights with Jack Hurley's aging and fading heavyweight Harry Matthews, Cockell won a couple of close ones and was finally credited with an eight-round knockout when Harry's aching and ancient back began to give way on him. Cockell hasn't knocked out anybody else recently except the venerable Tommy Farr, who happens to be the last Britisher to have had a go at the big title. Farr tried it with Louis eighteen years ago and scored a moral or a Pyrrhic or some kind of a nonvictorious triumph by remaining on his feet the full fifteen. This was hailed the world over as an accomplishment of rare significance, for the truth was that English fistfighting, especially among the big ones, had plain gone to hell in the twentieth century, and a British heavyweight who could maintain a vertical position over ten or fifteen rounds was credited with courage above and beyond the call of duty and qualified for a V.C.

Describing a man as a British heavyweight has become something less than a compliment in this century, which has seen such stand-up, knocked-down specimens as Joe Beckett and Bombardier Wells, vintage World War I, who were both flattened twice by Carpentier. That Frenchman didn't help Franco-British relations by scoring three one-round KOs over the London prides; the Bombardier stoutly hung on until the fourth the first time he was in there with the Parisian middleweight. A decade later there was Phil Scott, who boxed quite well but seemed to resent being hit to the body. Phainting Phil, they used to call him. More recently there was Bruce Woodcock, another Empire champion, who was being touted by his countrymen not so many years ago as a coming champion of the world. He also visited our shores and turned out to be a stand-up straight-left boxer with a chin of purest porcelain. Tami Mauriello dumped him in five and that was the last of *that* Empire champion except for a couple of appearances with Lee Oma and Lee Savold that would be described more appropriately in *Theatre Arts* than in a magazine devoted to competitive sport.

In the previous century it was altogether different. Prize-fighting owes its resurgence to the English, who were stirred by the remarkable courage and endurance and ferocity of such bareknuckle heroes as Daniel Mendoza, Tom Cribb, Tom Sayers, and Jem Mace. These were men who stood up for two or three hours and fought effectively with blinded eyes, broken arms, and injuries that could only be endured with superhuman pride.

In this century that sort of valor seems to have been inherited by such American champions as Corbett and Dempsey, Louis and Marciano. Whether our British visitor is of that mettle remains to be seen.

Along Piccadilly the London buffs may like to think of Cockell as a throwback to the glorious days when Britannia ruled the waves and a champion of England ruled the ring. But on Eighth Avenue, where feeling for the English prize ring tradition does not run high, my connection says they're laying 6 to 1 that Cockell is just another imported stiff.

The Fight

FOR YEARS I have pored over accounts of the English prize ring bareknuckle battles and tried to visualize what those fights were like. Daniel Mendoza, the heavyweight champion from the London ghetto, had introduced the art of footwork and some fancy blocking, but the average bareknuckle pug a century ago was a strong, squat, determined slug of a man who stood his ground like an ancient gladiator, dealing out punishment to the limit of his endurance and taking the full force of his opponent's blows without flinching. The prize ring was a test not so much of skill but of what the fancy liked to describe as "British courage." If a man had sufficient pluck—or "bottom," as they used to say—if he was a glutton for "facers" or belly blows, he could make a name for himself inside the ropes. He might be a feeble hitter or a sluggish performer, but as long as he fought on manfully to the bloody, insensate end in his hopeless cause, he was carried back to his barouche and cheered like a winner.

Except for the technicality of wearing eight-ounce gloves, Don Cockell's stand against Rocky Marciano in the fading daylight hours of a cool San Francisco sunlit day was a glorious—or appalling—throwback to this pre–Marquis of Queensberry condition. This was a bareknuckle brawl with gloves—and not a pleasant sight either—as an uncouth, merciless, uncontrolled, and truly vicious fighter (the unbeaten champion Marciano) wore down an ox-legged, resolute fat man who came into the ring with the honor of the British Empire weighing heavily—and consciously—on his massive, blubbery shoulders. He had promised his Union Jack supporters that he would not let them down, and the first words he mumbled through swollen lips after his fearful beating in nine rounds were an apology to his fellow countrymen for not having done better.

But the sad truth is that Don Cockell never will do better than he did against Rocky Marciano in the waning light of Kezar Stadium. American boxing writers had not underestimated him in unanimously dubbing him as a hand-picked opponent with whom Marciano would toy for a little while before he knocked him out. They had only underestimated his gluttony. He can eat thundering left and right hooks by the dozen, stagger around the ring like a Skid Row drunk, throw up between rounds from the force of the body blows, and then rise dutifully at the sound of the bell for another frightful three minutes of the same. Don Cockell was acclaimed by sportswriters on both sides of the Atlantic for his ability to absorb hundreds of Marciano's hardest blows, and one Englishman went so far as to write that "... this was the kind of extra courage which makes you proud to belong to the human race and to have been sired by the same breed as the boy who grew up in the back streets of Battersea."

The defeat, in which the English champion won only a single round, and that by a shade before Marciano had warmed up to the slaughter, has installed Cockell as a national hero. "It was really a victory," insisted the *London Star*. English Promoter Jack Solomons after the fight was talking of the rematch as a natural for London, where the sporting bloods have convinced themselves that their man could win if Marciano's foul tactics were prevented by a fair referee willing to enforce the rules.

British pride has always run high and perhaps never higher than in these embattled years when the sun finally seems to be setting on the second Elizabethan Empire. Every one of the visiting Englishmen I talked to, including Cockell, his high-strung, peevish manager, John Simpson, and the angry British newsmen in the tense visiting dressing room after the fight, seemed acutely and even painfully conscious that this was not just a scrap between a couple of heavyweights but between representatives of brawny America and dear old England.

The plain fact is that Don Cockell is not too much of a fighter, despite the fact that most of us thought he would only be around for five or six rounds and he managed to suffer on for eight or nine. He's just another brave bull who comes straight at you, holding and moving his hands fairly well until he gets tired; he doesn't hit nearly hard enough for the head-on style he uses, nor does he have any of the evasive footwork and headwork of a Walcott or Charles when they were at their best. He's just a light-hitting plodder, a sitting duck—and a nice plump one too—for any heavyweight with the guns to bring him down. If he were not the champion of the British Empire, and if the patriotism of fading glory did not steam up the prose of the British sportswriters, he would seem to be what he is—a willing trial horse, a dogged tub of fat.

You may give three cheers for his stoutness of heart; but even braver, it seems to me, are those who talk of a rematch, for one has to be a man of iron nerves—utterly fearless—to throw this defenseless warrior back into the pit with the most destructive heavyweight since Joe Louis and the most uninhibited one since Two-Ton Tony Galento used to swing fists, shoulders, elbows, head, and knees in the general direction of his victims. Tony even bit 'em once in a while and may qualify as the only cannibal now residing in Orange, New Jersey.

In the Cockell dressing room after the fight there was much to-do about Rocky's unmannerly tactics and such bitter attacks on American sportsmanship that we were more than ever aware of the difference between American fistfighting and British boxing. There is no doubting that the English adhere more closely to the rules. Their boxers are penalized for infractions that are overlooked as "just part of the game" over here. Fritzie Zivic, Sandy Saddler, Willie Pep, Jake LaMotta, and other topnotchers have gotten away with stuff that would probably get them banished for life from the English ring. It may have something to do with the difference in cultures. The British would seem to be more "civilized," while we still have one foot in the backwoods. Or, in Rocky's case, it would be more apt to say, in the jungle. Yet despite the rising tide of British indignation, I don't think Rocky fouled his hapless opponent deliberately. He goes into a fight like an old-time rough and tumbler who locks himself in a room with a man to see which one of them can stand it the longest. He lunges at you like a fullback, and when two big men collide in the middle of a ring heads are going to smash together. His punches are the equivalent of a home-run-happy slugger, and when he misses, his elbow is likely to catch you on the swing-around. He's a wild man when he's in there bombing for a knockout and he isn't listening for the bell at the end of the round. In this case the bell happened to be a dull antique, and the roar of the crowd and Rocky's obsession with annihilation could easily account for his hitting after the bell. Punching poor battered Cockell while he was down was another foul—in the old Dempsey overexuberant tradition—but, as Rocky tried to explain next afternoon, he had already started his swing and it isn't easy to suspend a punch in midair. Just the same, I thought Referee Frankie Brown might have warned Rocky occasionally—or even taken a round away from him for butts and low blows.

"Is Marciano the dirtiest fighter you ever fought?" Cockell was asked as he sat in his dressing room. He is a sturdy, proud, touchy man, who seemed not to like the fresh or direct questions of his American interviewers. Cockell resented this one. He rose and started to walk away. He alone of the British party had not complained.

Peter Wilson, who set the tone of indignation for the whole British contingent, summed it up for all of them when he said, "We still conduct boxing as a stylized sport under a formal set of rules. Here it is legalized cobblestone brawling. The methods used are unimportant. Winning is."

Thus, even in these days of NATO and Anglo-American brotherhood, the Revolutionary War crackles on.

If this one-sided match should be made again, even on Cockell's home grounds with a neutral referee, it is my humble, star-spangled opinion that Rocky will drape him over the ropes like wet laundry again, formal rules and all.

[May 1955]

111

A Champion Proves His Greatness

IN THIRTY YEARS of sitting near the fighters, I've seen some of the great natural matches—boxers in there with sluggers, punchers in there with defensive virtuosos, mean guys in there with boys you would gladly invite home for dinner. But Rocky Marciano and Archie Moore, in their memorable encounter for the championship of the world last week, provided a truly classic study in contrast. Their careers, their personalities, their backing, their styles of fighting were as sharply differentiated as mountains are from valleys, as water is from rock.

Contrast makes conflict and conflict makes drama, and the struggle at Yankee Stadium in the presence of a throat-tightened audience of 61,000 was a beautiful spectacle of pain and skill and endurance and die-slow courage and a resoluteness that makes champions and wins wars. The protagonists pitted against each other for the highest stakes in pugilism combined to make a nine-act play of violence that followed a tragic pattern. The Greeks would have understood the grim necessity of Marciano's triumph. And they would have wept for Moore, the oldest man ever to seek the laurels, who did almost everything he said he would do. Almost—therein lay his tragic flaw.

Before we review the battle, with its thrilling but inevitable ending, its moments of surprise and passion, let us quickly tick off the differences between champion and challenger that caught the imagination of the fans as have only two other rivalries, the Dempsey-Tunney and the Louis-Conn. Moore, as everyone knows, is a true master of self-defense, a science he has developed in twenty years of barnstorming. Marciano is the master of no defense, who moves in swinging punches like all the club fighters of all time, only more so. Moore is in the tradition of the tough colored middleweights, kept out of the big clubs, who roam the world in quest of eating money. Marciano's is the legend of the poor boy who hitchhikes to New York and strikes not gold but something of equivalent value in the person of Al Weill, later to be the Garden matchmaker. Weill was impressed by Rocky's strength, signed him to a contract, and placed him in the knowing hands of old bantam-weight Trainer Charley Goldman. Rocky delivered, and for the last five years he's been on the golden road (better known as the inside track), with every move thought out for him by one of the shrewdest and best-connected businessmen in boxing.

Archie, meanwhile, was fighting his way into old age on $300 purses in the tank towns. As if to shore up his confidence and his dignity, Archie is a boastful, somewhat overarticulate man who, on the eve of the fight, could elaborate on the subject of Marciano's inability to hit him. Rocky, on the other hand, belying his aggressiveness inside the ropes, is a modest and soft-spoken fellow who will say without apology: "You know how awkward and clumsy I am," and who would much rather talk about his Red Sox or about his father in the shoe factory and the fabulous eating contests in his Italian neighborhood than about his powers or his intentions in the ring.

As they climbed through the ropes a week ago, their differences were vividly revealed in their appearances. Rocky wore a blue cloth robe trimmed in white. But Archie Moore was resplendent in a robe of black brocade trimmed in gold, with Louis XIV cuffs and a brilliant gold lining. No Othello was ever more lavishly costumed. Archie had come through ulcers and years of tough fights and poverty to reach this moment of glory in the ball park, and his manner seemed to say, I am going to dress and act the part. He glared across the ring at Marciano like some South Sea emperor staring down an unruly subject. But Rocky doesn't play those games, he just comes to fight; and Archie's evil eye played no part in the events that followed.

The delay before an epic fight is always tantalizing. Most of the spectators have been waiting for the fight all week, talking it up all day, betting it, masterminding it, until they have brought themselves to an exquisite peak of anticipation. The crowd is both festive and tense and so much resembles the Pierce Egan descriptions of bareknuckle fight crowds that you know there is a consistent line of boxing enthusiasm up through the centuries. The impatient thousands cheer their old champions, Dempsey and Louis and Walker and Canzoneri, and then at last the ring is cleared and the two men are left alone to face the demands the night has in store for them. The significance of it presses on the crowd and it falls silent, grave. The stadium seems to hold its collective breath. Will Rocky, the 4-to-1 favorite, preserve his legend of invincibility? Can Archie Moore, the young old man of forty-two, make good his boast, "I'm a stylist, I can cope with any situation"?

So we have come to one of the good, nerved-up moments in heavyweight history. The champions touch gloves and are at each other, Archie moving nicely out of danger and jabbing as he promised to do, Rocky lumbering forward in his crouch. Marciano is starting slowly, as usual, but there is just a touch more finesse to his bulling ways than meets the back-seat eye. Weaving and bobbing, always moving forward, he is not as easy to hit as Archie had figured. He's catching punches on the shoulders and the gloves.

It's in Round 2 that Archie nearly lives up to his own descriptions of his abilities. Here is old-time boxing such as the good ones practiced before and after the First World War. Archie is feinting with his hands, his head, his shoulders—it is so good that he can't resist a little self-satisfied smile. He anticipates Rocky's lead and counters sharply—scientific fighting at its best. Rocky lunges in again and Archie times a masterful right-hand counter. Down, to the amazement of everybody including Marciano, goes the Rock.

There was blood on Rocky's left eye as he knelt on the canvas. Blood seemed to be oozing through the flesh of his nose. In my notes for this round I jotted, "Rocky cut, hurt, dazed." As the champion rose on the count of 2, I scratched out "dazed," replaced it with "startled." I was close enough to the ring to see their eyes and again there was a study in contrast. When Rocky unexpectedly had dropped, a flush of excitement and self-satisfaction had made Archie's eyes bright. Now he was watching Rocky carefully, perhaps remembering Walcott's mistake in not following through after felling Rocky in the first round the night Rocky got up and won the championship. Archie had announced publicly that if ever he had Rocky on the floor he would not let the champion escape. "Once I have my man hurt I know how to finish him," he liked to boast. Rocky was hurt but he was barging in again. He looked both wary and determined beyond your ordinary man's determination. It was a look that promised trouble for Archie Moore, and yet the Marciano fans held their breath and some later reported a feeling of pressure around their hearts because Rocky was clearly in need of recuperation and Archie was hurting him again with a wise selection of punches, stiff jabs, straight rights, and a well-executed left uppercut. Marciano's body seemed to shudder, but his eyes were sharply fixed on Archie and he kept coming in, landing a hard right to Archie's chin just before the bell ended a momentous round.

In years to come Archie may ask himself: "When I finally came to the moment I had been dreaming of for twenty years, what did I do wrong?" I think the answer is, nothing. The answer is that Rocky rose with his legs a little rubbery, but with his will to win challenged but unbending. Some unique power in him was refusing to lose, no matter how badly he might be outboxed or outhit. A boxing match is a test of will power, perhaps the supreme test; and in this vital department he excels any fighter I have ever seen.

In the next round we began to see the Marciano of the Walcott and Charles ordeals, a terrible figure immune to blood and pain, accepting hard blows casually, as if they were a trivial price to pay for the glory and wealth that ride with the title. Rocky was stalking Archie, missing three out of four but shaking the old campaigner when he landed. Archie Moore was employing all the skills he had accumulated and they were wonderful to watch. There were moments when he played with Rocky and made him look amateurish. That little smile would spread across his face as he slipped Marciano's blockbusters and countered with quick-handed combinations. But this round was a turning point, for it proved that no matter how brilliantly Archie boxed he could not stop the champion's forward progress. He could not prevent the champion from jarring him. The science of self-defense was inadequate to the problem of how to stop a human tank like Marciano from running over him.

It was a vicious Marciano that sprang forward in the fourth, a bareknuckle throwback hurling at Archie's head a relentless stream of clumsily effective punches. Archie knows a dozen ways to avoid a punch, ducking, slipping, rolling with a punch, picking it off; and over and over again he would bring his right arm up just in time to block a clubbing left hook.

But to boxing's science we may now have to add the Marciano law of saturation. You may get out of the way of nine punches but the tenth will break through and find you. Marciano, wild and clumsy though he may be, is such a voluminous puncher that the cleverest of his opponents has to be hit and hurt every so often. Rocky wears his men down like a hydraulic drill attacking a boulder. But the challenger was an elusive target in the fifth round, making Rocky miss and peppering him with straight lefts, reminding the audience once more of his boxing superiority. He was making all the right moves and the champion, after two strong rounds, seemed to be floundering. "Keep boxing him, boy, you can take him,"

Featherweight Champion Sandy Saddler shouted to his stable-mate as Moore moved back to his corner.

When the sixth round started, it was still a close fight. When the round was over, after Marciano had punched from bell to bell as if he were working out on a heavy bag, it was no longer. Archie was a battered, beaten pugilist. He had been knocked down twice, one eye had been closed, and the right side of his face was painfully swollen. His right arm was too weary to rise to the occasion of Rocky's vicious left hooks, and he had caught dozens of them as the champion turned on a demonstration of continuous punching that had to be seen to be believed. The Moore-Marciano fight may prove to the buffs that there is simply no defense for this kind of pressure. The tiring challenger rose gallantly to face his punishment. Only generous supplies of courage and defensive wisdom allowed him to stagger back to his corner. Oddly enough, Rocky was staggering too. Try punching a heavy bag for three minutes as fast as you can without stopping and you'll know why.

Archie Moore sagged onto his stool and there was Dr. Vincent Nardiello leaning over him, suggesting that the fight was over. But Archie is a prideful man. Pride was the only stake he had to hold on to through the frustration years. So he invoked it now, and asked for the privilege of being counted out. "Like a champion," he said. He did not want to be waved out of the ring on a doctor's certificate. And as if to prove his right to continue, he carried the fight to Marciano in the seventh with a series of slick combinations.

But the Rock is well-named, a discouraging man to fight, taking your best punches and then walking into you with both hands swinging. "He's a tank. A monster," people around me were saying. He knocked Archie down again, but Referee Kessler ruled it a slip. It didn't matter. Archie could sneak-punch and flurry, and it was a brave thing to see, but the sick-sad look of defeat had begun to shadow his eyes.

The last four minutes of the fight provided a cruel, crescendoing coda. Marciano was a battering ram and old Archie was a crumbling wall. "How long can he stand that punishment?" was the only question remaining to be decided. A merciless right hook drove the battered challenger back to the canvas, where he was still squatting, an abject figure of defeat, when the harsh bell prolonged the ordeal by ending the round a bare four seconds before the count of 10.

A dying tiger, still dangerous in his final few seconds of life, Archie fought back in the ninth, but Rocky closed in, broadsiding ponderous rights and lefts until at last the remarkable middle-aged light-heavyweight champion slumped down in his own corner, exactly where his stool would have been at the end of the round, a fatally wounded animal crawling back to its lair. There he was counted out, conscious but with the will to fight on beaten out of him at last.

It is a humiliating experience to be knocked into a stupor in public, and it was interesting to see how quickly Archie Moore reassembled the blocks of his dignity. Putting aside his agony and disappointment, he strode into his dressing room like a dramatic star coming in after the final curtain call. "Gentlemen, I'll be with you in a minute," he said with a jauntiness that belied his appearance. Then he was back, standing on a table like the Chautauqua character he is, insisting that he enjoyed the fight. "I think Rocky enjoyed it," he added. "I hope the public enjoyed it too."

Rocky talks more plainly. He didn't enjoy the fight. He just wanted to win it, as he had every one of his forty-nine battles. The experts still fault him for his lack of finesse, but right now we see him, a year or two hence, as the only American heavyweight champion ever to retire without a defeat. The old-timers talk of Sullivan and Jeffries and Dempsey. We may have another such immortal slugger in our midst. Are we too close to his shortcomings to recognize his incomparable virtues?

[October 1955]

118

The Comeback:
Sugar Ray Robinson

IN A PERIOD when the art of boxing was sliding into its decadence, Sugar Ray Robinson boxed like a throwback to the brilliant 1910s and '20s. In those days when you described a man as a great boxer, you didn't mean that he was merely an elusive footwork artist and rapid but delicate jabber like our Zulueta or Johnny Gonsalves. When you boxed well, you knew not only how to avoid punishment but how to deal it out strategically.

That was the way of Sugar Ray. I first saw him nearly fifteen years ago when he was only a year and a dozen fights out of the amateurs. But he was one of those naturals, like Joe DiMaggio and Ernest Hemingway. He had speed and grace and cleverness and power and endurance and passion. In his second year as a pro he had beaten Sammy Angott, Marty Servo, and Fritzie Zivic. His twenty-seventh fight, nearly fourteen years ago, was a return match with Zivic, and he let the fight game know he was ready for the welterweight title by knocking out the ex-champion.

Sugar Ray was a picture fighter in those early '40s. He had the long, slender, rippling-muscled legs of a dancer. If you wanted to box, he outboxed you, and if you wanted to fight, he outfought you. There was not a welterweight in the world who could touch him then; perhaps there never was. They wouldn't let him fight for the title because, held officially by a vincible champion called Red Cochrane, it was the personal property of the boys in the back room. To get work, Ray moved in on the middleweights. He beat Jake LaMotta in October 1942. Ray had to fight four more years and win thirty-eight more bouts before they finally let him try for the welterweight title. Red Cochrane had ducked him and retired. His successor as "champion," Marty Servo, had ducked him and retired. Now Tommy Bell, a colored welterweight trial horse, met Sugar in an "elimination" bout for the title. Ray was knocked dizzy in the second round. He looked all in at the end of four. It took him a few more rounds to pull himself together again. By the eleventh he was the Sugar Ray the Garden regulars had learned never to bet against. After five and a half years of dreary run-arounds, the welterweights had a champion who won his fights in the ring. It was a refreshing change.

There was that winter night in Chicago when Ray challenged LaMotta for the middleweight title. The experts had faulted Robinson as one great welterweight who was too frail, too slight, too short on ruggedness, ever to stay up there with the best of the middleweights. But that night in Chicago against the vicious bull of the Bronx he fought beautifully, fiercely, until the thirteenth round, when he hit Jake with enough combinations to drop a dozen middleweights. Jake didn't drop; he just stood there, a bloody, stubborn heap of flesh waiting for more.

Sugar Ray toured Europe, a golden boy with black skin. He was the darling of Paris. They mobbed his fuchsia Cadillac. It was a wonderful spring and summer in Zurich, Antwerp, Liège, Turin—until Randy Turpin, awkward, hard-hitting, a lesser playboy, took his title way in London.

I saw Ray, with a bloody eye, take the title back from Turpin with a passionate outburst in the tenth round in the New York return match. This was a rich, slipping, aging Ray Robinson. Good enough, though, to take the measure of the fading

Graziano and an up-and-coming Bobo Olson. Good enough to look like a shoo-in to turn the trick no middleweight champion has ever been able to do: win the light-heavyweight crown. After twelve rounds in Yankee Stadium he was so far in front of Joey Maxim that he couldn't lose unless he were knocked out. But it was 130 degrees under the lights on an airless summer night, and at the end of the thirteenth, with punchless Joey as an innocent bystander, Ray collapsed from the heat.

Retirement. Honor. Money. I'll know when I'm through, Robinson had boasted. But the big pay nights and the fickle idolaters sing a siren song.

Joe Rindone, who fights as if he were born to suffer, was chosen as victim No. 1 on Ray's retread hit parade. Joe obliged by getting himself knocked out in the sixth round. The durable, forward-moving, uninspired but unintimidated Tiger Jones was nominated as foil No. 2, but this sturdy second-rate Tiger forgot to read the script. He plain beat the starch out of the disenchanted Sugar Ray. Finally they put Ray in with the leading middleweight contender, the slippery and overcautious Castellani. Ray won on spirit and some two-handed flurries, but his legs were dragging at the end of ten.

And now the stage is set for Act III in the drama of Sugar Ray. In the same ring where he won his title gloriously, he aspires once more to rule the middleweights. It is a fight no fan should miss, if only because it belongs to the history of the ring, to the tragedy of a game that devours even the most gifted and the most canny of its children.

Maybe Robinson, off his timing and slower on his marvelous, dancing legs, can paste together his experience and passion and take the twenty-seven-year-old Bobo Olson out early. But the gamblers, who always went with this phenomenal winner (137 pro battles), are laying 3 to 1 the Sugar has melted away.

The vigorish boys were wrong. Not only did the original Sugar Ray knock out Bobo, first in two, and then in four, he would go on to regain his title, first from Gene Fullmer and then from Carmen Basilio, at age thirty-eight, when nearly all boxers are (or should be) in their rocking chairs.

Seven years later he was still at it, fighting no less than fifteen times in nine months, a forty-five-year-old losing to second-raters now, finally calling it a night after 202 fights, with only 18 L's, and all but two of those in his mid-'30s to '40s when he should have been home counting the money he blew in fuchsia Cadillacs, an entourage that would fill three limos at least, a life style à la Sinatra—only singers can go more rounds than the incomparable Robinson. Sic transit Sugar Ray, our twentieth-century nonpareil.

In Boston last week, however, age once more gave the back of its hand to upstart youth. It was like sitting through the same movie twice as Carmen Basilio and Tony DeMarco met for their title rematch. Carmen took a beating in the early rounds, Tony ran out of gas about the ninth, Carmen clobbered Tony into insensate submission in the twelfth. It was the same script as in Syracuse last June, when Basilio took DeMarco's spang-new welterweight title from him. It was a good movie, though, nicely cast if you like tough types, with plenty of action, suspense, and excitement. Running time was two seconds longer than the previous showing, but that may have been because the referee seemed a little slow in his counting.

The plot was actually better this time. The boys in the back room had shored it up with prefight talk that unless Carmen could knock out Tony the Boston officials would villainously vote their hometown hero back into the championship. As it turned out, Tony *was* leading on all the official cards (but justifiably so) when Carmen made them suitable only for framing with a succession of hard right smashes to Tony's head. Tony went down for a count of 8, got up, and wobbled into the arms of the referee. The referee took slow and exceeding care in wiping off Tony's gloves and then Carmen was on him again, with more rights, and Tony was down and the referee was stopping the fight for a TKO in 1:54 of the twelfth round.

Carmen added a last touch in the fadeout when he reported that he had injured his left hand in an early round. It will be ready, though, he added, when he meets ex-champion Johnny Saxton, probably in February. Saxton had better be ready too.

[December 1955]

Boxing's Dirty Business
Must Be Cleaned Up Now

JOHNNY SAXTON MAY BE an orphan, but no one can say he lacks for cousins in Philadelphia. Anybody who can clown his way through fifteen listless rounds and still be rewarded with a world's championship must have a covey of doting relatives in the Friendly City. I am still checking on the lineal connection between the new "champion" and his benefactors, Referee Pete Pantaleo and Judges Jim Mina and Nat Lopinson, all of whom gave the defending champion, Kid Gavilan, the treatment a GOP candidate expects in Mississippi. They voted the straight Saxton-Palermo ticket. The three officials, if not blood relatives of the hitless wonder, have at the very least a touching sentimental attachment for the Riverdale foundling who plays Cinderella to Manager Blinky Palermo's unshaven Fairy Godmother.

Blinky's champion "fights," as they used to say, "out of Philadelphia." He can't move far enough out to satisfy the nearly eight thousand fans who suffered through the gruesome, gluesome twosome between him and fading Kid Gavilan in Convention Hall the other evening. Blinky Palermo, a numbers man who traffics in fighters (Ike Williams, Billy Fox, Clarence Henry, Dan Bucceroni, Coley Wallace, etc.), operates out of Philadelphia. One of boxing's top-ranking ambassadors of ill will, a field in which there is always stiff competition, Blinky is frequently identified as "The Philadelphia Sportsman." It has become a sort of private joke, especially suitable to those papers who would rather not spell spade s-p-a-d-e. In 1951 a federal district court found Blinky guilty of contempt for refusing to answer questions before a rackets grand jury. Contempt is also the word for Blinky's attitude toward boxing fans in foisting Saxton, the human grannyknot, on them as Kid Gavilan's successor.

Johnny may never have known what it is to have a real brother, but he has certainly found the next best thing in Honest Pete Pantaleo, another Philadelphia sportsman, who handled the fight with such tender concern for Saxton's welfare that it is difficult for me to understand why there should have been such bitter criticism of him in the press. Extending a helping hand to an orphan boy trying to make something of himself is certainly a praiseworthy gesture. Statues of Pantaleo may yet be found in orphanages throughout America. A fitting inscription, to be engraved at the base of the noble bronze head of Pantaleo, might read as follows:

"For service to one of our own, above and beyond the call of duty, in donating the welterweight championship of the world to Johnny Saxton. Disregarding his own safety and placing himself in the greatest jeopardy by inviting the wrath of 7,909 onlookers and millions of irate TViewers across the nation, Pantaleo nevertheless persevered and proved the courage of his convictions by awarding Saxton even those rounds in which he failed to throw a single punch. Hail Pantaleo, boxing's Patron Saint of Orphans!"

The cost of this charitable project will surely be underwritten by Blinky himself. It is the least he owes Honest Pete. The debt can never be paid in full.

Not to be forgotten while we hand out these skunk-cabbage bouquets is the role of Commissioner Frank Wiener, who made quite a show of rushing to and fro, exhorting the "fighters" to cease their loving embraces and affectionate staring at each other. Wiener had already distinguished himself by announcing before the weigh-in that if Gavilan came in over the official weight limit, Saxton could still win the title by winning the fight. If the Kid won, the commissioner went on to explain, the title would be declared vacant. You and I, who aren't so courant with these things, may wonder why, if Gavilan was to be asked to turn in his title, it should be handed on a silver platter to Blinky's boy, who ranked fifth in the division, below the logical contender, Carmen Basilio. The only explanation that comes readily to mind is that it was Be Kind to Saxton (and Palermo) Week, and Commissioner Wiener was getting things started early.

Not since the days when Schmeling was winning his heavyweight title while reclining on his back after an alleged low blow from Jack Sharkey, or when Carnera was receiving his crown from the benevolent Sharkey, not since those sleazy days when talking pictures and smelly fights were in flower—well, I guess what I am trying to say is that Saxton can now share with Carnera the booby prize for being the most undeserving and unwelcome champion in modern ring history.

The bloodless and—except for Gavilan's earnest final round—nearly hitless mazurka was actually a fitting climax to a prolonged shell game that really began over a year ago when Carmen Basilio knocked Gavilan down and came within a lash of depriving him of the title that had made him the assistant Presidente de Cuba. The Kid rallied to win, but the smart boys looked at each other and decided that another good fighter was showing signs of wear and tear, no disgrace after more than a decade of active campaigning against Ike Williams, Ray Robinson, Billy Graham, Johnny Bratton, Tony Janiro, Tommy Bell, Paddy Young—the best of the welterweights and middleweights throughout the forties and early fifties. When your champion begins to have trouble making the weight and his best is a year or two behind him, you look for the fattest money match over the weight. So the Kid made a pass at Bobo Olson's middleweight title, which not only produced a pleasant pay night for Gavilan, Manager Angel Lopez & Co., but postponed the agony of paring down to 147 from an aging natural weight of 155. Then, when you can no longer escape the ordeal, you naturally look for the most money combined with the easiest opponent who can pass muster as an approved contender.

Bypassing Carmen Basilio, who had been waiting nearly a year for the rematch he had earned, Angel Lopez, who does the Gavilan business, made a private deal with Blinky Palermo whereby Blinky would guarantee Angel $40,000 if the Kid would put his title up for grabs, and with Saxton how else could you describe it? It seemed strange that there should be no provision for a rematch, a customary protection for champions.

I put this down on the raised-eyebrow page of my little black suspicion book. Was it an omen? Was Gavilan so confident of winning that he disdained the usual return-match clause? Or was he getting ready to abandon the welterweight class? The Pennsylvania Commission explained that it did not permit a return-match guarantee in a title fight. But after the what-shall-we-call-it, when Gavilan flew into a dressing-room rage and cried robbery, Lopez insisted that there had been a return-match guarantee after all. A secret agreement between him and Blinky. Seems as if there were as many secret agreements surrounding this fight as there were around the Treaty of Versailles. But Commissioner Christenberry cracked his whip for Basilio, somewhat belatedly, and said Saxton would have to meet the free-swinging Syracuse No. 1 boy within ninety days if he wanted to be recognized as champion in New York.

Was Gavilan really jobbed out of his title, as he so tearfully claimed, and was it a Carbo-Palermo double play? Paul John (Frankie) Carbo (not unacquainted with murder and commonly described as the undercover owner of Gavilan and dozens of other high-ranking fighters) had worked with Blinky before. They had been pointed out as the background figures the night Blinky's Billy Fox "knocked out" Jake LaMotta, said to carry the Carbo colors in the grand stakes. Christenberry, in a survey of boxing that will bear rereading, described Blinky as "next to Carbo the most notorious character in the combine." Why did Carbo and Palermo have dinner together at Dempsey's restaurant a few nights before the Gavilan-Saxton? And what was Paul John, alias Frankie, celebrating in a Philadelphia hotel after the Gavilan-Saxton?

These were some of the inevitable, unanswered questions as the song was ended but the aroma lingered on.

The fight itself was not fixed, in the opinion of this trusting soul. I can't get into the tail-chaser about who won which rounds because after the second I started scoring it with an N for nothin' happened. Saxton is a nothing-happens fighter who has perpetrated this sort of thing throughout his curious career. Two of his Garden fights were thrown out as no contests, although the Minelli mess somehow went into the record books as a KO for Saxton. Like this most recent fight, and the kazat-zky before it with Johnny Bratton, the only beating was the one inflicted on the spectators.

Gavilan was an aging twenty-eight, weakened from weight making, rusty from a six-month layoff, rarely using his injured right hand, and frustrated by a well-conditioned and accomplished spoiler. The Cuban was no longer the flashy Keed who fought in theatrical but effective spurts, incredibly hard to hurt and almost always good to watch. In recent years the spurts were shorter, the coasting periods longer. Came a night when the good fighter couldn't fight, especially in there with a stiff who wouldn't fight. Kid couldn't; Johnny wouldn't—that's the story if you only had money enough for a four-word telegram. The fix didn't have to be in. The fates have put the fix in, helped along by the wiles of Mr. Blinky and the Gavilan piecemen when they conspired to match a no-longer-boring-in Kid with an always-boring Saxton.

If Pantaleo had been a real referee instead of what he was, he would have bounced them both out of the ring after eight rounds and advised the abused paying customers to ask for their money back. Gavilan didn't earn his 40 Gs and Saxton didn't earn his championship of the world. If it had to be judged as a fight I would have called it for Gavilan because 1) you can have more fun in Havana than you can in Philadelphia and 2) Gavilan has been pretty great and deserves better than to blow his title in a hometown sleight-of-hand and 3) the Kid came on to win the last round in something like his old style, shaking Saxton up and providing the only real action in the fight. All the rest of the action was handled by the books, who were swamped with Saxton money throughout the day.

I don't know about the other ruling bodies, but the Schulberg Boxing Commission, which headquarters in New Hope, Pennsylvania, but has no working agreement with Frank Wiener, refuses to recognize Saxton as champion. It saw with its own eyes such welterweight worthies as Jackie Fields, Young Jack Thompson, Young Corbett III, Jimmy McLarnin, Barney Ross, Henry Armstrong, Fritzie Zivic, Ray Robinson— yes, and Kid Gavilan. In deference to these real champions, we declare the title vacant.

The Gavilan-Saxton turkey trot deserves a thorough airing. In fact, it may be time to ask again, as responsible sportswriters have been asking so long, whether boxing is going to be a legitimate sport or a dirty business? Jim Norris, the personable president of the IBC, as an honorable man and a true fight fan, should welcome an investigation of the dark underside of boxing. It can destroy the sport as the Black Sox conspiracy might have ruined baseball if an effective commission had not been set up to protect our pastime from its inside jobbers. To say this is not to attack boxing but to attack the boxing racket.

The boxing managers have their guild; the IBC is a powerful network of promoters from New York to San Francisco; even the veteran boxers are getting together. Maybe it's time to launch the Association for the Protection of the Poor Put-upon Fight Fan. The APPPFF. The middle P's don't stand for Palermo or Pantaleo. Won't stand for them, in fact.

[November 1954]

129

The Death of Boxing?

WAS THERE REALLY a *second* Sonny Liston–Floyd Patterson fight? In the rear of my station wagon lies a poster, already curling and fading with age, heralding that event or fiasco or nightmare miasma for the 22nd of July, 1963, in the sacred city of Las Vegas, mecca for thousands of religious fanatics who come to worship their ritual numbers, that first sweet 7, bountiful 11, and magical 21, and to exorcise the devils, snake-eyes 2, crap-out 7, and there-you-go-again 22.

You heard me, pal. Vegas. Where else but in that razzle-dazzle capital of Suckerland could you fill a large hall for a rematch of the felling of an apprehensive, thoroughly rehabilitated delinquent by a very tough prison-hardened man? With my faded poster five months out of date, I'm no longer sure if I really made the pilgrimage from my home in Mexico City to see that phantom fight. Vaguely I recall buying a seat on a plane destined for Las Vegas, but in retrospect no such geographical complex exists. I do not expect to find it again in the rolling sagebrush desert of the Southwest, but if your friendly gasoline station has added a handy road map of Dante's Inferno, you might come upon it suddenly on one of the lower levels. In that blistering July, had I been a victim of a Sodom-and-Gomorrah dream as I wandered between the bizarre training camps over which an angry, glowering Liston presided at the Thunderbird Hotel while the pensive, introspective Patterson showed his talent for speed of hand and melancholy interviews at the Dunes? Like the Sands, the Sahara, the Riviera, and the other sunless pleasure domes spread garishly along the Strip, the gladiators' headquarters were giant, nonstop gambling casinos that join hipster and square in a fevered fraternity devoted to sex-substitute games of chance played with round-the-clock patience and sublimated desperation.

As had been my avocation and *afición* for decades, I had come early to the fight grounds to study the contending champions as they prepared themselves for the impending conflict that was to decide the fistfighting championship of the world. I had watched the mighty Brown Bomber in poker-faced training at primitive resort camps, the rugged Marciano in his humble farmhouse isolated from the exhausting rounds of recreational activities at Grossinger's, the silky moves of Ezzard Charles in pastel sweatsuit at Kutscher's luxurious *Gemütlichkeit* in the Catskills . . . I thought I had seen the ultimate in exotic grooming for combat when Ingemar Johansson, the Swedish glass-jawed krone pincher, took over a superplush ranchhouse at Grossinger's and feasted on sumptuous smorgasbord and inept light-heavyweight imports from Stockholm.

But the training for the brief encounter perpetrated in Syndicateville, U.S.A., last summer—well, in the spirit of the wheel, the hole card, and the hard eight I'll risk a lowly dollar chip to a hundred-dollar blue that Vegas in July housed the goddamnedest training a fight buff ever or rather never hoped to see.

The ring has had its icon smashers, so gifted they were able to flout the physical demands of the sport, sharpening their reflexes and honing their muscles not in rigid training camps but in bistro and brothel. One of the great bareknuckle fighters of the early nineteenth-century London prize ring, Jewish lightweight Dutch Sam, boasted that he trained on gin. His son and worthy heir, Young Dutch Sam, scourge of the little 'uns, ran with the dandies to an early grave. In our fathers' day there was Harry Greb, the illustrious noncelibate who defied the taboos against *la dolce vita* on the eve of battle. The gin mills and the boudoirs were the Human Windmill's gymnasiums. Proximity as well as nature seemed to shape "Two-Ton" Tony Galento until any resemblance to a beer barrel was not coincidental.

Despite these playboys of the Western ring, there remains a traditional preparation for fisticuffing, a rigorous program of self-denial. The ground rules of this strenuous game have demanded over the centuries that the contenders retire to rustic retreats to devote themselves to the hard labor of running and bending and sparring and thinking. During this period of the hair shirt and the liniment rub, the pugilist was not only denied the joy of entering woman, he was rarely even permitted the preliminary joy of girl-watching. The true practitioner was a fastidious ascetic whose physical energies were turned inward, flowing back into himself, like a mighty river that reverses its current and pours upward into its headwaters. Thus, according to the mythodology of this ancient, noble sport, the pugilist does not dissipate his energies. He conditions his muscles, he builds his stamina, and from his self-imposed isolation he draws concentration and pent-up emotion ready to explode at the opening bell. The sex act is sublimated, its art and energies rerouted. The man intact, this reservoir of bone and flesh and nerve and blood, is ready to release full-force its dammed-up excitations.

Old wives' tale or physiological truth, the school of the abstemious has ruled the prize ring. Trainers of Primo Carnera used to laugh at their practical joke of tying a string around Carnera's penis while he slept so that an erotic dream would tighten the string, painfully, awakening him before a wasteful release of dammed-up energy. In poor Primo's case it was a futile precaution. Primo was as ponderous and helpless as a dinosaur. He came into the ring as Samson shorn. He was the champion who sprang full and overgrown from the fertile mind of the mob. The mob giveth and there stood, in all his bogus glory, the innocent champion Carnera. The mob taketh away, and there lay the broken body of the hapless giant. Today Primo is to be found in the happy hunting ground of wrestling, where they need to tie no strings around human appendages, since it is merely a marionette show for slaphappy sadists, with hidden strings and invisible wires operating life-sized muscle dolls.

But glove fighting had its dignity, at least in its finest hours, before descending into the decadence that now threatens to engulf it. One of its many attractions for me, in this impure world, was the monastic dedication. There is much about boxing that is ugly and abhorrent: the exploitation, the finagling and conniving, the shabby grifters ever ready to leech it. But the training period always had something immaculate about it, a tradition of physical discipline that conjured up Sparta and the Greek games. To watch Rocky Marciano rise at dawn brimming with good sleep and vigor, pumping his short, powerful legs over the Upper New York countryside, was an aesthetic pleasure. Similarly, in Vegas we left the crowded casino at four in the morning to drive out into the silent, night-enshrouded desert where Floyd Patterson was idyllically bedded down. The lights of the incredible gambling palaces flickered, but out at Hidden Well Ranch all was oasis serenity.

The sun was still just a promise of morning on the horizon when the gentle, unassuming Floyd strolled from his hideaway cottage, accompanied only by two strapping shepherd dogs. He tossed a red rubber ball down the dirt lane connecting the complex of ranch houses to a deserted desert road and moved with a fighter's practiced grace after it into the open desert country. He ran on and on, occasionally throwing the ball ahead of him to break the monotony of the long lonely run. Now the sun rose full but not yet hot on the desert-clean horizon and our man was silhouetted against it, jogging on with his black dog and his white dog unconsciously composing themselves into an artist's conception of how an aesthete of the prize ring should appear one week before a crucial contest. Driving alongside, slothful in a station wagon, I thought of *The Loneliness of the Long Distance Runner*. In that film, like the live drama we were watching, the preparation for the showdown was purity and grace and artfully lonely, and building to a climax that was agony and frustration, neurotic and perverse. To follow Floyd as he ran on into the rolling desert dunes in the softlit purple morning was to catch him in his proudest moment, when he was all concentrated, dedicated grace and energy. How confidently, it seemed, he paused for thirty seconds of piston-fast shadowboxing, ran backward a dozen yards and then forward again, into rising hills where our car could no longer follow, a lone figure of rare health and determination, with the big black dog and the big white dog panting with the joy of the effort and beginning to seem more tired than their poker-faced master.

Poker-faced but not a gambler, Floyd secreted himself at Hidden Well except for the training sessions staged with Vegas hoopla at the Dunes, where a thousand people a day paid their buck to applaud the quiet, modest monk working with humorless conscience to avenge the one-round humiliation he had suffered nine months earlier in Chicago. His body expressed confidence, but his mind seemed cobwebbed with complexities that should not foul the forward gear, the clear, simple thrust a pugilist—perhaps any artist or prime doer—needs to carry out his plan of action. When we asked him, for instance, if he thought Liston would knock him out again, Patterson stared at the floor and launched into a tortured paragraph replete with dependent clauses. He certainly hoped he would not be knocked out again; he would try not to enter the ring expecting to be knocked out again; however, no one can estimate in advance the effect of an opponent's blow on the brain, and it is always possible that the body wishes to react in one way while the mind, temporarily stunned or confused, reacts in another.

Before he was halfway through this convoluted oratory we

were all staring at the floor in embarrassment, feeling uncomfortably sorry for this bad boy gone good. In this modern world of contradiction and compromise you want your prizefighters strong and direct. You want a Floyd Patterson to say, "Hell no, he won't knock me out again. I come to fight. I'll beat his ass off." When we asked Sonny Liston if he thought Patterson would last longer the second time, he growled, "This time—shorter." Sonny was four seconds off the target, but they breed humanitarians in Nevada and there is a compulsory eight-second count of protection, even if the fallen fighter scrambles up to his feet before 8 as Floyd did, in his amateur eagerness to precipitate his own slaughter. From John L. Sullivan to Sonny Liston, eighty-one years and twenty-two champions, there never has been one so plagued with doubts and fears, the tentative tangle, as twice-disgraced Floyd Patterson. It is like asking Picasso if he thinks he is going to create any more immortal canvases and hearing him say, "Well, I'd like to, but when one puts his brush to canvas how does he really know whether or not the mind may misdirect it?" Or asking President Kennedy if he thinks the free world will fall and hearing him say, "Well of course we *hope* not, but who can foresee the gulf between desire and achievement?" There is an appealing integrity to self-deprecation, but it doesn't win ball games or civilizations.

Hemingway, to the point of being obnoxious, insisted on his preeminence as *numero uno*. He wasn't, always, but the thinking colored the doing. Patterson approached his Liston ordeal with a false-beard psychology. A man who hides from defeat behind a false beard has fallen, for all his virtues, into a sad state of torpor and confusion. The beard is a symbol of disguise, of trying to be something you are not, and Patterson may be boxing's first beatnik, a millionaire beatnik who makes a cult of defeatism. In his dressing room after he had again offered himself up with the resigned passivity of a human sacrifice, he sorrowfully announced that he would *not* retire, although he did not even feel worthy to challenge the loquacious upstart Cassius Marcellus Clay. Patterson should retire and cultivate his garden and his neuroses. He is fortunate that he had an honest manager, Cus D'Amato, whom he despises and whom he cut dead at Vegas. Cus did not job him out of his purses; he overprotected him like an indulgent father. As a result, Floyd is weaker and richer.

While Floyd was consulting his psyche in his desert retreat, Sonny Liston went through his violent calisthenics and cuffed his sparring partners around as if he was back schlocking recalcitrant Negro cab drivers for his old boss of the St. Louis Teamsters, John Vitale. After his workout, he would blow off a little more steam verbally abusing members of his entourage. He is an inarticulate, primitive, non-card-carrying Muslim, with a fearful suspicion of the white world and a prison-sharp "What's-in-it-for-Sonny?" philosophy. On the eve of the Vegas massacre, waiting for his call to the ring—a dressing-room companion told me later—he relaxed in contemptuous silence, sullenly clipping his nails. When it was time to move out into the aisle, he rose, stretched, and muttered, "Well, let's go down and cross the railroad tracks and stop in at the pay station."

Evening after evening, when all good fighters should be tucked into their quiet beds, Sonny would be at the crap or blackjack tables. Often Joe Louis, tragically reduced to a camp follower, would be at Sonny's side, playing for fairly large stakes with Sonny's bread. For those of us reared on the aesthetic of the ascetic, Sonny's social pattern was obscene. He is not just a naysayer but a f-u man. Shortly after training he could be seen around the Thunderbird pool ogling the Vegas bikini set. A few hours before the fight he was in the crowded restaurant of the Thunderbird casually dining with his wife. Mrs. Liston and certain small children seem genuinely fond of him, but he is the meanest and most hated man to hold the heavyweight title since Jack Johnson. He is keen-minded, illiterate, and socially scarred. The combination is apt to produce an authority-hating s.o.b. He is the only man I remember meeting who scares you with a look. There is a Father Murphy who flutters around him and is supposed to be rehabilitating him, but I think Sonny is forever trapped in his own resentment. I doubt if a million dollars will make him more lovable.

I've seen a championship provide a liberal education in social adjustment for antisocial personalities—acceptance, comfort, fame, they do work a difference. But it is sadly possible that it's too late for Sonny Liston to achieve anything more than the sodden satisfaction of clubbing men insensible with his abnormal-sized fists. In this day when the march of civil rights is raising the sights of Negro and white, Sonny is a throwback. It's not accidental that he has no connection with Birmingham and doesn't lock arms with Jackie Robinson and Belafonte and Floyd Patterson in the new civil war. Sonny marches and punches heads to his own drummer. He seems to pull his hatred around him like the toweled robe under which he flexes his massive muscles as he waits for the bell that sends him out to perform mayhem.

If Sonny Liston is the ex-con, hated, hating, the third point to the morality triangle is gaseous Cassius Clay, who talks better than he fights, a twenty-one-year-old Olympic champion who is everything that Floyd Patterson is not, brash, self-confident, flamboyant, the high-pressure supersalesman. While Sonny is the throwback, Cassius is the throw-forward. There is a great deal of talk about how much Cassius Marcellus Clay is contributing to "the game," selling out the Garden and doing for fistic glamour what poor butterfly Marilyn Monroe did for sex. The decadence that hung over the Liston-Patterson thing in Vegas pursues Cassius, our new clown prince, in another way. Cassius is tall and handsome and boyish and as articulate as a precocious college debater. He is a phrasemaker and a poetizer. In Chicago last fall he introduced himself to me as the coming champion of the world and pressed a poem into my hand predicting in eighth-grade verse his knockout triumph over Archie Moore "who will fall in four." The old Mongoose obliged, and in this day of Madison Avenue ploys a flashy near amateur became the ranking contender for Liston's title.

Cassius is as welcome to the fight game as is whipped cream to strawberry shortcake—he dresses and sweetens it up, but you know what happens when you eat too much whipped cream.

Cassius Clay is, I'm afraid, the fighter who most clearly reflects the flaws of the middle sixties. He is earning a fortune before he has mastered his trade. He may be the first fighter consciously to employ big-time advertising techniques. He is the perpetrator of both the big laugh and the big lie. Last spring in the Garden solid citizen Doug Jones exposed him as a rangy boy fast with his hands but totally ignorant of infighting and highly susceptible to a punch on the jaw. Even Patterson could beat him, and to put him in with Liston too soon may stigmatize the promoters as accessories to legalized murder.

But the big sell is on. In the days of boxing decadence Liston-Clay, with all these fancy ancillary rights, looms as the greatest spectacle since Elizabeth Taylor's entrance into Rome. Clay should prove himself against Patterson, or Eddie Machen, who went twelve against Liston with little pain. But boxing isn't that kind of sport. The fact that Machen was the logical contender catapulted him not to fame but to oblivion. Clay, green and vulnerable, is where the money is. Show business with blood demands his appearance in the arena.

In Vegas, Cassius Marcellus lay in luxury-hotel splendor at the Dunes, silk-pajamaed, attended by his brother–sparring partner Rudolph Valentino Clay. He ordered from room service like the new king of the new glamour sport of theater television he is. "How many eggs?—just get a great big platter and cover it. Bacon?—we'll take all you got down there, honey." He stretched. He laughed. It tickled him to think how quickly all this royal living had come to a poor kid from the back streets of Louisville. He called Liston a big ugly bear. He was laughing, but more about the money in his future than the fight. At ringside of the Vegas charade he climbed up to the apron and grimaced at Liston, then retreated in histrionic fear as Liston glared at him. There was a day when the heavyweight challenger carried himself with dignity. There was some sense of finality or seriousness to the affair. But sportswriters at Vegas were offended. The Louisville Lip, the self-propelled headline grabber, was making a mockery of an event that once was fought in earnest. This hamming at ringside was what the wrestlers tricked up. Next week's contestants glare and growl and maybe even take an openhanded poke at each other. Boy oh boy oh boy, the announcer licks his chops, these two brutes really hate each other. Fur is really going to fly, not to mention blood 'n' gore, when these two get a chance to settle their feud a week from tonight. . . . That's what Cassius Clay, who couldn't really lick Doug Jones and almost got knocked out by England's "Slow-Motion" Henry Cooper, is bringing to boxing. He may be selling a lot of tickets, but Elvis Presley brings a lot of money into the movie theaters and he acts about as well as Cassius Clay fights. Which is not to say that Cassius is a bad fighter. He is simply a promising, inexperienced boy, speedy of hand and foot, blasted off to stardom in an era when propaganda takes precedence over performance. Because boxing is basic and strips man down to his essentials, it has been a simple but effective measuring stick of social progress and retrogression. It has been a barometer of racial status. The Irish, the Jews, the Negroes, the Latin minorities have all dominated the sport in their upward struggle toward social acceptance. Now Cassius Clay beats his big drums and rolls his clever snares, singing songs not his mother but Mad Ave and the sellout wrestling prima donnas taught him. It may be telltale and ironic that the biggest pay night in the history of boxing looms in the same year that sees a mob-shadowed brute pitted against a salesman-boxer who is helping to transform the old game into the sappy circus for cheap-thrill seekers that wrestling has become.

As I returned last summer from that desert netherworld where Sonny Liston defied the old-fashioned rules of asceticism, and ascetic Floyd Patterson crapped out again, I wondered if boxing, in the hands of incompetents like the Nilons or opportunists like Roy Cohn, could survive. By coincidence my brother Stuart was producing-directing an hour TV special for David Brinkley on this very subject and our paths crossed at Vegas. He had interviewed Governor Brown of California who thought boxing should be abolished, and Norman Mailer who thought boxing should go back to bareknuckle to-a-finish brutality as an outlet for man's pent-up hostility, and Jersey Joe Walcott who saw boxing as an answer to the hungers of the underprivileged. I agreed and disagreed with all of them, and told my brother:

I've been a boxing fan for forty years. I find in no other sport the human drama, the intense interplay of individual skill, courage, and, yes, intelligence. A good boxing match—this may sound extreme—is not so different from a game of chess, only fists are moved instead of chess pieces, and in lieu of a board the game is played out on the human face, the human body. Man, shucked down to his basic materials, plays this dangerous game in the prize ring for million-dollar stakes.

But for all the great fighters who have earned millions, or attracted millions of dollars to the box office, how many retired millionaires do we find? Gene Tunney. Maybe with luck Floyd Patterson. A precious favored few. From the other end of the pugilistic telescope we find thousands of boxing's forgotten men. Some were champions like Beau Jack, a Horatio Alger hero in reverse—from eighteen-year-old shoeshine boy to forty-three-year-old shoeshine boy. Beyond the crown and the glory and the headlines and the all-time box-office record for Madison Square Garden, boxing's Metropolitan Opera House, lay humiliation and poverty. If Beau Jack were an isolated case, you might say Tough Luck—but this is much more than tough luck. For thousands of fighters, good fighters, winners—in the ring—wind up losers in life. Beau Jack, Johnny Saxton, Billy Fox, Johnny Bratton—no use to call the whole sad roll. They are meaningless ciphers to those who don't care for fights—and they are just as meaningless to those who know their names all too well but never gave a damn for their welfare or their future. Look at Benny Paret, the brave illiterate whom Emile Griffith killed in the ring for the welterweight championship. You can make a case for that death as a terrible accident. But try to make a case for the fortune that was stolen from Paret while he was shedding his blood for public amusement. Purses totaling $100,000 should have been coming to Benny during his twenty-fifth and last year on this earth. He should have amassed a small fortune. Like Beau Jack's millions, where did it go? Beau Jack, back at a shoeshine stand, where he started, would like to know. Mrs. Paret, living in a Harlem tenement with her small sons, is penniless, bitter, bewildered. The Sonny Listons playing the big chips at the Vegas tables, and the Cassius Clays in their fire-engine-red Cadillacs, reach out eager hands for all our materialistic goodies. But for every Liston there's an overmatched corpse like the late Ernie Knox, and for every Clay who flexes lovely muscles for his mirror and chortles in animal confidence, "I'm beeootiful," there's a basket case like the once-beautiful Lavorante, packed home to live out his vegetable years in Mendoza, Argentina, which, oddly, was the home I had chosen for my fictional, ruined giant, Toro Molina, in *The Harder They Fall*.

My forty years as a fight fan have been clouded with doubts and questions. When I published that boxing novel, the fight world—not all, but a vociferous and probably guilty minority—attacked me for what they thought was my effort to knock the fight game out of the box. The abolitionists thought they had an ally in me. But my real interest was to point up the plight of the neglected fighter—champion or club fighter—squeezed dry and then tossed on the dump heap, human refuse, expendable. The Beau Jacks, the champions shuffling out their lives as janitors, the basket cases like the unfortunate Lavorante, are a measure of boxing's dismal, unforgivable, perhaps fatal failure to provide for its own. It has been a gutter sport, a jungle sport, in which not the devil but degrading poverty takes the hindmost. There shouldn't be, there needn't be any hindmost for a boxer whose skill and guts and willingness to entertain have earned him hundreds of thousands, even millions of dollars in the ring.

Of all our athletes the boxer is the most exposed, the least protected. I'm not speaking now of an extra rope to the ring or more padding in their gloves. I'm speaking of more padding in their lives. Long-range protection. A ballplayer enjoys a retirement pension. A motion-picture veteran can turn to the Motion Picture Relief Fund, the M.P. Home. For half a century the fight game has cried out for these simple humanitarian needs. Think what just 1 percent of the gross of all fights over the years could contribute to the welfare, the survival of men who have given their youth, their health, sometimes their lives to boxing. A fund from which they could borrow in the difficult period of adjustment after retirement. A home for the mentally affected, the physically disabled. A pension to cushion old age. For years these reforms have gone crying into the wind. Too often in the hands of greedy men who treat fighters as chattel, in the hands of racketeers—or those contaminated by the American sickness of *what's in it for me?*—the fight game, despite the Floyd Pattersons, the Rocky Marcianos, and other happy examples of security, has been the slum of the sports world, and the boxers all too often are the athlete orphans of the Western world.

Boxing doesn't need politicians like Governor Brown to abolish it. It will abolish itself if it persists in its program of anarchy, chaos, and criminal neglect of the thousands who turn to it for escape from the dark corner of discrimination and want in which they find themselves trapped. I hope, for selfish reasons, because I enjoy it, that boxing is not abolished. I'd miss it, the brave, classic encounters. But I would rather miss it, see it abolished, than have it continue down the downward path to Beau Jack's shoeshine stand or the asylum where Billy Fox sleeps his troubled empty dreams. Boxing is at the crossroads—either it lifts itself or is lifted to some standard of conscience and regard for the boys on whom it feeds, or it will be nine, ten, and out, having lost through apathy and inhumanity its right to survive.

[January 1964]

142

The Chinese Boxes
of Muhammad Ali

CASSIUS MARCELLUS CLAY was minus six when quietly invincible Joe Louis was demolishing Max Schmeling and sending him on his shield to the land of the self-styled master race. The Joe Louis of Clay's childhood was another man, a balding, overweight ex-champion getting a boxing lesson from Ezzard Charles and a pathetic thumping from Marciano. Manager-trainer Angelo Dundee, a fixture in Cassius's corner from the first fight to the last, remembers Clay as a bubbling sixteen-year-old bouncing into the Louisville gym and begging to put on the gloves with Angelo's flashy light-heavyweight Willie Pastrano. Flying up from Ali's training quarters last March for the latest and greatest Fight of the Century, Angelo reminisced about his champion. In his voice was the awe one reserves for first meetings with the gods.

"There was something special about him even then," Dundee remembered. "Something about the way he moved, like the song says. Something about the way he talked. He's learned a lot, traveling around the world, being with people—he really feeds off people—little people, big people—that's his college. He doesn't learn from books—truth is he never really learned to read, but he sucks up knowledge, information, ideas like an elephant sucks up water. And he trumpets it all out just like an elephant, too."

"Do you go along with Ali's description of Ali? Is he the most unusual fighter you ever handled?"

Over the big Cuban cigar in the small Groucho Marx–like face the answer poured forth without a second's hesitation. "Not just a fighter, he's the most unusual human being, the most fascinating person I ever met—period."

In those hectic days before and after "The Fight"—the most widely attended single event in the history of the world—we were to enjoy an intimate look at the man who created the first $20 million rumble through the force of two unique qualities: his physical coordination and his metaphysical personality. A personality as changeable as a March weather report, a psyche simple one moment, complex the next, loving, suspicious, over-generous, self-protective, with flashes of brilliance lighting a dense thunder sky. We were privileged to sit with him in his introspective moments, get caught with him in the midst of crowds that threatened to crush him to death with their love, watch him handle rival hangers-on with the delicacy of a born diplomat, and see him swing from playful child to a man under all the pressures our hyped-up sports world and superstate Pentagon can bring to bear on a quixotic and sensitive nature.

We have said with conceit (in the old-fashioned sense) and also with conviction that, just as a people get the government they deserve, so each period in our history seems to create the heavyweight champion it needs to express itself on the plat-form where body language and social currents fuse. This seems to have been true of every true knight we have studied in the lists from American slavery's heavyweight champion Tom Molineaux upward. But never has there been a prize-fighter who seemed so to our manner born as Cassius Marcel-lus Clay a.k.a. Muhammad Ali. His career began, appropri-ately, in 1960, in the Camelot days, in the time of the Kennedys that welcomed the decade, promised it hope, and asked for sacrifices in exchange for solutions. The New Frontier. Already antique, the words ring with the sound of pewter respectfully aged and polished for Sunday visitors. Imagine a time before the Bay of Pigs, before Dallas, before Watts, before the attempted Americanization of Indochina, before assassination became an annual horror, Medgar Evers, John Kennedy, Malcolm X, Martin Luther King, Bobby Kennedy. . . . Before the credibility gap of LBJ. Before the Chicago Convention, before Kent State and Jackson State. Before Nixon promised to get us out of the war by invading Cambodia and Laos and North Vietnam.

As our only world-famous athlete of the Shook-Up Decade just past, C.M.C. a.k.a. M.A. received into his beautiful black body every one of the poisoned arrows mentioned above. Wounded by all those arrows of our social misfortune, he refused to die. Hate him for this or despise him for that, he is still our youth, our conscience, our Mark Twain of bitterness and laughter. Of all our champions, gloved and bareknuckled, from the end of the eighteenth century to the dawn of the twenty-first, he is, in his own words, "the most unusual." Taunted by the ofays, Jack Johnson taunted back. Accepted by whites who offered him the national laurels and social responsibilities that came with the championship, Joe Louis accepted back. Never quite an Uncle Tom, he was the Good Joe who knew his place. He was the hero but never the author of his allegory.

But the sixties were a whole different number. In a time of prodigies turning on their dads—or rather, tuning out their daddies—ready for the bell, ready to take on all comers in and out of the ring, was that prodigious brown descendant of Henry Clay: Cassius Marcellus Clay, the Fifth Beatle. Before we were prepared for impact—but what were we prepared for in innocent 1960?—the loud laughing mouth in the handsome Greek god of a head was shouting, "Here I come, ready or not!" And who except his fellow teen-agers could have been ready for the innovative style that was to revolutionize not only the heavyweight division but the heavy social order that it entertained?

Watching him dance around the best and biggest of the amateurs on his way to AAU and Golden Gloves titles, *cognoscenti* of the game were more amused than impressed. A heavyweight who prances around the ring like a lightweight? Look at the way he bends his dancer's waist backward to avoid being hit! A tough pro would move in and break his back when he pulled that kid stuff. That just ain't the way a heavyweight fights. But this was more than fast tactical footwork; it was excessive mobility, sometimes physically unnecessary, a new psychological weapon—hit and run, jab and dance, befuddle, frustrate, and tire the enemy before zeroing in.

Beatle V had begun to create his own pop culture in the ring. Archetype of the young athlete in the Age of Aquarius, he bounced happily to Rome for the 1960 Olympics, dazzling foreign challengers who could not believe a six-foot-three-inch will-o'-the-wisp. Or a bronze Mercury, for the eighteen-year-old original convinced an adoring audience that he was that earlier Roman deity incarnate, combining speed and grace with eloquence, wit, and a mysterious elegance.

Home to Louisville he came wearing his gold medal and his boyish grin, and the white world seemed united with the black in agreement with his own efflorescent image of himself: the prettiest, the wittiest, the greatest. He strutted the streets of his hometown and paused to admire his reflection in storefront windows. "Look at me—I'm beautiful! An' I'm gonna stay pretty cuz there ain't a fighter on earth fast enough t' hit me!" Then he would dance and throw his lightning combinations into the air, or in the direction of a half-scared, half-awed ten-year-old black brother—he has always been drawn to kids, and especially black kids, though this was still 1960 and the pattern was all ego-popping ebullience, a narcissism that might have been irritating but that was instead irresistible because it was so utterly without guile, because it spoke to you with the directness of the wild rose who says, "Look at me, am I not

146

beauty? Inhale me, am I not perfume?" You could no more resent the natural arrogance of the rose than you could the in-
souciant "Look, Ma, I'm dancin'!" of young Cassius Marcellus.
Of course a rose also has thorns, weapons concealed for its protection. That might have been a warning as to the deeper nature of the brown deity preparing for his pivotal role in the epic
drama of the sixties.

Scene 1, Act I, was deceptively harmonious, as truly made
epic dramas demand, festooned with integrated hero worship
and gratitude seemingly requited.

A group of well-to-do Louisville sports puts its money where
its local pride is and sets up a syndicate to sponsor Cassius's
professional career. In return for half the anticipated profits, it
pays him a comfortable weekly salary, with a down payment
on a tangerine-colored Cadillac, the first of a long line of exotic
chariots. His first pro test is a win over a tough white sheriff,
Tunney Hunsaker. Clay's fights are performances—put-ons
with blood. As he moves up into the big time, he rhymes his
predictions—"Archie Moore will fall in four"—and the ancient
light heavyweight, almost thirty years older than the quick-
footed bard, suffers the prophecy.

Next we see Clay at, of all places, The Bitter End, a hip
Greenwich Village launching pad for avant-garde talent,
where he sports a new tuxedo to engage in poetry competition
with a lineup of Ezra-Pounded bards, grooving to his impending Garden bout with tough and highly rated Doug Jones. In a
style all his own—call it an infectious boxing supplement to
the anti-over-thirty spirit of the oncoming youth style—he
laughs off all the old champions. Who's Liston? Louis who? To
a generation splitting from its elders and their traditions, he's
"The Greatest." Under that title he cuts a record of chatter,
doggerel, and song, and long before the hard-eyed experts of
the ring think he's championship material or ready for Terrible Sonny Liston, his LP is discovered by teen-agers, including
my sons, who find in his uninhibited ego-tripping nonsense
that indescribable pleasure of being different from us, yes, and

better than us. When my younger son was playing Clay's platter for the third consecutive time, I tried to cross-examine him as to what was so great about "The Greatest."

Across the generation net the answer was slapped back into my court in impatient monosyllables, "I dunno, Pop. I jus' dig 'im. I think he's cool. I dig the way he dances around those older fighters and makes 'em miss. And the way he rhymes and picks the round. He makes it more fun than in your day. And he's not a hypocrite. He knows he's 'The Greatest.' So why not say it? Why be a hypocrite? Be honest."

We retreated strategically, doing a verbal imitation of Cassius's defensive backbend, sensing the chronological lightning crackling in the atmosphere. We closed his bedroom door, and he went on singing along with Clay. The message was clear: The jib of "our" athletic heroes was cut to modesty. To every age its style, and "ours" (if we had to be consigned to the past) was for winners to hang their heads in mock self-deprecation. "Well, those guys in front of me opened up a pretty good hole and I just ran to daylight and got lucky, I guess." Did we ever hear a broken-field runner telling the press, "Look, I'm so shifty and so fast, it's impossible for the defense to lay a hand on me"? It's true that Joe Louis was asked one too many times how he expected to handle Billy Conn's speed and boxing ability; but when the fight was over, and the job accomplished, it simply wasn't Louis's or "our" style to speak the exuberant truth: "Look, I tried to tell you how great I was, and you chumps wouldn't listen. There's never been anything like me in the history of the world."

Truth, man. Don't hide behind a lot of well-gee-whizzes like your daddies. Come to think of it, a whole new generation coming of age in the early sixties thought of the preceding generation as slower, dumber, less musical, less honest, more hung-up, less where-it's-at. Every generation wants to devour its predecessor, and we have only to go back two generations to conjure the Jazz Age of Fitzgerald and *College Humor* when bare knees, rumble seats, ukuleles, bathtub gin, wild parties, and free verse were creating a new life-style almost as horrifying to the people who grew up in the nineteenth century as the present youth culture is to the parents of Woodstock Nation. The key to that sentence is *almost*. Maybe it's because we're still going through it, but the intensity with which that Now generation wants to rip off daddy and mommy (*vide:* the latest "youth-oriented" epic at your neighborhood moviehouse) makes the Scott-Zelda rebellion seem as dangerous as a game of Post Office.

If the child of our times carries a flower in one hand and a stick of dynamite in the other, it is because he is an Oedipus who has read one book too many of Marcuse (or Che or Fanon) and is ready to lay down his guitar and his strobe light to fight for something he defines dimly but deafeningly demands—a better world, an environment that will contain and harmonize our nuclear genius.

And where does this bring Cassius Clay (as he still called himself in his antechampion days)? To Las Vegas in the hot July of 1963. President Kennedy is still safely in the White House. There are some fifteen thousand U.S. Army "advisers" still noncombatant in Vietnam. Liston, first a homeless St. Louis waif, then a tough old jailbird, later a Teamster goon, is heavyweight champion of the world. Yet to burst on the American consciousness is a black intelligence burning with scorn for "the collective white men" and "the so-called American Negro"—Malcolm X.

Cassius Clay has come to Vegas as the heir apparent to the heavyweight throne. He has just butchered the British and Empire champion, Henry Cooper, in five rounds after having been saved by the bell himself at the end of four. Proximity to disaster hasn't dampened Cassius Clay's love affair with Cassius Clay. "He thrives on the precipice," says faithful Angelo Dundee. "He could give Norman Vincent Peale lessons on the power of positive thinking." And it's true that the clout of the Cooper hook that put him down has served only to convince young Clay that the most powerful punch in the world can deflect him but momentarily from his climb to the top of the mountain. He is twenty-one years old, and one of his room- mates is Destiny. The other is his brother Rudolph Valentino Clay.

When David Brinkley and his TV producer, Stuart Schul- berg, call on the Clay brothers, they find them stretched out on their luxurious beds, bare-chested and barefooted, wearing ex- pensive slacks. "Da-vid Brinkley!" Cassius cries out, in that natural comedy style that makes his emphatic pronunciation of names laugh-provoking without being insulting. "Da-vid Brinkley, you're my man!" Cassius is on the phone to room ser- vice ordering breakfast. "Orange juice, a couple of jugs, a box of corn flakes. And milk. Can you send three quarts? And eggs— scramble up a nice batch for us, say about two dozen? Two or three rashers of bacon and a loaf of toast. What, service for six? No, ma'am, this is breakfast for two!" The recent conqueror of the British Empire and his brother Rudolph Valentino fill the room with their laughter. Then Cassius turns to Brinkley with those large eyes framed like a movie star's between butterfly brows and high cheekbones. "Say, David, will you do me a favor, let's do the 'good nights' together." And the super- charged contender lapses into a more than passable imitation of Chet Huntley. "This is Cassius Marcellus Clay in Las Vegas. Good night, David." And Brinkley responds in his patented sign-off. "And this is David Brinkley. Good night, Cassius." Clay breaks up. He pounds his brother in joy. "Hey, David, that's out of sight!"

Watching him roll his marvelous brown body and bark with laughter like a frolicking young sea lion, who would guess that this would be the same man who was soon to frighten, infuri- ate, and finally confront the white power structure of America? But looking back on the twenty-one-year-old Cassius with the hindsight gained from observing and visiting with the twenty- nine-year-old Ali, we now know that within the beamish boy who bantered with Brinkley lurked the racial anxiety, produc- ing anger as causatively as boiling water releases steam. We follow joyously flamboyant Cassius Clay through his visit to Vegas for the Liston-Patterson "fight." And since everything about the transformation of Cassius the Caterpillar into Muhammad the Butterfly is instructive, we wonder at the meaning of his existential acts. He invades the casino where Liston is playing blackjack, calls him an ugly bear, invites him to an impromptu match to settle the title here and now, laughs at the scowl that had frozen the blood of men who had thought themselves brave.

Onlookers were merely amused by the brash kid with the big mouth who seemed to have borrowed his publicity buildups from the wrestlers' division of the classical school of acting. What was dangerous about Cassius was not immediately appreciated: the intensity, the concentration, the determination with which he played. It was this that separated the fools of Shakespeare from mere Middle Ages merrymakers. Wise kings listened to inspired fools while foolish kings laughed at the exterior apparatus of their jokes.

The best of fools was a set of delicate Chinese boxes, and just such a fool was Brother Malcolm's "so-called American Negro," a series of ingeniously fitted personalities, each larger one concealing and protecting a smaller one within until you finally come to the true resilient core. Many hundreds of years of slavery and now more than a century of hypocritical "freedom"—a democracy with the black man still locked into the steaming cities while the white man retreats from his day's work to the flowering suburbs—this is the historical imbalance that conditions all but the most profoundly integrated (or whitened, Ali might say today) black man to take refuge in his Chinese boxes as a fox hides in the hedge from the hounds.

I may have more black friends than 95 percent of white Americans, and sometimes I feel I have succeeded in reaching the box within the box within the box—but I never leave the room without a feeling that the brothers left together will now continue to remove black Chinese box after Chinese box until at last they are left sitting around in their naked souls, like a game of spiritual strip poker that reveals all to each, an exclusive deal played in a private club off limits even to sympathetic white players who would win the game.

What has all this to do with Cassius Clay in pursuit of Liston's title and his subsequent odyssey? To our minds, a great deal. We are preparing ourselves not to be surprised when a young man, making of each boxing bout his parable, exchanges one image for another as dramatically but also as easily as an actor changes costumes between scenes.

And make no mistake about it, they were scenes in a drama that young Cassius knew he was playing, an allegory in the Brechtian manner that he was consciously authoring and acting out. On many different levels—the physical, the psychical, the religio-political. From his training camp for the first Liston fight Cassius waged an intense campaign of psychological warfare. The old bus Cassius had bought to move his entourage was painted red and white with "World's Most Colorful Fighter" emblazoned across the top, and covered with signs broadcasting his low opinion of the champion: Bear Hunting Season. Liston Will Fall in Eight. Big Ugly Bear. . . . Cassius would invade Liston's training camp, hose him with a torrent of insults and threats—poetically alone in America in thinking he could supplant the brooding, dangerous Sonny, who was expected to spank the obstreperous Cassius as a stern papa would whup a wayward son. The odds on Liston were 8 to 1. Of the press who were on the scene from every continent, we remember not one who gave the strident challenger a chance.

But Angelo Dundee, who somehow managed to remain uninvolved in the psychological high jinks and the gathering morality play, had warned us that Cassius had the style to outbox and defeat the ponderous, aging Liston. An odd group had believed in Cassius Clay. Our teen-aged son David, who sent me twenty-five dollars he had saved from allowances to bet on youth vs. age; Drew "Bundini" Brown, an ancient mariner and saloon-keeper with a gift of gab, almost as seven-tongued as Cassius, who was called "assistant trainer" but was really the guru-in-residence; and an unobtrusive black man who was quite possibly the most remarkable man, black or white, then living in America. This was the acknowledged spokesman for blackness in Harlem, the scourge of Uncle Toms and Negro civil rights leaders who spoke of integration and gradual improvements. This was the rising star of black militancy, the ex-hoodlum, thief, dope peddler, and pimp who finally, through the teaching of Elijah Muhammad, had come to understand his life of ghetto hustling as the painful preparation for his eventual role as liberator of his more than twenty million brothers suffering a living genocide in white America. Born Malcolm Little, he was known in the street as Big Red before he became even better known as Malcolm X.

In tracing two centuries of major prizefights, we can see how inextricably they are woven into our social fabric. From Molineaux to Louis, our champions were heroes of related acts that served as parables of cultural change. But B.C., Before Clay, they had only dimly recognized their roles. Now it was A.D., After Dallas, which Malcolm X had called "America's chickens come home to roost." There was a keen black hatred of all white institutions in Malcolm's mind when he made the statement that Elijah used as the official reason for silencing him, pending his excommunication from the Black Church. The headline, seemingly a crass postmortem on the catastrophe in Dallas, had been taken from a context in which Malcolm had been discussing the atmosphere of racial hatred and social violence that the white man had created in America, a rabid intolerance that finally had struck down the Chief of State himself. This was too tragically true. A liberal white President had no business driving in an open car through a hate-filled Texas city where his enemies were articulate and armed. Camelot was in ruins, the boiling volcano in Harlem was getting ready to erupt again, and Malcolm X, in the moment of greatest travail in a life that sensitively reflected all the nightmare distortions of the American dream, was counseling the

153

challenger along lines either totally unfamiliar or anathema to the sports world.

Malcolm was not a fight fan; indeed he hardly knew who Cassius was when he met him and Rudolph at the Detroit mosque several years before. Cassius impressed him then simply as a likable, friendly, clean-cut, down-to-earth youngster with a contagious quality.

But in The Fight of 1964, Malcolm was convinced that Cassius had invited him to Miami to help the young fighter prove to the world the superiority of Islam over a white Christianity that had brainwashed the Negro community to accept inferior status and servitude. Molineaux had fought merely with his fists. Johnson had fought with his mocking smile and his wicked tongue. Cassius would fight with weapons never before carried into an American ring, his faith in a non-Western religion, as well as his growing awareness that, while he might be part of a minority 10 percent in the United States, he was also part of a global family of nonwhites among whom Caucasians were in turn a minority doomed to eventual defeat. While Cassius was rattling his bear trap and playing the loud-mouthed fool, while white Miami was either disgusted or entertained by this shrill showboating, a new philosophical and social confrontation was taking place that would prove as crucial to the middle sixties as was the Louis-Schmeling debate to the late thirties.

"This fight is the truth," Malcolm told Cassius. "It's the Cross and the Crescent fighting in a prize ring—for the first time. It's a modern crusade—a Christian and a Muslim facing each other with television to beam it off Telstar for the whole world to see what happens." The mystical reformed master hustler with the razor-blade mind was convinced that Allah had brought Cassius to this moment in order to prove something to black men with stunted egos who thought they needed white spiritual advisers.

Those who attended the wildest weigh-in in the history of the heavyweight division thought that Cassius was more in need of psychiatric than spiritual assistance. Minutes before he burst into the ring at the Miami Beach auditorium we could hear the threatened promise of his arrival, like thunder before a storm. Then he and Bundini exploded into view, furiously pounding canes in angry rhythms on the floor and shouting their tribal slogan, "We're coming to rumble. . . . Float like a butterfly—sting like a bee! Where's the ugly bear? . . ." For an hour the demonstration went on, with Cassius screaming, lunging at Liston, shaking his fists, bulging his eyes. Cool and seasoned Jesse Abramson of the *New York Herald-Tribune*, trained to report without involving his emotions, was for the first time shaken at a weigh-in. "I think they should call it off," he said to us. "He's in no condition to fight tonight." Most experts decided that Cassius was terrified and suffering from manic hysteria at the prospect of having to enter the ring with the dour-faced champion. Liston did his best to fix him with "the look," a baleful stare he had perfected during many years in prison. But Cassius would not be transfixed like Floyd Patterson. Screaming like a banshee, pounding the stage with his feet as if possessed, he kept up this bizarre performance until his blood pressure had bubbled over the 200 mark and observers were convinced that the next stop was the psychiatric ward.

While reporters were asking the local boxing commissioners if they were considering calling off this unequal contest between a seasoned old champion and this hysterical boy, Cassius was back at his motel being examined by Dr. Ferdie Pacheco, who found his blood pressure miraculously normal. "A case of self-induced hysteria," diagnosed Pacheco. As Malcolm said, it was a case of mind over matter. There wasn't a man in the world Sonny Liston was afraid of. But was this towering dark screamer a human being or a whirling dervish?

What we were seeing, along with all the other innovations Cassius was bringing to the climactic ritual of the heavyweight championship, were the new tactics of confrontation politics. Already a cult figure to the young, he was applying to the traditional ceremony of the ring the outlandish behavior of an Abbie Hoffman, a "crazy," against which the old-fashioned prison aggression of Sonny Liston could not aim its cold inner fire. Old-time boxing purists were disgusted, but there was Muslim method in his madness. In that hour of simulated rage he had cried, "You're the chump and I'm the champ! It is prophesied for me to win! I cannot be beaten!"

In the fight that night, a macabre affair haunted by goblins and doubting Thomases, Cassius confounded his army of skeptics by making Sonny Liston suddenly look very slow and very tired. The old bull was winded after two rounds, punching ponderous gloves into the spaces that Cassius had occupied a moment before. At the end of seven rounds Liston hulked in his corner like a rejected Buddha, a worn-out god with a hole in his cheek toppled from his throne by a new religion—while the irrepressible standard-bearer of this new religion leaped around the ring proclaiming to the world he had just conquered symbolically for Islam, for Harlem, for Birmingham, for South Chicago, for a billion dark-skinned rooters around the globe, "I am the king! I am the king!"

Next morning at the press conference we discovered another of the Chinese boxes that make up the complex called Cassius Clay. Or so he had been called until that morning when he announced, in a voice with the volume now turned so low he was barely audible, that he was giving up his "slave name" and from now on would be known as Cassius X.

He chided the reporters for almost unanimously picking against him and informed them that he believed in the religion of Islam, that he believed Elijah Muhammad was its apostle, and that this was the religion believed in by more than 700 million people throughout Africa and Asia. Now reporters in the back of the room were calling "Louder," whereas the day before they had feared that Cassius's vocal gymnastics might burst their eardrums. When he stepped down from the platform we asked him about his immediate plans, and he told us he thought he would travel to Africa, the Middle East, and

156

Asia. "They will all want to see the new champion of the world who believes the way they do," he said so quietly you had to lean toward him to hear it all. "And I will talk with the leaders and the wise men of those countries."

Of the past eight heavyweight champions, six had been Negro, but this was the first black champion to proclaim his blackness, to say to the white world, "I don't have to be what you want me to be," the ideal practitioner to tap out on the heads and bodies of his opponents the message: Black Is Beautiful.

[February 1972]

In Defense of Boxing

AS MUCH AS I love boxing, I hate it, and as much as I hate it, I love it. Every sensitive *aficionado* of the sport must bring to it this ambivalence. For make no mistake about it, at its worst, professional boxing is a cruel sport, just as, at its best, it is exhilarating, artistic, and, yes, ennobling. A natural rivalry for the championship of the world between two gifted professionals, tuned to perfection, is, in this opinion, a sporting event surpassing all others, from Super Bowls to Kentucky Derbies. No wonder it has had a grip on our imagination from the original Greek Games to the most recent Olympics, with its crop of new *Wunderkinder* hoping to replace Sugar Ray Leonard and the other overnight darlings of Montreal.

Write this off as macho nonsense if you will, but from his primordial beginnings man has fought with his fists—as he came later to club, dagger, sword, gunpowder, and, finally, atomic bombs. With gloves and seemingly civilized rules, the dual instincts of throwing punches and smartly defending against them has been recognized and ritualized as a sport, even a "science"—the "Sweet Science" being no misnomer for a game that has produced such master boxers as Willie (The Wisp) Pep, uncrowned welterweight king Billy Graham, and the two Sugar Rays, Robinson and Leonard. Those who abhor the fight game see it as a brawl between two mindless brutes trying to bash in each other's skulls. And it is sadly true that a fight between

158

two stiffs who are all muscle and no talent illustrates just what is base and heartless about boxing in general, and maybe the human race in particular, just as a dramatic confrontation between Sugar Ray Leonard and Thomas (Hit Man) Hearns (as well as Hearns and Marvelous Marvin Hagler) brings into play a chess game of mind and body that may make boxing the most thoughtful sport of them all—in which moves are thought out as far in advance as Willie Mosconi's at the billiard table.

Still, this year, when boxing in our international satellite society is reaching larger audiences than ever before, the game that has fascinated writers from Hazlitt and Byron to Hemingway and Mailer is on the ropes—and at least one organization, the American Medical Association, would like to count it out. At its recent convention in Hawaii, the AMA called for a ban on boxing—amateur as well as professional—on the basis that "boxing is the only major (so-called) sport in which the intentional purpose is the physical harm of the opponent, and that chronic brain damage is the almost inevitable result of a ring career."

Devoted friends of boxing rushed to the attack. Asked Bert Randolph Sugar, former editor of *Ring* magazine, "Why have they singled out boxing, making it the litter box of sports, when football has a weekly casualty list that looks like a Vietnam body count and auto racing possesses the charming aspect of having spectators catch the car instead of the ball?" Quick to answer his own question, the irrepressible Mr. Sugar suggests that boxing is made a whipping boy because it has no recognized spokesman, no national commissioner, no Pete Rozelle who can defend the weekly double column of football injuries, no Blue Book breeders of thoroughbreds to defend the fatalities and injuries to horse and rider that make horse racing a sport as dangerous to life and limb as automobile racing, another of the eleven sports listed ahead of boxing both by the ESPN cable network and the National Board of Insurance Underwriters on the index of injury, violence, and death.

Lack of a commissioner, a Peter Ueberroth, a Federal Commission of Boxing to establish and enforce rules of safety and preventative "medicine" through thorough pre- and postfight testing, is one of the reasons—and an authentic one—for the prevailing "open season" on boxing. José Torres, the articulate and intensely human ex-champion who headed the New York State Athletic Commission, was only half kidding when he said that "more human suffering may be caused by doctors' malpractice and failure to make house calls than from boxing per se." And knowing opponents of the AMA, such as Dr. Ferdie (Fight Doctor) Pacheco, may accurately describe the AMA as a political organization representing less than 50 percent of the American medical profession, with a reputation for furthering economic self-interest rather than socially beneficial medical programs. Still, while accusing the AMA of overkill in urging prohibition of both amateur and professional boxing, Pacheco acknowledges that brain damage can be a consequence of prolonged activity in the prize ring and that the reports of the *Journal of the American Medical Association* should be studied and heeded. But Pacheco also views the AMA as "political, opportunistic, and manipulative." Why didn't they look into other dangerous sports? Like Torres and other well-informed critics of the AMA, the Fight Doctor believes the answer to his challenge lies in the fact that the medical lobby is taking on a sport that can't fight back. It is vulnerable for reasons both legitimate and illegitimate. If it had a reputable body that could fight back, that body would also be overseeing a sport that cries out for policing, that is now a plunder ground and sometimes a killing ground, a multimillion-dollar sports business run without rhyme (now that Ali's gone) or reason, ethics or long-range plan. Instead of a single authoritative body, there's a bunch of fistic politicos: the WBA, the WBC, the IBF, the USBA, the NABF . . . with rival champions and conflicting top-ten contenders, with rival safety rules and jurisdictions, all pretending to preside over the one sport to attract nearly all its participants from ghetto America, the *favelas* of South America, the slums of Mexico, the Philippines, and the

Far East. Football, baseball, basketball, hockey players would never tolerate the anarchy in which the boxer is asked to practice his exacting, exciting, and sometimes dangerous profession.

Without boxing scholarships to lever him into at least a minimal college education, the average fighter is a young hopeful from Spanish Harlem or the mean streets of Detroit or the gang-hardened alleys of Chicano East Los Angeles. With dreams of becoming an overnight millionaire like Sugar Ray Leonard, Larry Holmes, and Thomas Hearns, he eagerly accepts the rigorous dedication of mind and body demanded of a professional boxer. Or, we should correct ourselves, *should be* demanded. For every careful, caring Cus D'Amato, who taught his boys (like champions Floyd Patterson and José Torres) to protect themselves both in the ring and outside the ropes, there are the "meat merchants" ready to take healthy, hungry boys and throw them to the wolves. In contrast to ringmen in the class of Ray Arcel and Gil Clancy are "brave" managers who beg ringside doctors not to stop a contest in which their "boy" is suffering deep cuts and near-concussion, and greedy promoters who not merely promote their spectacles but own the champions. This includes the seemingly respectable television networks that sign potential stars such as the recent Olympic champions to lucrative long-range contracts, and then fatten their records on set-ups, tankers, greenhorns, or washed-ups who should either not be licensed at all or never be allowed in the ring with gifted and protected opponents who cuff them about at will. With the exception of NBC, which at least has the ring-wise Pacheco making the matches and calling most of the shots, the networks are as guilty of "meat merchanting" as the most cynical of the old-time managers with their "Get-in-there-they-can't-hoit-us." And even Pacheco was heard to mention on a recent "show" that one of his contestants was hopelessly outclassed.

"Fighters are a dime a dozen, but managers go on forever," is the slogan of this hardened tribe who go on managing kids who get knocked out six times in eight fights—and if you think this is exaggeration, thumb through a Ring Record Book.

Threading through the pages full of power and glory are records like that of Marcus Dorsey, a Houston middleweight, knocked out ten times in seventeen fights, winning only his very first fight. Or Al Byrd, a North Carolina heavyweight, knocked out in eighteen fights in twenty-four starts. Or Irving Booth, knocked out in all seven of his first seven fights, in the first or second round. Where are the commissions, the promoters, the managers who should be telling these sacrificial lambs in wolves' clothing to go home and forget it—the world of Holmes, Hagler, and Hearns is not for them?

In this climate of neglect—with too many meat merchants and not enough Cus D'Amatos and too many no-talent "Christians" thrown to the lions—the public cry for abolition or reform comes only when an exhausted Duk Koo Kim is inadvertently beaten to death by Ray (Boom Boom) Mancini, or a drug-abused Willie Classen, stopped in two of his previous fights, is allowed one more, fatal round with then-undefeated Wilford Scypion. Instead of waiting for tragedy to strike again, it behooves defenders of boxing not to shrug off but to take a good, hard look at the charges of the AMA.

According to its high-sounding Council on Scientific Affairs, its own study of thirty-eight boxers, as well as a study in the British medical magazine *Lancet* of fourteen Finnish boxers, and a further study by six physicians published last May in the AMA *Journal*—all based on CT (computed tomographic) brain scans, electroencephalograms, and neurological tests—a significant number of those boxers suffered from chronic encephalopathy, cerebral atrophy, and, in about one-third of the cases, a condition described medically as *cavum septum pellucidum*. This abnormality has been discovered in tests both of Muhammad Ali, and of the best white heavyweight in recent years, Jerry Quarry, who fought all the tough ones of the sixties and seventies, Joe Frazier, Muhammad Ali, Ernie Shavers, Ken Norton. . . . Jerry is not at all the punchy stereotype with which enemies of boxing like to belabor the sport. He's not walking on his heels, and his speech isn't slurred. Articulate and responsive, he's an effective TV colorman at ringside. But when he volunteered to participate in a series of tests sponsored by *Sports Illustrated*, along with Tex Cobb, who took an unmerciful (and needless) beating from Larry Holmes, and a club fighter named Pacheco (no relation to Dr. P), his CAT scans and psychoneurological results were subnormal.

Without overloading readers with statistics and medicalese, it's the AMA conclusion *that boxing is deleterious to the human brain*. But not all experts agree. Dr. Bennett Denby, the neurosurgeon at New York University Medical Center who advises the New York State Athletic Commission, studied 125 CAT scans of fighters knocked out last year and found no evidence of brain damage caused by boxing. While the jury is still out, there is no point in denying the *possibility* of brain damage, especially from the accumulation of blows over a number of years. Just as there is little point in defending the boxing status quo by citing the number of fatalities in auto and horse racing, tobogganing, hang-gliding, and so many other dangerous sports. Yes, Pat Ryan, the starting quarterback for the Jets, was sidelined for the rest of the 1984 season after serious concussions suffered in two successive games. Of course, the 280-pound linemen blindsiding a star quarterback are trying to do more than stop the passer; consciously or subconsciously they're trying to whack him out of the game. Nor is it of any value to a brain-damaged veteran of sixty or seventy fights to argue that Ron Turcotte, a little gem of a jockey, is paralyzed from the waist down, as is Daryl Stingley of the New England Patriots. Or that major automobile races are advertised on TV by featuring again and again deadly crashes with cars rolling over, slamming against walls, and trapping their drivers in fires. Bodily harm, intended or accidental, attends every sport of violent contact. But we who follow boxing have an obligation to deal with our own sport. If a jockey keeps falling off his horse, he is disqualified. But for the fighter who gets knocked

163

out almost every time he climbs through the ropes or shuffles through his bloody career as a hopeless loser, there is no Thoroughbred Racing Association to rule him off the track.

It is not the findings of the AMA—alarming if still inconclusive—that we question, but its conclusions: to abolish both amateur and professional boxing. In the first place, these are two different sports, the first limited to three rounds, with headgear, and the referee ready to step in practically with the first sign of a bloody nose. The professional main bout goes anywhere from ten to fifteen rounds and is a test of endurance as well as courage and skill. This kind of prizefight has been banned again and again.

A fight to the finish was outlawed in England throughout the bareknuckle days of the nineteenth century but flourished just the same with such natural rivalries as champion Tom Cribb vs. the American slave champion, Tom Molineaux, and Richard Humphries vs. Daniel Mendoza, "the Jew," drawing tens of thousands, from bluebloods to scalawags. Forbidden in the United States as well, the Manly Art responded to an insatiable urge all over the country. "The Great" John L. Sullivan had to go all the way to rural Mississippi to face a major rival, Jake Kilrain. If Gentleman Jim Corbett had to meet San Francisco rival Joe Choynski on a barge to avoid police interference, so be it—they fought it out. Wherever boxing was banned, there was always some state or territory beyond the law where natural rivalries were settled with impunity.

After winning his bareknuckle championship from Paddy Ryan in the wilds of Mississippi, Sullivan went all the way to France to defend his title against Charley Mitchell. Only the oldest of old-timers remembers that New York banned boxing completely about eighty years ago. And what were the results? Did boxing disappear? No, like booze in the twenties, it flourished in speakeasies—only they were called boxing "clubs."

Instead of a ticket, you bought a "membership"—oh, man's ingenuity is endless when it comes to something he (and she) is unable to resist. In the years of boxing's "banishment" there were many more fight cards in New York than there are today. Every borough had its club or clubs, with professional boxing every night of the week. But it was totally without supervision. There were no weigh-ins and no safety precautions. Lightweights were thrown in against middleweights. There are grim stories of battered bodies being found in the river or abandoned in alleys after brutal club matches that mindless referees never bothered to stop.

Finally, boxing was welcomed back to respectability again under the Walker Law (the famous Mayor Jimmy), allowing ten-round fights without awarding decisions, a sop to reformers who reasoned that without official decisions at the end of the contests, the gambling element would be eliminated, along with their fixes and underworld coups. So this became the era of "newspaper decisions," with the gamblers as involved as ever and paying off on the round-by-round tallies of the boxing writers.

Unfortunately, this group had no more of a lock on public virtue than commission judges, who have made their share of strange and suspicious calls over the years. And so, finally, boxing was "normalized" in New York again, with the hope that a state athletic commission could keep it as clean and safe as this demanding contact sport will ever be.

But New York is only one state, faced with the problem that it has forfeited its championship franchise to Las Vegas, not to mention Latin and European rings on the TV satellite circuit. There was a time when a champion sanctioned in New York enjoyed credibility as a champion of the world. But the fact that New York rulings have no effect in Maine, Mississippi, Arizona . . . that some states have their own commissions, while some have none at all—and that boxing may be the one sport practiced in every part of the globe, North and South America, Europe, Asia, and Africa—makes an American ban on boxing an exercise in self-righteous futility. Not only would the ban lead to a mushroom spread of "speakeasy" boxing clubs from New York to San Diego, but American fighters would become a commodity for export to Buenos Aires and Mexico City, Monte Carlo and Rome, Tokyo and Johannesburg. . . .

So the AMA "ban on boxing" can be written off either as a publicity ploy (why did they hold up until after the '84 Olympics their vote to outlaw even amateur boxing?), or a futile cry in the wilderness of the fight game. To cry for abolishment is a cop-out, really, for everybody knows that boxing is no closer to its end in 1985 than it was in 1885, when John L. Sullivan was king. The plea from this corner, then, is not to join the AMA lobby in its grandstand move but to take its most cogent facts to heart and work from there. Decades overdue but now more urgently needed is a federal boxing commission, not a body of dodo politicos or anything-goes boxing apologists but people who care about boxing and know about boxing, who love boxing without being blind to its faults and who want to lead boxing out of its jungle chaos into the world of legitimate sport.

Challenged by the AMA, boxing needs a Judge Kenesaw Mountain Landis, who was appointed to reform baseball after the Black Sox scandals of 1919. It needs a program of protection that is uniform from state to state, via a master computer with a data base of all boxers' performances and medical histories—so that "opponents" who have no business in the ring could no longer stumble on from state to state, with nobody checking and nobody caring.

Such a commission, staffed by professionals, would insist on much more than the routine physical examination, which in many states is a perfunctory knee-jerk exercise. There should be CAT scans and EEGs and neurological tests before and after every bout. Cerebral atrophy may not be totally avoidable, but at least thorough before-and-after exams would identify potential victims. Boxers over thirty should be monitored with special care, for it seems axiomatic that the older a fighter is and the more blows he absorbs, the more susceptible he becomes to cerebral abnormalities.

A promotion that exploits an over-the-hill Ali, or the comeback of eye-injured Sugar Ray Leonard, or encourages a brave but punched-out ex-champ like Vito Antuofermo to return to the ring is not going to welcome a federal commission with strict standards for all the states. Big-time promoters have been a law unto themselves and laugh off their critics as do-gooders and bleeding hearts. Too often the prevailing attitude is "boxing is a gutter sport—trying to reform it is like trying to reform hooking on Eighth Avenue." But the history of the modern prizefight, all the way back to seventeenth century's James Figg, is studded with reform—from bare knuckles to gloves to thumbless gloves; from fights to a finish to thirty rounds to twenty rounds and now a limit of twelve to fifteen; the use of mouthpiece and groin protector; the judgment of doctors and referees to stop unequal contests. . . . The trouble often lies in the enforcement. When what proved to be fatal injuries were being inflicted on Benny Paret, Jimmy Owen, Willie Classen, and Duk Koo Kim, officials more sensitive to their dilemma might have stepped in and saved their lives. The brutal shutout that Larry Holmes pitched against Tex Cobb could have been stopped after five or six rounds and simply called "no contest." Two men parrying each other's blows and trying to box, think, and will their way to victory make an exhilarating contest. One man beating on a defenseless opponent round after round makes it brutal and boring.

Along with computerized medical records based on CAT scans, EEGs, and the recently developed MRIs (magnetic resonance imaging), a federal boxing commission should also appraise the fitness of referees and cornermen in whose hands lies the safety of thousands of young competitors, most of them hoping to fight their way out of the oppressive social conditions into which they were born. Without exception, they are willing to take their chances, brain damage and all. "It's my one shot at moving up, man—only way outa the ghetto," says a hungry, quick-fisted black kid at the Bed-Stuy gym who admits that if he weren't here, cleaning up his act and accepting the discipline, he'd be out there with his jobless, street-hustle brothers dealing drugs, squeezing Saturday-night specials. "Like, my fights are in the streets, and my roadwork is outrunning the cops."

A featherweight novice from Spanish Harlem agrees: "Talk about brain damage, man. You get it *out there* a helluva lot faster 'n you get it in here!" As long as those conditions motivate kids like these off the streets and into gyms from Bed-Stuy to downtown L.A., no AMA is going to stop them.

So let's step up to realism and give them what they need. Not the rhetoric of abolishment but the reality of reform. Including a long-needed and studiously avoided pension plan, plus a retirement home/hospital along the lines of the Motion Picture Relief Home. Two percent off the top of every multi-million-dollar promotion could underwrite this plan. This fight fan/reformer trial-ballooned these ideas thirty years ago, and all he has to show for it is a plaque from Notre Dame for having done the most for boxing that year. My predecessor was Bishop Shiel, my successor Rocky Marciano, with whom I held a press conference to push our reform. It's a handsome plaque, but I'm still waiting for the improvements it symbolized.

Congressman Henry B. Gonzalez of Texas has already opened the next round in the battle to ban boxing by swinging into Congress with a bill calling for the sport's abolishment. There are a lot of poor white Texas kids and brown-skinned Chicanos in his constituency. So we'd advise the honorable Henry B. to move for our federal boxing commission. Let him help set it up soundly and promptly, so that these boys—his constituents—would be protected against both an unsupervised, multimillion-dollar fight industry and the bootleg "club" operators ready to step in should the legal rug be pulled from under some four thousand pro boxers—plus countless amateurs—by the good doctors of the AMA.

[April 1985]

168

Journey to Zaire

IN THE CONGO (now called Zaire: rhymes with My Ear) the old African hands like to quote a native proverb:

"Only when you have crossed the river can you say the crocodile has a lump on his snout."

And now that I have flown across the equator by way of Iceland, Luxembourg, and Trier, Germany (thanks to the topsy-turvy logistics of Video Techniques, which masterminded our press charter flight), to see a Festival of Music that failed to fest, and the Fight of the Century that failed to be fought, I have an amendment to that ancient African saying:

"Even *after* you have crossed the river, you still may not know if the crocodile has a lump on his snout."

From Joe Louis's days I've flown to the scene of championship fights. But today I'm recalling the flight from California to Miami to see young Cassius Clay challenge the sinister Sonny Liston, the 10-to-1 favorite, and the hysterical scene at the weigh-in when Cassius and his resident guru, Bundini Brown, first introduced the slogan, "Float like a butterfly, sting like a bee," carrying on like banshees, with Clay's eyes bulging, his mouth screaming and blood pressure doubling. Officials were being urged to call off the fight because Clay was so emotionally disturbed that he should not be allowed in the ring with a killer like Liston. That night he climbed into the ring cool and self-contained, darting in, out, and around the lumbering Liston who, as veteran fighters are wont to do, went from middle age to senility between rounds.

Next morning at his press conference, the multifaceted Clay, by far the most complex and provocative of all the champions I've known over the years, had undergone another personality change. Now the new champion declared his faith in Black Muslims and, taking the lead from his mentor Malcolm X, announced that henceforth he would no longer use his "slave name" Cassius Marcellus Clay but would be known as Cassius X.

When I asked what kind of champion he intended to be, his answer was unexpected, touched with pomposity, and yet, with hindsight, a reliable projection of the man. "I want to use my championship as a calling card on all the great leaders of the world," he said. "I want to travel to all the great capitals. Boxin' has brought me to where I am but I know there's a lot o' things more important than boxin', even than being the Greatest, the champion of the entire world."

Ten years ago I could not have foreseen that this spirit of defiance, intellectual curiosity, and the search for roots would lead all of us on the strangest journey of my forty years of fight-going, the journey to Kinshasa.

On Ali's last weekend before his departure for Zaire, I drove to his self-designed complex of log cabins on a mountain top in the Amish country. No frills at the camp, just good solid cabins, solid benches to sit on, solid food. The only decorations are enormous rocks, the size of three Bubba Smiths put together. Each bears the name of a former champion, Sonny Liston, Rocky Marciano, Archie Moore. There is a smaller rock for Angelo Dundee, the veteran trainer-manager to whom Cassius first turned for help when Dundee was managing champions and Clay was the teen-age amateur pride of Louisville.

Ali was in high spirits. He looked fit and was proud that he had been in camp all summer, training harder for this fight than for any bout since he was allowed to fight again four years ago.

170

"You wanna watch me run in the mornin', you'll have to get up *real* early."

The call I had left for 5:30 a.m. seemed to come two minutes after my head touched the pillow. A quick cold shower told me I was awake, and after a hot coffee and Danish in the kitchen with Bundini Brown, who somehow was philosophizing before the sun was up, we drove down the long curving hill with Ali and turned into a green rolling valley where Ali said to his sidekick Gene Kilroy, "Okay, stop here." He got out of the car and started running along a deserted road between dairy farms. He ran in heavy field boots, not jogging sneakers, and a thick elastic belt drew the excess liquid and fat from a body now pared down from over 230 to 218. On he ran, mile after mile, while we chugged along behind him, with the September sun beginning to light the day. Occasionally a curious cow or a horse would come to the fence along the country road to watch him pass. For almost half an hour he ran, occasionally backward, sometimes pausing to whistle punches into the sweet morning air. When he finally came to the end of his self-appointed marathon, he did a little more shadow boxing to taper off, attracting a small audience of early rising farmers and their children.

"I'm ready," he assured these rural neighbors who had never seen a prizefight but to whom the peregrinating Ali had become a welcome sight.

"Just ran half an hour and I'm not even breathin' hard. Tomorrow I'm leaving for Africa! The rumble in the jungle! George Foreman is in big trouble. I'm goin' over there as the champion of the people and I'm comin' back as the official champion of the whole world."

"If you think Evel Knievel made that jump, wait 'til I beat Foreman's rump!"

I wasn't sure these simple country folk knew exactly what he was talking about, but they seemed as hypnotized as his most ardent fans in the ghetto.

That afternoon, after going eight spirited rounds with four

sparring partners, Ali showered and dressed in the meager quarters off the gym where he also slept, and then perched himself atop a pile of logs. A sense of well-being and the excitement of going to Africa, "back to the homeland," had raised his usually ebullient spirits even higher.

"If you think the world was amazed when Nixon resigned, wait 'til I beat George Foreman's behind."

Then he grew serious. "It's much more than a sports event. It's a symbol of the Black Awakening, with black American stars like me going back to our African roots. Stars like Stevie Wonder and Diana Ross and James Brown and Aretha Franklin, all those beautiful black people goin' home to share their experiences with the black musicians who never left. And all the black people of Africa and the leaders of a young black country bigger'n all of Europe 'n India put together! That's the real story. It'll make history. The first comin' together of Afro-Americans and their African brothers."

His eyes widened in amazement at the enormity of this impending phenomenon. "Let's get it on!"

After two days of zigzagging over oceans and across continents, we were finally deposited in downtown Kinshasa, at the Hotel Memling, where the heat impresses you like an affectionate ghost, while invisible bugs cuddle up for comfort.

Meanwhile, a journeyman heavyweight named Bill McMurray had sliced the invincible George Foreman over the right eye. The fight had been postponed! For a week, a month? Nobody knew. Foreman & Co. were barricaded behind locked gates and armed guards, as inaccessible to the press as Nixon at San Clemente.

Next morning I was on the road to N'Sele, about forty miles from Kinshasa, where Ali and his retinue were set up in style in the presidential villas provided for visiting dignitaries. The road was narrow and jammed with traffic leading out of town, but then it widened to the only four-lane, divided highway in all the 900,000 square miles of Zaire. The land was cracked with heat and looked more like sand than life-giving earth. It

was a country thirsty for the rains that would come in October
and beat down relentlessly for the six months of the monsoon
season. We passed small villages with one- and two-room
houses of cement block. The women along the road were tall
and stately, dressed in colorful ankle-length wraparounds.
Walking like models, they were carrying incredible loads on
their heads, sacks of potatoes, baskets of laundry, even wood.
Occasionally we would pass a small stream where black children were swimming. Every few miles there were huge road-
side signs in green and yellow, clearly lettered in English:
"Ali-Foreman—You Are Our Brothers. Let the Best Man Win."

At the entrance to N'Sele, which is also a large experimental
farm and the meeting place of President Mobutu's Popular
Revolutionary Movement (the country's only political party), I
was surprised to find that we entered through a pagoda-like
archway. It seems that this luxurious retreat for the President, his advisers, and visiting heads of state was built as a
gift from the Taiwan government. At the end of a long driveway, we came to a dead end. And there it was, the mighty
Congo that Stanley had marveled at and that Conrad had so
vividly described when he first saw Kinshasa (then
Leopoldville) as a village of grass huts and wooden shanties
more than eighty years ago.

I was anxious to see how Ali was taking the postponement,
but the river held me. It was so wide, four miles across, that
Brazzaville on the opposite shore was a grey-purple haze. An-
chored at the bank in front of the large villas was the presidential yacht, actually a four-decker riverboat. In front of it
was a companion vessel, the Mama Mobutu, which runs up
and down the great river, passing out medicines to the villages
and taking on patients in need of more serious medical attention. What I had not realized was that this giant of a river, second only to the Amazon, was choked with hyacinth. Clumps of
hyacinth, even small islands of them, floated in slow motion
down to Matadi and the sea. A grey, torpid silence hung over
the river. I stared at a narrow boat in which fishermen were

drifting upstream against the downflowing current, and wondered if it was an illusion caused by sunstroke or jet-lag. But
these fishermen knew the peculiar currents that would carry
them against the flow of the river. I longed to follow it as it
twisted its way like a two-thousand-mile cobra into the heart
of darkness, the rain forests, the trackless savannas, and the
lush valleys where ancient Africa still lives. Day after day,
during my weeks in Zaire, I would return, walking the mile-
long promenade in front of the villas, to watch the river. A few
times I watched it from the top deck of the Mama Mobutu,
where I had accompanied Ali's old Cuban trainer, Luis Sarria,
whose gout had flared to an unbearable extreme in the oppressive humidity. Waiting for the doctors to treat the taciturn,
long-suffering Sarria, I kept looking down at the purple flowers, no two clumps the same size or shape until suddenly I realized that almost an hour had passed. I couldn't believe it. I
was intoxicated with hyacinth and heat and a mysterious haze
that seemed to conceal and at the same time intensify the sun.

At the villa, I found Ali, surrounded by familiar faces, installed in a spacious house with marble floors, plush couches
and easy chairs, elaborate chandeliers, an ample kitchen and
pantry, and two large bathrooms. There were two framed
blow-up photos of President Mobutu, as there are in every
villa, every home, every store. In his leopard-skin hat (the
leopard, not the lion, is the king of the jungle in Zaire), his
piercing eyes measuring you through horn-rimmed glasses, his
jaw thrust forward, this ex-journalist turned general who then
proclaimed himself president, is a man to be reckoned with.
When John Gunther, researching *Inside Africa* twenty years
ago, asked the Belgian governor-general, "Who runs the
Congo?" the answer was unhesitating: "I do." Now President
Mobutu could give a similar answer. Democracy is still a
stranger to the Republic of Zaire. But Mobutu could argue that
all the wealth of a country rich in diamonds, copper, and cobalt
is no longer siphoned off to the Belgians. If some may be siphoned off to secret bank accounts in Switzerland, millions

174

more are being reinvested in the internal development of Zaire. And where there was only a single native lawyer and a handful of university students twenty years ago, now there are four thousand students at Kinshasa University alone, and Zairians are beginning to fill the middle-class and professional slots that were once the exclusive province of the tiny Belgian minority.

In his villa, Ali was a restless tiger. He had honed himself physically and psychologically to a fine edge, pointing his entire year toward the night of September 24. Now he would have to ease off, put on weight so he could carve it off again, timing himself to the bell. That's not easy when the opponent has the hole card—Foreman has the cut and the advantage of deciding when he'll be ready. Ali suspects the cut may just be a Foreman ploy. He had blown up with idleness and success. He wasn't ready. "It won't be no week, it'll be a month, maybe more," Ali grumbled, no longer the ebullient long-distance runner I had followed at Deer Lake only a week before. Then he shifted emotional gears. "I've got to turn a negative into a positive. Poor George is goin' to come into that ring knowin' he's no superman, knowin' if a sparrin' partner c'n cut him, I c'n jab-jab. [He illustrated with vicious lefts that missed my chin by inches.] I've got to keep runnin'. I've got to keep my edge. I've got to hold this whole thing together. I think Foreman is just stallin' for time. He knows I'm ready and he ain't. Well, I'll wait him out. I don't know what I'll do with myself, outside of trainin'. Wish I knew French. I don't understan' what they're sayin' on television. I wish they'd show some Westerns like we have back home."

Ali was back in his homeland but he was homesick. He missed Deer Lake. He missed Chicago. He missed his new custom-built bus in which he could go streaking down the turnpikes of America talking on his mobile radio to truckers with code names like Girlwatcher and Sneaky Pete, often rednecks who became instant pals when they realized that Big Bopper was actually Muhammad Ali. As he talked out his homesickness, I realized how intensely American he was, as American as Gerry Ford and Mickey Mantle. Africa was a dream, a loving and lovely dream, a distant remembrance of things past. Muhammad Ali was still Cassius Clay, the kid from Louisville, the child of Little Richard, Tutti-Frutti, and the American Dream Machine.

I walked down the row of villas calling on various members of the Ali entourage, and it was comic relief to greet the same faces I had seen at the primitive cabins of Deer Lake now ensconced in palatial villas.

The sparring partners, lacking Ali's patience, imagination, and incentive, were going up the wall. Another month in this God-forsaken splendor? Nothin' to do but stare at them weeds in the water. They wanted out. Even the ever-patient Angelo Dundee, who had seen his fighters through a hundred crises, was wondering out loud how he'd get through another month of splendid isolation in equatorial heat. Angelo isn't a player who runs to town to find the action. He stays close to his fighter. He minds the store. He's ready with the smelling salts, the Q-Tips, the adhesive, and all the other medical tricks of his specialized trade. He's ready to slap Ali sharply on his thighs if he starts leaning back against the ropes, inviting Foreman's pile-drivers. He's ready for the fight. But if tropical rivers and African sculpture don't turn you on, what do you do with yourself on an experimental farm near the equator?

I found a mutiny mounting in the press room. Carpenters were hammering and sawing away, belatedly building phone booths for reporters to phone in their stories. Newscopy was being torn from Telex machines by overzealous Zairians who objected to what they considered slurs on the country, the fight, and its management. They even ripped out the simple truth—that the Foreman cut may have been a blessing to the government of Zaire because telephone and Telex communications were nowhere near ready to service the reporters from all over the world who would be on hand when and if the fight took place.

176

That evening I dined with friends from the American embassy and Zairian acquaintances who had been educated in the States. I passed on to them the mood of the press and suggested that if the local authorities didn't want to totally alienate them, why not call a meeting, admit this was a situation they'd never coped with before, and ask the reporters to bear with them as they worked out their difficulties?

This simply is not done in African countries, they explained. It would mean a loss of face. No one admits mistakes, and since there is a rigid pecking order in the political structure of Zaire, with no one willing to report to his superior that anything is amiss, the chances were that President Mobutu knew nothing of our problems. He had kept his word. The soccer stadium had been enlarged to a capacity of 62,500. Streets repaired and widened, new street lights installed. New buses in circulation. The fighters enjoying the most luxurious hospitality the country could afford. And at this very moment, famous musical stars from America were on their way. Kinshasa, Zaire, was on the map, which was the main purpose of the government's $12 million investment in the face-lifting. Not to mention the $10 million guaranteed the fighters by a mysterious Swiss company called Risnelia, in which President Mobutu was said to be involved.

I returned to the press room next morning expecting another battle report from our writers in their struggle for free speech in this vast, recently chaotic country held together by authority. Instead I heard that Tschimpumpu Wa Tschimpumpu, director of the press for the Foreman-Ali Commission, had called a conference for 10 a.m. to "straighten everything out."

I called my friend at the embassy who hurried over to the meeting to see this miracle for himself.

He needn't have hurried. The meeting began at 11:45. Meanwhile, handsome hostesses in flowing gowns and exotic hairdos mollified us with excellent Simba beer. Finally, Tschimpumpu—a name that was to be constantly on our lips—made his entrance, a young man with savoir faire, genuine charm, and ready wit. He began with an apology for any inconveniences the press may have suffered in their first few days. My embassy friend turns to me in amazement. In the two years he's been stationed here he's never heard such an apology. Tschimpumpu assures us that President Mobutu was a journalist himself and understands our problems. Somehow our unease must have reached the president's ear, otherwise citizen Tschimpumpu would have never taken it upon himself to offer excuses.

What we are experiencing is a confrontation of cultures, Western vis-à-vis African, the first baby steps on both sides in an effort at accommodation. Having assured us that "there would be no 'probe-blems,'" that additional telephone lines would be installed in time, and the Telex machines unmolested, he went on to lecture us on the sensitivities of the new republic. "The country is no longer to be called the Congo because we do not want to be reminded of colonial days. Our great river is no longer the Congo River but the Zaire. The name of our president is not Joseph Desire Mobutu, but Mobutu Sese Seku. We have all changed our names from the French Françoises and Pierres handed us by the Belgians to the true names that reflect our African heritage. Is it too much to ask that our president's name be spelled correctly and fully? We are a young country but we are a proud country. We need your understanding and your help." Then he flashes an ingratiating smile. "If anyone disappears, or is eaten, please let us know."

Momentary laughter. Then reporters begin to shout: "This means no more censorship?"

"And the phone won't be banged down if you hear something you don't like?"

The free-for-all of a presidential press conference is unknown in Zaire. Still Tschimpumpu smiles and charms his way through the extraordinary session, announces that The Fight will definitely be rescheduled for October 29. To which Foreman's fast-talking trainer Dick Sadler adds, "If George's eye is ready."

178

The festival-night seemed to reel from disaster to disaster. Five hundred American musicians, technicans, advance men, male and female groupies swarmed into the Intercontinental Hotel, accompanied by sixteen camera crews who were to shoot five hundred miles of film. But Stevie Wonder and Aretha Franklin were no-shows, and James Brown, said to have been guaranteed $100,000 for his appearance, finally went on at 4 a.m. to an audience of three hundred, two hundred of whom could not be awakened even by Brown's musical histrionics. The old star, Etta James, on the comeback trail, never got on at all and went back to her hotel in despair. Ali's dream of black Americans and their African brothers coming together to make music still remains just what it was back in Deer Lake—a dream. On the first night of the festival, overpriced from $3 to $20, there were five thousand people looking very lonely in the vast soccer stadium. The following night there were only fifteen hundred. Our black American musicians found the Zairian music boring. The few Kinshasans on hand were mystified by the sophisticated sound of the Jazz Crusaders and the Appalachian poetry of Bill Withers. Only Miriam Makeba, who spoke French, sang the songs of her Black South African people, and moved in her theatrical gown like a wicked angel, was able to establish any rapport with her audience.

Maybe, I wondered, as I watched the talented Pointer Sisters bomb with the rest of the talented American stars, you can't go home again. You can only dream of home. Of course there are African echoes in the soul music of America. But the ears of the Zairians seemed deaf to them.

Towering Don King, the ex-numbers boss who had had plenty of time to dream while doing time in the pen for inadvertently killing a runner with his fists, had conjured up this festival, just as he had sweet-talked the fighters into signing for $5 million each before finding the source of that munificence. In a flowing robe incongruous to modern Kinshasa, he had presided over the plush lobby of the Intercontinental.

Now, with the music festival in ruins, and the fight in jeopardy, our Emperor Jones was suddenly incommunicado.

On the eve of my departure, I drove back to N'Sele to say goodbye to Ali, who asked me to stay for a soul-food supper. The headliners who came out to clown with him are back home in their recording studios, and a sense of loneliness hangs over the villa. He wishes I could get in touch with Sidney Poitier and other movie stars who might send him some new American flicks to pass the time. He still nurses the bitter feeling that Foreman faked the cut to give himself more time to get in the kind of shape Ali was in when he arrived.

"But I'll wait," he says, "I'll keep runnin'. Keep jumpin' over that cactus, and it gives me a good feelin' when the kids pop up and shout, 'Ali, Ali, buma ye!' (Lingolan for 'Kill 'im, Ali.')," a phrase heard on every street corner in Kinshasa.

After supper I said, "Take care." He answered, "When you comin' back?" and then I was on my way to D'Jili Airport, with a last look at the hyacinth moving through the moonlight on the river.

One more time I made the seemingly endless trip from Kennedy Airport to Paris to Kinshasa, and out to the Presidential Villa at N'Sele.

There was our ever-ebullient Ali, with wife-to-be, the gorgeous Veronica. And the familiar team, the white Kilroy in a sea of black faces, the outrageous Bundini Brown, the tall serious "Blood," the tough, stammering, dependable Pat Patterson, the dark, silent, Cuban conditioner Luis Sarria—each one a colorful stone in the complex mosaic called Muhammad Ali.

There were other white, invaluable faces in the tumultuous black sea—Angelo Dundee, as capable a trainer as ever worked a corner, and "Fight Doctor" Ferdie Pacheco, who loved Ali as fervently as anybody in camp, but beginning to have his troubles with Black Muslim detractors.

Ali, as always, was above the internecine jostling for position near the throne. And as always, along with the fun and games at which he excelled, Ali was approaching the fight with all the attention of a football coach for the Super Bowl, of which the impending Ali-Foreman would be the fistic version.

Ali had discovered that despite his imposing string of knockouts, Foreman had endured two ten-rounders with an aging light-heavyweight from Argentina, Gregorio Peralta.

Night after night Ali ran the Foreman-Peralta tapes in the spacious living room of the Presidential Villa. Night after night his impromptu comments provided a spirited narration: "Now look at that! There's that li'l ol' man (Peralta was about thirty-five and weighed 185) layin' back on the ropes and Big Go'ge thinks he's killin' 'im but all he's doin' is gettin' arm weary!

"Oh, if that li'l ol' man c'n do that to 'im, givin' him shoulders and elbows 'n gloves, 'n pullin' back from punches, what d'ya think I'll be doin'?"

Now Ali would jump to his feet in excitement and demonstrate his strategy. "Five, six rounds, Big Go'ge is so tired, his arms is so heavy he can't lift 'em any more and then I come on—pow! pow! pow! and Big Go'ge is down, can't get up he's whupped! An' everybody's screamin' Ali! Ali! Ali . . . ! Oh, le's get it on!"

And so it came to pass, on the night of October 30, 1974, or more accurately at the unlikely hour of 4 a.m., in the unlikely setting of the soccer stadium in the capital of Zaire, the "Rumble in the Jungle" ended precisely as our mercurial black prince had predicted.

Moments after the dramatic finish, a tropical downpour flooded the ring. Back at the villa an hour later, the exuberant champion and this writer fought an impromptu match by dawn's early light. And if I didn't have the series of photos to prove it, I wouldn't believe it either.

[October 1974]

Leonard-Duran

ON THE EVENING of the battle a downpour soaks but seems
not to dampen the spirits of the $500 ticket holders, who look
like a strange hooded fraternity wearing black garbage bags
over their heads.

The ring is an island in a furious sea of Panamanian flags.
Roberto Duran and his countrymen seem to have taken over
Montreal. From my local connections, I learn that the French-
speaking citizenry, still scratching their way toward indepen-
dence from English Canada, identify with Duran as a
flag-bearer for the aspirations of a small Latin nation.

But Duran doesn't need the advantage of a partisan crowd.
When the bell sends him out to do what he seems to have been
born for, he wastes no time imposing his will on the fight. He
comes charging forward like a small but angry bull, greeting
Leonard with a vicious left hook just a mite low, Duran's way
of telling this upstart opponent who is boss.

By the second round the pattern of the fight is established.
Duran will keep moving forward, full of sneaky little moves,
his head bobbing, his hands feinting, slamming hard lefts to
the body, or pushing Leonard back until the champion is
pinned against the ropes. Leonard, unintimidated, fights back
with commendable vigor and courage.

Before the second round is over, the swarthy challenger with
the scraggly beard nails the clean-shaven champion a tremen-

dous overhand right. Leonard goes back but not down. Somehow he weathers that punch and the others that follow as Duran pursues him with the kind of primitive snarl that has gone out of fashion.

It looks as if former light-heavyweight king José Torres's prediction is on the mark—Duran inside of three. But Ray is answering the big prefight question—can he take a punch?—with a surprising affirmative.

Later he will admit that his head did not clear until the fifth. He is unable to use his boxing skills because Duran simply refuses to let him fight at a distance, continually crowding him and cutting off the ring. "All right, if you won't let me fight my fight, I'll fight yours and beat you at it," Leonard seems to be saying back to him with his fists.

Leonard couldn't jab and he couldn't move side to side like a Jersey Joe Walcott or the first Sugar Ray, but he was proving he was no fragile Golden-Gloved wonder. He could sure as hell fight—long on bravery if short on ring savvy, actually standing there or leaning there, trading shots with Duran, something none of the experts thought he was up to.

There had been nice boxers like Esteban DeJesus and Ray Lampkin who had been able to box their way around Duran for ten rounds, but invariably the hands of stone got to them by the eleventh and twelfth. Duran thrived on combat as his opponents wilted under late pressure.

But with Leonard, incredibly, this was not to be. His confidence grew as the fight surged on into those dangerous double-digit rounds. It was Leonard who was coming on from the eleventh, reaching down for those mysterious extras like a true champion and almost matching Duran's big second round with a mighty thirteenth, in which he landed a classic hook that made Duran shiver and hold for the first time.

Leonard had the range now and was landing bombs. But Duran had a stouter chin than the Wilfred Benitez whom Ray had stopped in his other title fight. It would have been an even more decisive round for Sugar Ray if the ring-wise Duran had

183

not met the challenges with the resolve and ferocity that have been his trademark.

To the final bell they fought without quarter—in an ironic turnabout Duran a better boxer in his own shifty alleycat way, Leonard forced out of his style but proving a better two-handed banger than any of us would have expected him to be.

When the decision was handed up, it was close, only a point or two on official cards and most of our unofficial ones. But at the final bell, Duran had thrown his arms in the air in an instinctive signal of victory and Leonard was looking down at the canvas as if he knew he had lost. Unaccountably, Mrs. Leonard fainted dead away. Her husband had not taken the kind of savage beating the stone hands had meted out to scores of victims. But the pressure had been relentless.

In the immediate aftermath, young Leonard, neither bloodied nor bowed, was making sounds about retiring with his millions to safer professions. But tomorrow he will be seen on the Wide World of Sports telling Howard Cosell that he is ready to pursue Duran to any ring in the world to win back his crown.

Of course, the Mexican left-hooker, Pipino Cuevas, who holds the WBA version of this title, would make an engrossing opponent for either one if he gets by tough Tommy Hearns, if only the two international commissioners would stop their bureaucratic nonsense and unify the titles again.

But if or when Duran and Leonard meet again, with Pipino, Hearns, and still youthful Benitez in the wings, I'll be ready to climb on another plane, no doubt reminiscing at the bar with Norman Mailer, José Torres, Blackie Lisker, and the rest of the *cognoscenti* about Leonard-Duran I—when two dedicated little millionaires went at each other in a $30 million spectacle that actually measured up to its hype.

WALKING INTO P. J. CLARKE'S after the Tuesday night "fight," I was accosted by nonadmirers who had read my pieces on previous days, praising the alley-dog determination of Roberto Duran that had brought him seventy-two victories in seventy-three bouts.

"Hey, Budd, you owe me money!" they challenged. "Becuz of you we bet Duran."

Fighting Phil Rafferty and all my friends, forgive me. If I misled you, I am ready to cut the gloves off and hang 'em up for good.

I wish I were a Rockefeller (or maybe a Duran) who could pay a token dollar to every believer who put his money where my mouth was—which is more than Duran did with his fists.

As I went to sleep, instead of counting sheep, I found myself counting the number of fights I had seen since my old man started taking me to them two a week before I needed two digits to count my age. I finally fell asleep at two thousand. But with the exception of Sonny Liston quitting to Cassius Clay in Miami in 1964, I could not call back a single fight in which a champion had done an *el foldo* like Duran's dump to Leonard in New Orleans.

Was it fixed? I consider myself an expert in this unhappy field. The fight crowd never quite forgave me for writing *The Harder They Fall* in which a prototype of the mob-controlled Primo Carnera was limned. When Blinky Palmero's Johnny Saxton "defeated" Kid Gavilan in the Johnny Friendly town of Philadelphia, there was a full-page ad in the *New York Herald-Tribune* signed by this writer headed: "Boxing's Dirty Business Must Be Cleaned Up Now!"

The scandal in New Orleans is not going to be cleaned up by the earnest pleas and honest writers who love the sport but loathe the boxing *business*. Fights can be dumped in a dozen ways. Sometimes everybody but the fighter knows. Sometimes *only* the fighter knows.

Roberto Duran—the game chicken—dumped Tuesday night.

Having consulted with Dr. Ferdie Pacheco and other experts in sports medicine, I am absolutely convinced that Duran was telling the truth when he cried, *No mas, no mas!* He was suffering from a shoulder twinge, stomach cramps, and a severe case of salsaitis. If you don't know what that means, I suggest you find ex-*campeon* Roberto Duran on a private beach and ask him. Guaranteed he will punch back harder than he did against Ray Leonard Tuesday night.

Champions have obligations to paying customers and loyal bettors. Cramp or no cramp, ex-macho Roberto, give 'em back their pesos. And in the meantime, if there is a shred of honor left in the boxing commissions, hold up and give to the poor the $7 million this *pollo* flucked away.

[July and November 1980]

Ali-Holmes

Prefight

WRITERS—fiction writers, dramatists, poets—have been attending and describing epic fights all the way back to Homer with his classic blow-by-blow account of Epeus vs. Euryalus. En route to Las Vegas for Muhammad Ali's outrageous $8 million crack at usurper Larry Holmes's heavyweight championship, I count myself a member of a hardy club that includes such nineteenth-century literati as Conan Doyle, William Hazlitt, and George Bernard Shaw, and in our own century of violence, Jack London, Ernest Hemingway, Nelson Algren, Norman Mailer, and Joyce Carol Oates.

What draws writers to fighters? I remember Rocky Marciano asking that question in the kitchen of the old farmhouse he was using for training quarters at Grossinger's when he was preparing his farewell appearance against Archie Moore. Like writers, fighters perform in public, and when they come out of their corners they are naked and alone. In those corners are managers, trainers, and cutmen to give advice or lend first-aid for the cuts and lumps that fighters consider fair exchange for money and glory. In lieu of the Angelo Dundees and Freddy Browns, writers have agents, editors, and publishers. The critics who score writers' fights may cause them to cry "I was robbed" with all the outrage of a Marvin Hagler after his Vito Antuofermo fight.

But there is another reason for the fascination that drew Hazlitt to the Gas Man, Shaw to Tunney, and Mailer and this writer to Muhammad Ali, who dominated the fight world of the sixties and seventies as had Joe Louis in the thirties and forties. Not only is the fighter in there under the lights, naked and alone when he fights for the championship of the world, but his quest is also more dramatic than the Yankees' or the Steelers' because it is a now-or-never, one-time thing. If the Yankees blow the pennant, they'll be back next year. If the Steelers falter, they can always regroup.

What gives the Fight for the Championship its epic quality is the awesome finality of the outcome. Sonny Liston goes down before young Cassius Clay and he's really down and out. It's all over. A one-day legend after Miami and Lewiston, he's back in Vegas—not much better than he was on the bum in St. Louis—looking for favors from the wiseguys. Foreman blows the big one to Ali in Africa, and then what should have been an easy one to Jimmy Young, and he's out of fighting and on the Jesus circuit. Fighting for the prize focuses down on one night, one round, a fatal second when the mind loses touch with the punches it controls or means to avoid.

Contrary to popular conception, boxing is a mental sport. While quarterbacks, pitchers, and infielders making the double play have to see a game in their heads before they can execute it on the field, the fighter—we're talking about champions, not the Ron Standers of this world—must be chess players who make their moves according to strategic plans of action. Try to think of a prizefight as a chess game and you are a little closer to it than if you try to compare it to a bloody brawl in an alley.

Ex-middleweight Roger Donoghue, who taught Marlon Brando the fighter's moves in *On the Waterfront*, has explained how a boxer offers "pieces of himself," sometimes exposing his chin and letting an opponent land glancing blows that build false confidence. What you're really doing is drawing your opponent into a trap. When he strikes again you are ready for the counterpunch. His mistake is your opportunity. As in tennis, it is a game of forced errors. But as exciting as McEnroe and Borg can be, no matter what the outcome at Wimbledon and Forest Hills, you know they'll be back on the tube again and again.

Just as chess is simulated war, the Fight for the Championship is more like war itself in its impact on winners and losers and its irrevocability. When Leon Spinks upset a mentally unprepared Ali three years ago, Spinks could afford to smoke thousand-dollar bills and drive $20,000 cars against the traffic up one-way streets. Now a fickle public seems unaware that he'll also be climbing into the ring at Vegas Thursday night, just another fighter on the card against another would-be, Bernard Mercado.

The drama of the fight game lies not so much in success stories as in failure stories. Think of "interim champ" Jimmy Ellis, who won the tournament to find a successor to Ali when the title was heisted because Ali said no to the Vietnam War. Today Jimmy works as a one-eyed sparring partner for the aging/ageless Ali.

Or remember Buster Mathis, that giant butterball with remarkable agility, who looked like a coming champion of the world until he crossed the tracks in front of oncoming trains— the Frazier Freight and the Ali Express. Today fat Buster is just another strong boy in overalls loading trucks in Grand Rapids, Michigan. I remember the night he ran out of gas in the twelfth round against Ali in the Houston Astrodome. Following fighters all my life, I had always found it more revealing to go first to the loser's dressing room. I found Mathis sitting on a bench in a gloomy vestibule, all 260 pounds of him sobbing, "It's all over . . . it's all over . . ."

In the winner's dressing room, amid the jubilation of Ali's entourage, Ali the Compassionate was saying, "I wanted them to stop it. I didn't want to hit him anymore. I didn't want to hurt him."

189

That was almost ten years ago, in what might be called Ali's middle age, after he had lost the first fight of his life (Joe Frazier I), and was cranking himself up to winning his title back again.

The Fight (The King Is Dead)

HERE IN LAS VEGAS, this glittering, easy-come, easy-go capital of the Western world, where the losers outnumber the winners a thousand-to-one, Muhammad Ali joined the silent majority at last.

True, your average loser doesn't walk away with eight million spondulicks (which he will share with his partners Herbert Muhammad, the Internal Revenue Service, and an entourage that will be out Monday looking for new ways to live in the manner to which they have become accustomed through the providential Mr. Ali). But losing is *losing* and, even with his record jackpot, the most theatrical and controversial of all heavyweight champions has bowed out uncharacteristically— not with a bang but a whisper.

After last night's pathetic performance—no jab, no legs, more dope than rope—the song is ended, but no member of Ali's believers would like to think that the memory of the Holmes fiasco will linger on. The ghetto children, who took heart from the float-and-sting of their black butterfly, and their white counterparts would like to remember the razzle and the dazzle that befuddled Liston and the heart and mind that conquered Frazier and Foreman. Not a single note of that honey melody was to be heard in Ali's round-after-round catching as a sharp, serious, credible new champion, Larry Holmes, pitched his shutout against the battered ghost.

There are two kinds of champions, commission-appointed and popularly acclaimed. Last night, even for the last of the diehards, Larry Holmes became the heavyweight champion of the world. Now this writer knows how Jack London felt when he picked Jim Jeffries over Jack Johnson and how the sentimentalists wept when they hung with Joe Louis against Rocky Marciano. This corner had voted against the logic and with the myth. But the moment comes when reality prevails against dreams, romance, and dancing old-fashioned two-steps with the past. It is as painful as it is healthy to admit, "The king is dead . . ."

Before I began writing this requiem, Joe Louis was wheeled down the aisle to ringside. The bell for Round 1 of Holmes-Ali was yet to ring. Here are my notes, verbatim: "Joe Louis wheeled in—mouth hangs open—eyes staring—what is he seeing? He holds his head in his hands. An attendant wipes spittle from his mouth. His head sags. He sees nothing. The crowd cheers as Ali comes down the aisle. Louis doesn't see him. Doesn't hear the cheers."

Our Joe Louis, the greatest before "The Greatest," destroyer of Billy Conn and Maxie Baer and Max Schmeling, slumped beside me in his wheelchair. After the early rounds of the fight last night that Louis was attending without seeing, a fight in which Larry Holmes established immediate dominance and exposed Muhammad as an old man, we found ourselves calling on the Lord of this cruel sport to spare us the sight of a wheelchair for Ali.

If the live gate was a record 6 million, with another 45 million in theaters around the world, the paying customers, many of whom felt they were rope-a-doped, were cheated of the most furious exchange of the evening.

From where I sat near Ali's corner—by coincidence in almost the same relationship to his corner I enjoyed in his victory over Liston in Miami sixteen years ago—it looked as if Angelo Dundee wanted to stop the fight when he saw that Ali was no longer able to defend himself. Another round or two and this prideful warrior might have been as damaged as his ex-doctor Ferdie Pacheco thinks he already is. The faithful Bundini Brown backed Ali's wish to go on with the ordeal. Bodyguard

191

Pat Patterson tried to separate Angelo and Bundini. Then Patterson looked down at Herbert Muhammad, sitting directly in front of me. Herbert had not been able to watch the fight for at least the previous two rounds. Herbert gave Patterson a little hand signal and then buried his head in his hands.

The Holmes-Ali fight was over and so was Bundini-Dundee.

In the silence of the crowd, subdued by the disappointing spectacle, Sylvester Stallone, a rocky-eyed optimist, found something glorious in the effort Ali made and in the glory that had come to Larry Holmes. While I pretended to agree with him, because he spoke dramatic logic, my heart still belonged to the old music. That music had stopped now. Holmes and Stallone were dancing to a different bongo. And while we look before and after, and pine for what is not, is it not time to welcome new champions who pay their dues?

[October 1980]

The Welterweights: Sugar Ray and "Hitman" Hearns Walk with Legends

THESE WERE GLADIATORS who climbed through the red, white, and blue ropes, before a star-studded crowd, in the shadows of the pretentiously, but aptly, named Caesar's Palace. Only Sugar Ray Leonard and Tommy Hearns, two welterweight champions determined that there should be only one, were gladiators with a difference.

Thanks to the technology explosion, the wonder of the satellite beaming a prize fight to almost 300 cities, 55 countries, and—they say—250 million people (grossing a possible $40 million), our modern gladiators were paid way over gladiatorial scale—$8-to-10 million for the winner and now undisputed champion Sugar Ray Leonard, with an estimated $6 million to console poor Tommy Hearns as he heads back to Detroit's Kronk Gymnasium to nurse his wounds, rethink his mistakes, and plan his revenge.

A title once held by fighters of legend like Henry Armstrong, Barney Ross, and Ray Robinson was claimed last night by a worthy successor in a fourteen-round battle of wills and skills that ranked with the great ones we've seen in this division over fifty years.

As these two young men of contrasting backgrounds, styles, and personalities climbed through the ropes in a burst of energy and showmanship, the tension at ringside was almost unbearable. If there was a tension scale like a Richter, this was a 10.

Music from *Rocky* blared, Caesar's Palace flags waved, and an expectant crowd almost evenly divided cheered their champions, tall Tommy Hearns in a robe of white satin; the graceful, now revved-up Sugar Ray, dancing around the ring. Music up. Then silence. The bell. An animal roar, and The Showdown—as it had been hyped and indeed turned out to be—was our only reality. Nothing in sports equals this moment when two perfectly matched athletes—after months of sparring, running, bag punching, calisthenics, and tactical planning that prepare young bodies and minds for this terrible test—move toward each other at last.

For round after early round, Leonard gave a credible imitation of Ali on defense in his prime. Desert heat still lingered in the dusk, and Hearns, who never had gone more than ten rounds (and only three times, at that) in his short but explosive career, tested his suspect stamina. Leonard's strategy was dance and move away, side-to-side, in a boxing ballet meant to frustrate his tall, baleful, dangerous, but less experienced opponent. Hearns's face—long and angular, Aztec in its impassivity, lack of expression becoming an expression to remember—was a study in combative concentration as he pursued the elusive Sugar, using his freak seventy-eight-inch reach to score with whipping jabs and occasionally crisp right crosses.

Five rounds with Leonard hardly throwing a punch—was he giving the fight away? His answer was abrupt and violent in the sixth round. In a dramatic shift of gears, he was on the offensive now, reverting to the style of the first Duran fight in Montreal, catching Hearns with furious left hooks and left-right combinations. Big rounds for Ray. It is Hearns who is going backward now, eyes weary and worried. He's ahead in rounds, but Leonard the boxer is outslugging him. Hearns is jarred and staggered.

You could almost hear the frantic instruction from Hearns's corner. "Now *you* dance and box, don't let him nullify the physical advantage. Make distance your ally. Jab, jab, time the distance, shoot the right to the bruised left eye."

Thus the battle swings back to Hearns. There are brilliant, brutal exchanges, but Tommy has the range and has regained poise and confidence. With only three rounds to go, he's at least two points ahead, possibly three, and the damaged eye of Sugar Ray Leonard is beginning to offend the squeamish.

And then, just as in the movies (maybe they hadn't played that *Rocky* theme for nothing), a desperate but self-composed—make that *self-possessed*—Sugar Ray reaches down as all the great ones do and comes up with an explosive rally that turns the tide one more time. Vicious lefts to the jaw and body, combinations that buzz-saw a tiring Hearns into the ropes. Terrible punches that make us tremble. Valiant but overwhelmed, Tommy Hearns is falling out of the ring. When he climbs back, the eyes are glazed. *Queer Street* they call it in the cruel vocabulary of pugilistica. Hearns fights back, but the air is out of the balloon. Leonard smells blood, smells victory, moves in. Hearns is about to fall when a referee more merciful than most moves in to grab the wounded Cobra. When he turns to raise the hand of the best welterweight in the world today, those in the $500 seats knew they had gotten their money's worth.

Old-timers were comparing it with Robinson-Basilio. New-timers were looking forward to Leonard-Hearns II. It could be World War III.

[September 1981]

The Gerry Cooney Story

Black Day for White Hope

WHEN I FIRST met Gerry Cooney, he was a kid, an over-grown twenty-four-year-old who had won his battle with adolescent acne and knock-kneed awkwardness. He was an odd mix of shyness and teen-age prankishness, with a dark Irish ambivalence toward the public recognition thrust upon him after he cast a white shadow on the black world of heavyweight champions.

Since the Joe Louis–Ezzard Charles–Joe Walcott days, there have been only two Caucasian interruptions to the steady march of Afro-American heavies—the indestructible Rocky Marciano and the not-so-indestructible Ingemar Johansson. Along came Patterson, Liston, Ali, Foreman, Frazier, Norton, Holmes, Weaver, Spinks, and Tyson. Even the contenders, the overweights, the momentary champions were black—Page and Thomas, Witherspoon and Tubbs, Berbick, Tucker, and Dokes.

For a generation, honkies have been relegated to trial horses and rugged losers like Jerry Quarry and George Chuvalo. White Hopers barely had time to learn his name before Duane Bobick was exposed in less than a round by Ken Norton.

So, in a sports/business that has never outgrown its traditional ethnic rivalries, there is still an appeal to primitive emotions most fans have overcome in baseball and football.

Cooney, in the early eighties, was a very hot ticket. On the eve of the Norton fight in the Garden, sensing the left hook would do to this aging Kenny what it had already accomplished with two other prestigious senior citizens—Jimmy Young and Ron Lyle—we talked about the fame and fortune that was about to descend upon him like a flash storm.

One day he's just a big kid commuting from what was then blue-collar Huntington to the traditional grime of Gleason's Gym in downtown Manhattan. But before his fast-talking manager could say "God bless America," Gerry is training in posh Palm Springs, with movie stars taking the place of the beery aficionados who had seen the good ones come and go at the old gym that stank so sweetly of blood and sweat and dead cigars.

Almost before he knew what hit him—because he hadn't been hit that hard or that often in an upwardly mobile career that had never taken him beyond Round 8, with nineteen of his twenty-five fights not even going four—the six-foot-seven-inch boy-next-door was in there for a mere nine million bucks with Larry Holmes, a true heavyweight champion. Holmes had gone fifteen with a vintage Norton, a punishing twenty-three in two bouts with Shavers, who had been left for dead by both Weaver and Snipes, and had proved himself a fistic Lazarus who could not only rise from the dead but bury them in his place.

Having paid his dues, Holmes broke out in verbal hives at the sight of the young, white Gerry-come-lately upstaging him on the cover of national magazines, and getting parity on the pay night, despite the fact that this Long Island honker had been an awkward kid in the Golden Gloves when Larry was punching and getting punched for a living from San Juan to Manila.

Holmes got even in that pivotal fight with Cooney five years ago, jabbing him mercilessly (though whoever heard of a merciful jab?) and setting him up for the straight right hand until after awhile Gerry's face became a sickeningly easy target for the champion's right-hand rifle shots.

Anyone who questioned Cooney's readiness to climb through the ropes against Holmes was on solid ground. Less solid were those who questioned Cooney's heart. Heart, or courage, or bottom as it used to be known in the bareknuckle days, is a necessary ingredient of every sport. As they sang in *Damn Yankees,* "You gotta have heart . . . miles 'n' miles 'n' miles 'n' miles of heart . . ." But since boxing is the most personal, naked, one-on-one sport ("a chess game with blood," we once described it), heart, grace-under-pressure, true grit are not only exposed but revealed on a giant magnifying glass under blinding lights. And so in this intensely personalized sport/combat, the contestants are more inclined to hypersensitivity than most athletes in other fields.

In a lifetime of watching and knowing professional fighters, I've been struck by their kinship with poets rather than tobacco-chewing outfielders from Georgia or teen-age wonders at Wimbledon. "I'm not hurt, just embarrassed," a friend of mine told me after the referee stepped in to save him from further punishment. In the dressing room at the Garden, Archie McBride, a heavyweight I co-managed, stared at the floor after being stopped by Floyd Patterson in seven and mumbled, "I'm okay. I'm okay. I just feel bad you and all your friends had to see me like that."

When Floyd Patterson lost his title to Liston in the most humiliating way a champion can, KOd in one, he donned a disguise complete with false beard and sneaked out of Chicago like a serious bank thief on the lam. Losing fighters have been known to go out and get drunk, or in these days snort a line, or hole up in a brothel or a monastery.

So what Gerry Cooney did after the Holmes fight, after his corner decided to abort Larry's moving in for the *coup de grace* in the thirteenth, wasn't a total break with boxing tradition. Gerry went off and hid.

Cooney Questions Career After Losing to Holmes

AFTER THE HOLMES FIGHT, Cooney wanted to be alone or with his in-group high school buddies. He felt he had let the "Cooney-Country" people down. He brooded, he drifted, a fistic Hamlet asking himself into the night, "To fight or not to fight?" And getting no answers. He was famous, even in defeat, and an overnight millionaire, but—son of tough Tony Cooney, who had trained him and his older brother, Tommy, to be fighters before their teens—he didn't know where he was going, or who he was.

His sabbatical from boxing went on for months, and months that grew into years. His diehard fans began to wonder—was Gerry Cooney hanging them up at age twenty-eight? Was the last White Hope (although that peg truly revolted him) packing it in because he had enough bread and couldn't get his head together after losing to Holmes? Some boxing writers were on his back, and some of the Cooney-lovers were losing patience, too. He could have challenged Mike Weaver for the WBA title, or Dokes, when "Dynamite" or "Cokeamite," took Weaver by a suspicious one-round KO and then "successfully" defended that title via a highly questionable draw. Into such bathos had the once-vaunted heavyweight crown descended. Gerry would have been a lively candidate to pick up the pieces. But it seemed as if the heart that had carried him through thirteen bruising rounds against the crafty and vengeful Holmes was no longer where his hard-minded father had wanted it to be—in the prize ring.

And when, after twenty-seven months, he finally decided to put on the gloves for real, it was only half for real. It wasn't against Snipes or Berbick or even a Quick Tillis. No, for this auspicious comeback, his cautious manager Dennis Rappaport and his surrogate father, trainer Victor Valle, chose a former sparring partner, Phil Brown, whose main interest in the fight

199

seemed to be what corner of the ring would be most comfortable for a declining figure. And when even that "fight" was postponed again and again, due to well-publicized and chronic injuries to knuckle, shoulder, and eye, the Anti-Cooney Club grew rapidly. Nor did things improve when Cooney made short work of another journeyman, George Chaplin.

When Gerry followed up that stirring victory not with a challenge of a top-rated contender but with yet another retirement, even the most loyal Huntingtonian was taking down the green flag and hoisting the white. "Forget Cooney, he's got his millions, he's in the disco, he's a joke," a bartending ex-boxer exploded at the mention of his name.

A few weeks ago, at a spacious but Cooney-cluttered condo at the brand-new super-yuppie spa at Great Gorge in upper New Jersey, Gerry nodded philosophically at the criticism that's shadowed his curious career since the Holmes fight, just three bouts (lasting less than seven rounds) in five years. In that same period Spinks has fought fifty-three rounds, including two fifteen-round razor-thin wins over an aging Holmes, eight with the hard-hitting Jim MacDonald and three years ago a bristling twelve for the light-heavyweight title with our ring-wise Long Islander Eddie Davis.

"Did you see what one of the columnists wrote about me the other day?" Gerry said softly. "That if I were George Washington we'd still be part of the British Empire because I'd have said it's too cold to fight in winter? That hurt. And I said something to the writer I shouldn't have said. I guess I shouldn't let it get under my skin. But in a lot of ways, while it may have looked as if I just took the money and ran, these have been tough years for me. They can laugh at the injuries and the postponements, but the knuckle problems and the shoulder weren't excuses. They were frustrating and they took time. Training, and then having to stop and heal and then start again, and stop again—it can drive you crazy. I'll admit I had moments when I started asking myself, 'Maybe I wasn't meant to be a fighter.'

200

"And there were so many other distractions. I honestly think if I had won the Holmes fight I wasn't ready for it. I was still a kid—it's taken me these years of frustration and trouble to grow up and feel like a man. The writers, they have a right to write whatever they please, but sometimes they just ask the obvious questions they already know the answers to, and don't take the time or the trouble to go deeper."

Brotherly Love Takes Its Toll

BACK IN HIS CONDO after a hard run, Gerry didn't hide from a hard question about his brother.

"Okay, my brother. It's easy to write a line about having family problems. That goes in one ear and out the other. But I wonder how well the writers would be doing their job if their brother was on hard drugs—if it was driving their family crazy—if they opened a restaurant-bar where the brother would go to the cash register to put in his arm. When you're in training for a fight that's all you should think about. But even getting ready for the Holmes fight—the night my father would've dreamed about—that's when my brother Tommy got into the heavy stuff.

"I know they keep saying, 'Excuses, excuses,' but how can you keep your mind on fighting when your brother comes into the house we grew up in, wants money again, and in front of our own mother, goes in the kitchen, gets a knife, and slashes his wrists!" Gerry puts his head down and relives it. "It was a nightmare. I had to call the police. He's in a rehab now and doing okay. But it's tough, it's tough, I hope he'll be okay. But those things take energy, the energy you need to be a fighter.

"Another thing. Fighters who get into big money aren't prepared. So many things come at them. So many distractions. I think there should be some kind of education for fighters, so they know what to do with the rest of their lives.

"And there's so much b.s. in the fight game. Like King trying to corner the market on the heavyweights. Witherspoon fights Smith and Carl King manages one of them and co-manages the other. But King doesn't control Spinks, Butch Lewis does, and Dennis [The Menace] Rappaport kept me independent. Believe me, I like boxing. I love to fight. I really wanted Holmes again—I learned a lot in that fight, what not to do, and press him more when I had him hurt, like in the tenth, and how to move away from the right hand.

"They say all things come to those who wait. I was overconfident for Holmes. Now I'm confident in a more mature way. I've got to win this fight. Winning now means more to me than it did then. So it isn't Holmes, but it's Spinks who beat Holmes. And if Holmes was the champion, no matter what all those commissioners say, then it's not just hype to consider this a fight for the heavyweight championship. I've got to win this fight."

"And Mike Tyson?" (Now the WBA-WBC champ.)

There is a pause. "Tyson can punch. I'm still not sure how well he takes a punch. But first things first. I'll make my statement with Spinks. And then see what happens."

In the plush ring at the Spa, where Yuppies commute fifty miles in their Mercedes to get expensive, carpeted health, Cooney goes ten rounds with three willing but run-of-the-mill sparring partners. He strolls the ring between rounds and, contrary to some reports, he's sweaty and a little bloody but not winded forty minutes later. Only one of the sparmates does a partial simulation of the smaller, much more mobile Spinks, and Gerry is not the most fleet of feet, though his hand speed is there, and the dangerous left hook, and the determination to prove he's more than hype and hoopla and soon-to-be $2.5 million richer.

He'll have to jab and hook, think and move to catch Spinks. I watched Cooney with three illustrious veterans, the slippery Tippy Larkin, the tough/smart Fritzie Pruden, and the old Jersey middleweight, once Marlon Brando's double in *On the*

Waterfront, now a U.S. marshal, Billy Kilroy. While diplomatically critical of his footwork, the consensus was that if Cooney can catch him and bang him to the body, Spinks will be hit harder than at anytime in his unbeaten career. "Holmes wobbled him," said one of the three, "and Gerry can topple him."

That just could happen in an early round, as Spinks has always been a slow starter, and Cooney has to go after him. He has to jab and remember to move his head to the right, so it won't be an inviting target for Spinks's right hand. Victor Valle seemed to be still teaching his almost thirty-one-year-old student that bit of wisdom in their workouts at the Spa. Both fighters are curiosities. Cooney the banger whose hands are faster than his feet but who fights back when stung or hurt. Spinks who seems neither boxer nor slugger, who doesn't move side to side with the grace of a Holmes or Ali or the earlier Ezzard Charles, but gives you lots of jerky movement, an unorthodox busybody who boxes to his own drummer, and that drum has a disconcerting way of changing rhythms. It's Cooney's left hook predictability against Spinks's constantly shifting and awkwardly clever unpredictability.

Cooney could knock him out, he's so much bigger and stronger. Spinks could jiggle and flurry, gadfly and busy his way to a decision. Spinks could punch and slice and accidentally butt Cooney's Irish version of a Roman nose, as a sparring partner did. The Cooney punch, plus Spinks's shifty experience, would make one helluva fighter.

But they'll be *two* fighters in Mr. Trump's ring tonight, Cooney with his place in boxing history on the line, and Spinks with his nontitle title at risk. Cooney and Spinks have both said they can't wait to get it on. I wish I knew who was going to win, so I could tell you in advance.

Our hunch is with the punch. But, unlike his brother Leon (to whom Ali once loaned the title for six or seven months), this Spinks thinks. Even without Howard Cosell, it could be a Monday night to remember.

Requiem for a Heavyweight

THE TITLE OF THE FIGHT—since fightbiz and showbiz are more and more interchangeable—was "The War at the Shore." Only, just short of five rounds of nonstop, nonclinch, take-no-prisoner intensity, a new title popped up on our screen for Michael Spinks's dramatic victory over the greatest heavyweight to fight out of Long Island since John Morrisey tried it in the nineteenth century.

So credit the winner-and-still-champion Spinks the Jinx with writing a new title to the unexpected five-round war: *Requiem for a Heavyweight*. And, putting vanity aside in this moment of emotion, after watching the brains and heart of a true fighter overcome the size and starboard power of an almost, a Could-Have-Been, and now it never will be the War at the Shore wound up with Cooney at the Shore retitled *The Harder They Fall*.

Boxing may be the most misunderstood of all sporting events. It would seem, unlike baseball or basketball or even water polo, that it is a confrontation of brawn, physical brutality, matter over mind. Wrong. Victory is not to the strongest or to the fleetest, it is to the man who has the unique gift of matching brain to body and hand movement, who is able to think two or three moves beyond his hurt. That ability separates the men from the boys, and in the climactic meeting between the ongoing Spinks and the no-going Cooney, it was the two-hundred-pound Spinks, the punching man's thinker and finally the thinking man's puncher, who proved himself the man, and Cooney, who should have destroyed him in four, finding himself outfought, outmanned, alas no longer a contender but a six-foot-seven boy suddenly over his head at the shore.

Now, with philosophy behind us and the technique of a very interesting contest ahead, let's, in the style of that extravagantly paid sports commentator, "go to the videotape." The picture we see shows a scowling and very serious Gerry Cooney going forward and pressing, jabbing, but (in the notes of this ringside table) "not too effectively." He's throwing lefts, but

Spinks is moving smartly away from them and then, deciding he has to do something, moves in and smacks Cooney's still inviting jaw (the same one that appealed to Larry Holmes five years ago). Round 1 to Huntington, but this is no Ken Norton, no standing target like Eddie Gregg. Ringside reporters turned to each other in agreement: "This is a fight."

It's still a fight in the second round with Cooney so-so jabbing and scoring with lefts softened by Spinks's knowing movements away from Cooney's predictable one-at-a-time left-hand shots. The fighter-thinker Spinks (you feel-see-think-see this with him at ringside) tells him to send Cooney a message: you think you're winning this fight, you think you're bigger and stronger, so *wham!*—my notes read: "three-punch combo—one, two—flush—Gerry's nose, Gerry's jaw." The round goes to the slower, shorter, lighter, smarter Spinks who says, "I'm here! I'm here!" even as blood begins to trickle from a torn right eyebrow. If Pierce Egan, who might have been doing this piece for the *Post* if it had been around in the late eighteenth or early nineteenth century, would have said for Round 3, "Spinks comes out gaily." A worried and slightly confident Cooney catches him with glancing left hooks, but the fighting mind of Michael brings him in and out. Cooney fights back awkwardly, ineptly, bravely, but once again the writers turn to each other because they are concerned with the entertainment value of a close fight and not with the futures of the contestants after this match, or maybe that the careers of one or the other is over. "This is a fight!"

The fourth round is the key, and it looks as if the key is in Cooney's hand, and he's ready to open all the doors in Trump's Plaza Hotel, Casino, and Roman Colosseum. Spinks is retreating, Cooney is coming forward, Cooney is winning, and he's not fighting an all-out knock-about as he did against the Nortons and Ron Lyles and Jimmy Youngs. He seems to know what he's doing. Spinks goes back to his corner on what appear to be weakening legs. One more round . . . the bigger, stronger banger is ready to take him out in five.

Only, wait! Round 5 tells us what boxing-fighting-mental-physical-heavyweight fighting is all about. Just when you think Cooney is coming on, Spinks and his ring-wise corner know what Michael has to do to save and win this fight. We were close, but not close enough to hear what Eddie Futch was telling Spinks, but it must have been, "Look, Michael, you know he's wide open for right hands, you know you can catch him with combinations that will confuse and bemuse and abuse him. Forget legs, forget tired, get off first and take him out. He discourages. He's brave, he takes a punch, a fair punch, but give him a bunch of punches and . . ."

And Round 5 is two minutes in and Big Gerry Cooney is in very big trouble. He's forgotten everything he's learned in all those months from Victor Valle, or maybe he's remembered what he's disremembered that Victor Valle forgot to tell him.

Anyway, with fistic fate thumbing its nose at all the experts—those who had Cooney winning early or Spinks winning by decision late—with two handfuls of seconds left in Round 5, Spinks is beating the deleted out of Cooney, hitting him with so many punches only a computer can count them. And Cooney is down. And down again. And a very nice boy/man or man/boy from Long Island is not only down but out of the fight game and into the rest of his life. While Michael Spinks, the fighting man's thinker, the thinking man's fighter, goes on to better things. Like the other Mike—Tyson.

So, if Tyson bonecrushes Tony Tucker and Tyrell Biggs and Frank Bruno and all the other million-dollar nonentities Jim Jacobs has lined him up for through 1987 into 1988, somewhere down the road we may see the heavyweight fight that brings us back to the good old days of one heavyweight champion. Like Louis, Marciano, Ali, and Holmes. Out of the alphabet soup, HBO, WBC, WBA, IBF . . . we're down to an ultimate two now—and it only takes two men when their names are Tyson and Spinks.

[June 1987]

The Eight-Minute War:
Hagler-Hearns

IN THIS AGE of hype and hyperbole, maybe we have to watch the fat adjectives and the easy-come superlatives—but banging this out a few minutes after Hit Man Tommy Hearns got hit by so many thunderous right hands that his knees wobbled, his eyes glazed, and Marvelous Marvin Hagler left him for dead, let's throw caution out the window (just as Hagler did) and call this the most furious eight minutes of all-out fistfighting seen by this old ring-goer in fifty years.

And if you want to go back another twenty-five, that's all right, too. Because old-timers (and new-timers who have seen the old films) came away from this one with their own knees trembling, convinced that they had seen the most ferocious first round since the first three minutes of the legendary Dempsey-Firpo fight, when champion Jack Dempsey was knocked through the ropes, and both men fought each other to a standstill, until in a handful of minutes only one man was standing, Dempsey, and the Wild Bull of the Pampas was down and out but never forgotten.

Hagler-Hearns belongs in that select company of Greatest Fights of the Century. And the fifteen thousand who were lucky enough to see it live Monday night—and the two million in theaters around the country—will be talking about Round 1 as long as boxing remains the savage and exciting sport it is, and boxing nostalgia lives on. Officially it was all over two minutes and one second into Round 3, but to those of us at ringside, the fight was won in that explosive and unexpected first round, when Hagler sprang from his corner, caught Hearns in a flurry, and had him backing up before the fight was thirty seconds old.

Suddenly and almost immediately, all those physical advantages that Hearns's boosters had been describing all week—height, reach, speed, punching power—were taken away from him by a champion who fought like a man possessed, possessed of pride, relentless ring smarts, and a will that was stronger than Tommy's. If a battle as furiously fought as was this one can also be described as a psychological victory for Hagler, it's because he willed his way through Hearns's long and snaky left jab and his vaunted right hand.

To his credit, Hearns fought back, forced to sacrifice the game plan and fight for his life.

Fight back he did, with his own wicked jabs and own right hand that cut the hairless one high on the forehead. With blood spurting down to make a grotesque red mask of his face, the champion pressed on. Time and time again, in the first round and the second, Hearns would go reeling backward, with Hagler in pursuit, as if Hearns were a mugger surprised by a victim who refused to give up his wallet and instead turns on and runs his tormentor down.

Hearns had been tormenting Hagler all week, with his short but showboating training in the posh Caesar's Palace Pavilion, predicting a third-round knockout, while Hagler, true to his blue-collar background and character, was putting in his hard and lonely work in a downtown gym. Tommy was surprisingly accurate in predicting a three-round fight. Not even more surprisingly, it was the tall, racehorse-trained challenger who would fall in three.

In the prefight analysis, we had mentioned a possible chink in Hearns's shining armor, a failure of nerves or a tendency to panic when the pressure became so overwhelming that his skills deserted him. By the end of that already historic Round 1, that's exactly what was happening as he tried to ride out the storm with evasive moves that failed to evade. When they both connected—and there were too many punches to keep track of as in a normally hard fight—it was Hearns who showed the hurt and Hagler who poured it on.

Though he fought back in spurts, Hearns was clearly weakening, off balance, his discipline gone as a bloodied but oh-so-unbowed Hagler roared, or rather, warred on. On the cap he had been wearing all month was a dirty three-letter word: WAR, and that's what we mean about no tripe to the hype because Hearns was fighting to survive and Hagler was fighting as if his country had been invaded, or—since he's a home body—as if a dangerous thug had gunned his way into his house, a thief whose violence had to be taken away from him by brutal counterforce.

There was an anxious moment when referee Richard Steele called time for a closer look at Hagler's cut, a moment when there might have been an ironic turnabout with Hearns winning by TKO a five-minute fight he was clearly losing. But Steele waved the aroused champion back to the fray, and the champion showed his appreciation by banging Hearns with a thunderous right hand, followed by combinations to head and body that carried a mean message: "I own you! I own you!"

Poor Tommy Hearns, looking so swaggeringly dominating in the countdown days to Monday night's drama, had a sad look on his face that said, "I agree. I agree." Down went the Golden Boy in the golden trunks, as the bloodied-face winner—and still champion—was carried around the ring on the shoulders of his handlers in a scene reminiscent of *The Great White Hope*. There have been a lot of fight movies put down by this critic because the nonstop blow by blow à la *Rocky* looks like an exaggerated melodrama. Monday night we saw the real—not the reel—thing, and although it was only an eight-minute movie, it moved us to emotions true fight fans will never forget.

When this writer was a few years younger he used to ask his father, "Dad, did you really see Luis Firpo knock the great Jack Dempsey out of the ring?" One of these years I expect to be answering a similar question from my five-year-old. "Yes, Benny, it really happened, just the way you heard about it, a great champion imposed his will on a famous challenger in the opening round."

[April 1985]

Sugar's Sweet, Marvin's Sour

THIS WAS THE FIGHT that only Angelo Dundee, and the loyal adherents of the new world middleweight champion, described with any accuracy.

Sugar Ray would be too fast for Marvelous, they assured the Haglerians. He would frustrate his stronger, harder-hitting opponent with body moves and head moves, move in, throw punches in quick bunches, and dance away from the heavy artillery. He would neutralize Hagler's aggression, outsmart and outcute a champion who had successfully defended his undisputed title a dozen times, hadn't lost in eleven years, and was edging into the golden circle of middleweight immortals like Sugar Ray Robinson and Carlos Monzon.

That was Sugar Ray's scenario, and to the wonderment of some and chagrin of others, it *played*, at least through the first half of a technical fight when Sugar Ray, boxing with old-time skill laced with caution, was able to run, flurry, score points, make the old champion miss, and make those of us who had foreseen an early Hagler knockout look as if we should find another line of work.

For those who are drawn to boxers who run and hide, land punches that sting rather than jar, Sugar Ray was proving to be their darling. But in the fifth round, Hagler seemed to decide that enough *was* enough and began to press the elusive comeback artist with bodypunching that hurt. He won the round big, and the closer followers of the game were convinced that the tide was turning. Sugar Ray was slowing down, and although Marvin wasn't speeding up he was pressing on in a way that made us feel that sooner or later the tires would go flat on Sugar's bicycle.

Round 9 had echoes of Hagler-Hearns' tumultuous Round 1, with Hagler finally nailing and hurting what seemed a slowly melting Sugar. But to his credit, Leonard would flurry back, refusing to let his weary legs and arms quit on him as nature would tell him to. He wasn't winning, but the crowd—and apparently the judges—were giving him an A for effort, an A+ for being there at the end of ten, somehow still dancing, but with the heavy feet of the marathon dancers shuffling on and on in the old Depression days.

Dancing, running, surviving, showboating, playing to the crowd, that oh so fickle crowd, Sugar Ray was still there at the final bell. Our old middleweight champion, not bloodied or bowed, but simply frustrated, had won a close decision on this reporter's card. But two of the three judges found for Sugar Ray, choosing light over heat, or glitz over true grit. It was one of those subjective decisions that had boxing writers in fierce debate, and at least in one case a New York writer and a Washington writer almost ready to fight Round 13 themselves.

It was that kind of evening, with a now bitter Marvelous Marvin telling us, "I can't believe it. I rocked him, I hurt him, he fought like a girl, a split-decision should go to the champion, I felt at the end of the fight I won it, but Pat [co-manager Petronelli] said, 'No, no, this is Vegas.'"

The truth is, a somewhat befuddled and maybe aging champion let the early rounds slip away from him, didn't press with the savagery of the Hagler we know, and leaves this glitzy and unpredictable town "with a terrible feeling in my mouth."

If there's a rematch, let it go fifteen. Maybe then the better man will emerge victorious. But for the moment, the king is dead, long live the king.

[April 1987]

Historic Night in the Ring: Holmes-Spinks

IT WAS A NIGHT to give heart to the underdogs of this world to dream the impossible dreams.

It's a once upon a time fairy tale of a light-heavyweight champion not considered with the great ones—Conn, Moore, Foster—who accomplished Saturday night what no light-heavyweight champion had ever been able to accomplish: lift the crown from the heavyweight champ.

Going up against that undefeated heavyweight champion, even one clearly on the skids, Michael Spinks was not only a 5-to-1 underdog to Larry Holmes but given no chance by any of the boxing writers I checked with through the day—with one exception. Our fearless leader, Jerry Lisker, called it in advance loud and clear: Spinks!

As far as Holmes had obviously slipped from the form that made him a credible successor to Ali, I thought he'd have enough left—the straight jab and the hard right—to handle the strong and actively unorthodox Spinks. In the early rounds that seemed the smart pick, with Holmes moving forward and jabbing, no longer brilliantly or punishingly, but doing enough to establish control.

Then things began to happen. Spinks things.

Larry was looking slow and puffy and Michael was taking

heart. At times Michael's style was to walk away. At times he backed off and dropped his arms. At times he cried out that Holmes was giving him the elbow. But there were also times when he startled Holmes by suddenly moving forward and throwing punches in bunches. They didn't hurt Holmes, but they made him unhappy.

That became the pattern of the fight: Holmes puffy-faced, jabbing tentatively and unable to throw the right hand that had pumped defeat and retirement into the face of Gerry Cooney.

Except for the well-timed flurries when Spinks shifted gears and drove the old champion backward, it was no Louis-Conn, not exactly pregnant with dramatic movements. As both contestants admitted in the postfight press conference, neither one was hurt or in trouble at any time.

What was most spectacular about this fight was its historicity: unanimous decision for Spinks, two of the cards by a single point—which tallied precisely with what this writer scored, ditto Dick Young and other boxing mavens.

It's been boxing tradition that the close ones go to the champion, as Louis was helped in the first Walcott fight and later Ali and Holmes. This fight did live up to its History Hype in this respect: Holmes was grounded in his quest to match Marciano's record of 49-0. With all his riches, his "$99 million in the bank," he will now live in the record books as 48-1.

How the triumphant Michael Spinks will fare in the confusing world of the fragmented heavyweight championship should give a welcome zest to the game this year. Meanwhile, the disingenuous and appealing conqueror laughed off the hard questions at the press conference: "Look, don't ask me about tomorrow. Let me enjoy tonight!"

It was a night to remember, not round by round but for the historic passing of an old champion and the crowning of a new. And for one Ripley element: of all the brother acts in boxing, only the brothers Spinks (Leon and Michael) have become heavyweight champions of the world.

So Leon's was a fluke and short-lived. More power to the little brother who stood in his shadow. Michael brings a welcome new energy to the lackluster heavyweight division—the long-shot breaker of the jinx that has frustrated light-heavyweight champions from slick Philadelphian Jack O'Brien to power puncher Bob Foster.

Sad to see a final champion come up empty. Good to see a hard-working young champion bang his way into the golden circle.

Boxing as metaphor for life, its surprises and its inevitability, moves on.

[September 1985]

They Fall Harder When They're Old: Tyson-Holmes

WE PICK UP exactly where we left off in our appraisal of the Mike Tyson–Larry Holmes "fight" on the day of their encounter for the heavyweight championship of the world that was hyped by the black Don (King) and the white Don (Trump) as "heavyweight history."

It would be, we feared, not so much an athletic contest between the new champion and the old champion dreaming those comeback dreams. Instead, it would be a ritual, a sacrifice of the old, tired ex-champion with nothing left against a new, powerful, relentless, remorseless twenty-one-year-old who has everything left. Tyson thundered right hands that drove Holmes back into the ropes and, finally, into that inevitable retirement beyond that first, iffy, semiretirement never-never land in which Larry Holmes drifted for almost two years, coming back for the farewell pay night that brought him $3 million and brought us to the conclusion, once again, that age thirty-eight is the dividing line beyond which lies boxing senility.

We have mentioned, in our retrospective on the comeback attempts of ex-champions, that it was no fun to watch an ancient Joe Louis outboxed, outpunched, and outpunished by his successor, Ezzard Charles. And there was agony rather than exhilaration in the ten-round pounding of our black prince, Muhammad Ali, at the hands of the finely tuned Larry Holmes eight years ago.

Last evening, at the posh Imperial Ballroom at the Trump Plaza, where five hundred celebrities from Barbra Streisand and Kirk Douglas to John McEnroe and Tatum O'Neal had gathered, the only celebrity I felt an urge to embrace was Ali. His face looked a little puffy, he was walking slowly, and you had to lean forward to hear the whisper that once had been a roar of defiance, triumph, and irrepressible humor. As we hugged each other in a way that concentrated twenty-five years into a moment of shared highs and lows, Ali whispered: "Too old, just gettin' too old. . . ."

We could describe the abbreviated Tyson-Holmes fiasco blow by blow, but that would be as much an exercise in futility as was Holmes's aimless attempt to challenge Tyson's claim to the first undisputed heavyweight championship of the world since Larry himself held that proud title.

Ali, the super champion become the super victim, said it for all of them. "We're gettin' too old. . . ." Larry Holmes, finally coming out for the first round after McEnroe and mother Tatum had to be introduced to an impatient crowd of sixteen thousand for the third time, faced the young tyro Tyson with a look in his eye that sent an unmistakable message to his brain: "Gettin' too old."

Young, confident, unforgiving, Tyson came out fighting, and old, anxious, tentative Holmes came out retreating. Where once there had been the stinging jab, there was now a long left hand that pushed out in anxiety. Something in Larry's demeanor was saying: "Please don't hurt me." My notes for Round 1 read: "Holmes has nothing. He runs, but not on legs with any plan. Simply falling back in disorder. No jab, no right, no legs, *nothing.*"

The Larry Holmes of the Ken Norton fight and the Earnie Shavers fight and who defended the title twenty times with skills that brought him to the threshold of greatness, that

Larry Holmes was simply not in the ring with Tyson last night. He looked like Larry Holmes, or maybe his slower, thicker brother. He answered to the name of Larry Holmes, but the performer, or rather the nonperformer, who showed up to fill the bill was an imposter who had no business being in the same ring with a black angel/monster of aggression who may still lack the finesse of a Joe Louis but who restores to the heavyweight division a sense of unity, dignity, and finality that's been lacking ever since Holmes put down the mysterious Gerry Cooney six years ago, and then started his slow, tortuous descent to the pathetic disarray he brought to his less-than-four-round farewell to boxing.

[January 1988]

Spinks's Magic Act
Is Not Enough

THIS MORNING, waiting for the bell that finally brings together the undisputed but beleaguered heavyweight champion of the world, Mike Tyson, and the also undefeated, unpredictable and mischievous challenger, Michael Spinks, there's a sense of relief in the press room that at last you can write about the impending contest, the long-awaited confrontation between the two best heavyweights in the world, with a combined record of sixty-five wins, most by KO, and losses none.

So many major fights have fizzled as major disappointments—a Holmes or an Ali revealed behind the screen of hype, a Cooney suddenly coming apart under pressure—that one hesitates to say what we're about to say: Let's try to forget for one hour tonight, to put aside the emotional and economic melodrama of The Tyson Story, the complex battle for the mind and heart (and bank account) of the twenty-one-year-old throwback to the old days of fistfighting brutes—and focus on what may happen tonight!

Brute force, a power-puncher goes after the kind of opponent he's never met before, a guile guy, an artful dodger, a thirty-one-year-old who has been through light-heavyweight wars with Yaqui Lopez and Dwight Braxton and Eddie Davis and then mysteriously moved up from 175 pounds to 200, Saturday afternoon weighing in at 212¼ with his trousers on, though we didn't get to check his pockets—maybe weights, more likely just money.

Anyway, he is the only growing boy of thirty-one, and he's not growing bigger. He's growing smarter, with the invaluable Eddie Futch as full professor in charge of Fistic Strategy, though Spinks has a knack for thinking on his feet, an Actors Studio type who may not know the whole script but has an instinctive gift for improv.

In all the years I've been following this sweetly brutal science, I've never seen one quite like Spinks. Stick-and-move-move would seem the logical approach to neutralizing Tyson's talents. But Spinks isn't that kind of boxer. No Billy Conn. No early Ali. No Ezzard Charles moving with grace from side to side. Just a lot of zigging and zagging, refusing to accommodate you by simply presenting himself in front of you with jiggle steps, a kind of juggler of the ring who suddenly jabs and throws an uppercut from a funny angle that shouldn't work, but sometimes does for exactly that reason. It's so unexpected, so unorthodox.

Michael Spinks is no take-out puncher, though he stiffened Cooney. He didn't stop Braxton or Eddie Davis, and in thirty rounds with a depreciating Larry Holmes never had him in the kind of trouble that Mike Weaver and the other heavy hitters had him in when he was younger and faster.

But for a guy who can't punch and can't box, at least in the classic style we call boxing, Spinks does something else: somehow, until now, he finds a way to win, in his own style. A survivor original. And if this sounds as if we've written a preamble to vote for a Spinks upset of Cus D'Amato's little street kid grown up to a hard rock 218, you're wrong.

No matter how many different directions Spinks tries to move away from Tyson or toward him, no matter how many distractions, how many public airings of private dirty laundry have interrupted his training, how much he misses the guiding hand of surrogate father D'Amato and assistant surrogate, the late Jim Jacobs, no matter what angry "I've got a contract" Bill Cayton says about Don King, Robin Givens, and in-house, or rather in-castle mother-in-law Ruth Roper, no matter if he's only 50 percent of the 100 percent he could have been if he had totally dedicated himself to preparation like the great champions he reveres, no matter.

There has to come a time in this fight (say between rounds 4 and 7), when Spinks runs out of improvs, when the quickness of hand surprises old Michael, and when he realizes for the first time: "Oh mother, that's how a real heavyweight really hits!" He will be hit as he's never been hit before in all his amateur days and his dozen years of professional fighting, and he will go down and out fighting, unless a merciful Futch stops him from coming out for more, as he did with Joe Frazier in that fateful fourteenth of the Ali Thriller in Manila.

So on goes Tyson, on to Evander Holyfield a year from now, on to more astronomical gates and astronomical troubles. One can't help feeling that for this man-child in this gilded world, with his $4.5 million dollhouse, his Bentley, his Rolls, his woman, and his business controllers, the worst is yet to come. Anyone who comes from where he's been and loves to raise pigeons can't be all bad. We pray not.

So on to the fight. Once and for all. Bless the loser, and may God help the winner.

The biggest fight of all may still be Tyson vs. Tyson.

[June 1988]

The Second Coming of George Foreman

OKAY, LAUGH AT ME, tell me I'm a true child of the Hollywood studio where I was raised, that I've been to one movie set too many, prematurely convinced that all of life can be defined as one great movie.

Well, if you've been following Big George Foreman as long as I have—from the Olympic Games in Mexico City twenty-three years ago, to his disastrous night with Ali in Zaire (the "Rumble in the Jungle") six years later, to a pilgrimage to his Church of the Lord Jesus Christ in Houston and his horse-and-cattle ranch in rural northeast Marshall, Texas, just a few weeks ago—you can't help feeling that the George Foreman Story is the sum of every fight movie ever made, from *The Harder They Fall* to *Body and Soul* to Wallace Beery in *The Champ*. And come Friday evening, April 19, the forty-two-year-old ex-heavyweight champion of the world, in his "Second Coming" after an unprecedented ten-year retirement, is casting himself as a black "Rocky"—if not a black Lazarus—ready to challenge the twenty-eight-year-old undefeated king of the heavyweights, Evander Holyfield.

When Jersey Joe Walcott won the heavyweight crown from Ezzard Charles at the age of thirty-seven, that feat was considered a geriatric miracle. And the venerable Jersey Joe had been in there with toughies year after year, including twenty-six memorable rounds with Joe Louis. When Jim Jeffries came out of five-year retirement as the "Great White Hope" in his futile attempt to remove the belt from the lithe black waist of Jack Johnson, he was an ancient and creaky thirty-five, "a mere shadow," as we boxing guys say, "of his former self." So if old George, who reigned in '73–'74, can beat the socks off young Evander when they square off at Trump Plaza, he'll not only earn a niche in the Guinness Book of Records, he'll strike a blow for middle age that hasn't been equaled since *Life Begins at 40* became a runaway bestseller almost sixty years ago. Not to mention picking up a cool $10 million, not a bad paynight for a preacher who eschews the lifestyle of a Jim Bakker.

If you buy the premise of "George Foreman: The Movie," let's flash all the way back to young George, the Teenage Terror, establishing his identity as a big-fisted Lord of the Jungle of Houston's Fifth Ward, where the shy, overgrown drop-out found he could excel in the University of the Street: survive or die. A powerful hitter who found an outlet for pent-up energy in flattening anybody in sight, George somehow drifted into the Job Corps, where a fellow named Doc Broadus talked him into putting on the gloves with this blunt invitation: "You're big enough and ugly enough."

The gym was a revelation. On Front Street, in what George still calls "the back of Houston," it was a world of handguns, knives, drugs, muggings. As an accomplished street fighter, like his younger counterpart, Mike Tyson, whom he may eventually tangle with in the first $100-million fight (if he beats Holyfield), Big George was on the way to the slammer or the cemetery when amateur boxing gave him a reprieve.

In a brief amateur career he had all the finesse of a slaughterhouse worker pounding a mallet on the unprotected skull of a steer. Down they fell and up went George. With hardly a dozen fights he's in the Olympic tryouts. Four wins and he's our heavyweight entry in Mexico City, four more and the big

Black Power, Black Prince, Black Magic. Poor George—how could the undefeated heavyweight champion of the world be defined so pejoratively?—scowled and glared and treated the press as if it were his enemy, which indeed it was. Ali, whose gift for public relations matched his boxing skills, had an appetite for press conferences not unlike Jack Kennedy's. Somehow he managed to make the big black bopper from the backstreets of Houston a great *white* hope, or dope, and poor George didn't help matters by going everywhere with a pet police dog. Apparently nobody had told him that the breed was a symbol of oppression used by the Belgian police to intimidate native troublemakers.

Everywhere Ali went he was greeted by Zairian cries of "Ali, *boma yé*! Ali, *boma yé*!" (Ali, kill 'em!) I stayed with Ali at the Presidential Villa some twenty-five miles out of the capital, took early morning walks with him, and little black children would literally pop out of the bush to shout their *boma yé*'s. If George was the champion of the world, you'd never know it from the loving throng around Ali and the hostile silences or jeers George couldn't help provoking. George was floundering—in search of a persona. The battle of identity was a shutout for Ali.

Ali wasn't working on psychology alone. Boxing was a science, too. The only opponent Foreman hadn't knocked out in a hurry was an aging South American light-heavyweight by the name of Gregorio Peralta. Night after night Ali ran Foreman's Peralta fights, twenty rounds of them. One night he shouted, "Look how that old man's laying back on the ropes! George outweighs him by thirty-five pounds and he's leaning on him and throwing them big heavy punches—and nothing. Peralta's giving him shoulders and elbows and gloves. George's getting tired! If Peralta can do that, what can I do? Six rounds and George'll be so punched out he won't be able to lift his hands."

Ali choreographed that fight like Balanchine. It was a helluva fight, but if you had been with Ali you knew the ending, like running a movie you've seen before. Down and out in eight went George. Three o'clock in the morning. Tropical rain. "Ali, *boma yé!*"

That morning going back to the Presidential Villa with Ali, and even sparring a celebratory round with him, I saw it through Muhammad's eyes, as a Conradian morality play. Flash forward to Foreman's ranch in Marshall, and I'm seeing it for the first time from the point of view of the dethroned and virtually deboned ex-champion:

"I felt deshelled in Zaire. Like a fish being cleaned. Ali taking the whole deal. It's like having your backbone removed. Back in the dressing room it came down on me. Hey, I lost my heavyweight title. Like being raped. I couldn't adjust to it. Devastated. I didn't want to go home. Couldn't face my people. Went to Paris, Georges Cinq Hotel four, five days. Then all the way to Hawaii. Had all the money I wanted. Bought everything in sight. Only thing I couldn't buy was peace of mind."

George had put Don King in business with the Ali fight, but naturally King Don had Ali now, and while he was still Foreman's promoter, he made no effort to get him the rematch George felt he deserved. Nineteen seventy-five and '76 were listless years, with George toying with five journeyman heavyweights in one night, almost getting flattened by Ron Lyle before putting him away in a messy display of The Manly Art of No Defense, an anticlimactic take-out of Joe Frazier again, three easy wins over what the fight game dismisses as "tomato cans," and then another big scene in the George Foreman Movie, a dreary exhibition in the heat of San Juan in which George ran out of power and stamina like a sixteen-cylinder Cadillac sputtering to a stop with the gas gauge on empty. Jimmy Young, a shifty, ring-wise spoiler who seemed to have outpointed Ali for the title the year before, made George look clumsy and aimless.

George still blames the loss on the machinations of Don King, who can machinate with the best of them. King had a CBS deal pending, says George, and there were complaints that Foreman was dumping the tomato cans so fast there wasn't enough time for commercials. He was urged to "carry" Jimmy Young, George explains that humiliation to this day. But in the stultifying island heat he lost control of the match, until at the end he was stumbling around like the drunken wino he had been in his youth.

Now for the movie. Everybody figures this is curtains for George, another has-been shuffles off into the wings. But the airless dressing room becomes George's road to Damascus. I had heard the transcendental story from others, but at the ranch George was reliving it. Even this skeptic was moved by his recital of revelation:

"I felt something come over me like I never felt in my life. I felt bombarded. I tried to tell myself, 'It's no disgrace, I showed I could go twelve rounds. I could go home and retire right now—and *die*.' Where did that come in? I kept hearing a voice saying, 'I don't want your money, I want *you*.' That *voice*! I knew it was God in the room. I felt a giant hand reach down and pick me up. 'I'm dying for God,' I think I was screaming. 'Tell everybody I'm dying for God.' I felt blood on my face and on my hands. Crucified! I jumped up and kissed everybody in the room. 'I love you! I love you!'

"I used to make jokes about religious people. I figured the church was just for poor people singing songs. And all of a sudden I was one of them. Gil Clancy, my trainer, thought it was heat prostration and I went to the hospital, but the heat went away but God was still with me. I quit boxing [in 1977] and started preaching on streetcorners. On the same corners where I used to break heads just for the hell of it. Now I was loving those people, the way Jesus loves us. At first they laughed at me, Crazy George, maybe one too many punches, but my mind was clear as a bell, working better than ever. I saw what I had to do, build my own church, and a youth center, where kids could work out and live clean, study, and get off the streets. Put $300,000 of my own money into it. That's one reason I decided to go back into boxing after a ten-year layoff, to make some money to enlarge the Community Center and keep the church going."

Whether you're a fan of Born-Agains or not, these eyes have seen the Second Coming of George Foreman, not only at peace with himself at the ranch on the outskirts of the little town where he was born, but at the Youth Center, and the Church of Our Lord Jesus Christ, where I attended a service on a recent Sunday.

Outside an unpretentious stucco building, children in their Sunday best were gathering with their neatly dressed parents. The atmosphere was friendly and relaxed. Mostly blacks, along with a few Latino families and three or four Caucasians who also lived in the neighborhood. I talked with Charley Shipes, whom I recognized as a welterweight contender back in the '60s, and with George's younger brother, Roy, whom he put through Berkeley, and a young, well-built nephew, Charley Dumas, an instructor at the Youth Center who assured me in a surprisingly soft voice that George would be along to preach—even though he had flown in from a press conference in Washington, D.C., just an hour before. I turned around and there was George, driving up with two of his nine children, the four-year-old Leola and two-year-old George (George IV, as he's known), with newborn George V in the arms of his young wife, Joan. All of George's sons are named George, with nicknames to differentiate them. Big George was singing a snatch of a song to his kids as I came up and reintroduced myself. How pleasant he was, warm, friendly, happy—I couldn't help mentioning how different he was way back in Zaire when he was outdoing his police dog in growling and glaring. "I don't even know that George Foreman," he laughed. "Don't wanna know him. Sorry I'm late. Been doing interviews with Holyfield. Having fun. Come on in."

The service was appealingly low key. No rolling and hollering. Two little girls with bright-colored bows in their hair sang "What The Lord Has Done for Me," with George backing them discreetly on tambourine. Then Charley Dumas's sweet-voiced "Let It Shine," to his own guitar accompaniment and George as the rhythm section on tambourine.

Then it was George's turn to take center stage, and a modest turn it was. Talking quietly, confidentially, in the low-key style of this place where there are no crucifixes, figures of Christ, or any religious adornments—just a few humble baskets of flowers. This suburb of Houston is called Humble, pretty well-named for the simple goings-on that Sunday morning. George talked about trying to give children a conscience, through the example of Jesus Christ, "so maybe they won't steal your purse." And he thought that "there's gotta be more to life than just living. Habits gotta change here on this Earth. If you don't spread it [good will] here, you're not gonna spread it nowhere else, honey." George's sermon turns out to be a lot of down-home common sense. There are no pictures of Jesus in this church "because the painters who made the pictures were only using models. He's blond, he's got long yellow hair, all that stuff. You tear the pictures off the wall, you're not tearing off Jesus. Even Michelangelo and da Vinci were painting models. Those were just boys they knew, not Jesus."

In his big, baggy black slacks, black leather vest and loosened purple tie, George's enjoying himself up there. He makes them laugh out loud at cults and superstitions. "You wear crosses around your neck, that's ignorant. You don't need no crosses to believe in Jesus. Jesus has never been a God—he's a man. A good man. Jesus ain't God. But what he died for—we gotta live for."

Charley Dumas picks up his guitar and softly backs George up on a closing hymn, as George spreads love from his tambourine.

"I come every Sunday," says a grey-haired white woman on her way out into the noonday sunshine. "And I bring my fourteen-year-old grandson. First time he came, he didn't even know our preacher was a fighter."

But up at the ranch, in the small but smartly appointed

gym, you can see that George is a fighter, again. What began as a laughingstock when he looked like an overstuffed giant sausage, all 260-plus pounds of him, knocking over big, brave and defenseless tomato cans four years ago, is getting more serious now. Since his return in 1987, he's won twenty-four fights (twenty-three knockouts, one decision). Now, knocking off glass-jawed Gerry Cooney in two, or tenth-ranked Adilson Rodrigues in another two, doesn't necessarily qualify him to become the first forty-two-year-old champion in the history of the heavyweight division, but ready or not, he's earned a shot.

One thing Big George has won for sure is the identity debate. In the press conferences it's George, with his born-again preacher skills and his down-home wit, who takes the play from beautifully conditioned and well-behaved Evander Holyfield. And while Evander's manager, Lou Duva, is quick-minded, the '91-model George Foreman can beat him to the one-liners. It's almost as if the once-sullen Sonny Liston the Second has become the graceful, articulate, people-loving, and press-caressing Muhammad Ali.

Whether or not this movie ends with another miracle—the comeback victory of George Foreman—is anybody's guess. The ring *cognoscenti* fall back on that tried and occasionally true cliché—"When he hits you, you go. You gotta give him the puncher's chance."

And as Big George was saying, back at the ranch, "One thing about Evander, he doesn't mind getting hit." Big grin. "That's the kind of fighter I like."

Evander's cagey brain-trust, Lou Duva and George Benton, may have something to say about that. But win or lose, this 260 pounds of fighting preacher has proved what gifted novelist F. Scott Fitzgerald denied when he wrote, "There are no second acts in American lives." Not only is The Second Coming of George Foreman a helluva second act, it's giving us a happy ending that you only see in Hollywood fairy tales like *Pretty Woman.*

[April 1991]

231

Foreman-Holyfield:
The Bigger They Are,
the Harder They Don't Fall

AFTER THE VIETNAM and Watergate '60s and '70s, and
Boesky, Milken, and the takeover boys of the '80s, America's
been hungry for heroes. The Japanese and the West Germans
were outproducing and outselling us. "Say No to Drugs" was a
vapid slogan mocked every day from Harlem to Hollywood. It
seemed as if, since that terrible day when JFK went down in
Dallas, and the proud Lyndon Johnson quit, and Nixon retreated from the White House as "an unindicted co-conspira-
tor," something had gone awry with our American Dream.
Drugs and the deficit. AIDS and recession were our front-page
news. The Greedy '80s seemed to be giving way to the Noxious
'90s. Ten more years of gloom and doom?

And then all of a sudden, up from the abyss fight-fan–novelist Jack London wrote about, came a brace of heroes, the articulate General Schwarzkopf, the first black chief-of-staff, Colin
Powell, and—after his astonishing twelve-round set-to with
Evander Holyfield—the Reverend George Edward Foreman,
who came within one heavy right-hand punch or two of remov-
ing all those resplendent (and redundant) heavyweight belts
from young Holyfield.

When the bell ended Round 12 a few minutes after midnight on the morning of April 20, with Big George very much on his feet and the younger, more agile champion doing the clinching and begging for the bell. Holyfield may have had the WBA, the WBC, and the IBF titles still in his column, but somehow the three biggest capitals in our alphabet got away from him— USA.

Before the fight, after every round, and when he stood face-swollen but unbowed waiting for the demanding final three minutes of a fierce-paced and constantly competitive fight, Foreman heard the chant of eighteen thousand doubting fans he had turned into believers, "George! George! George! . . ." And in a record number of pay-per-view living rooms and bars, George's new constituency was chanting along with them. No question that an able and finely trained Holyfield won on points (our arithmetic on the silly ten-point-must system wound up 115-112). He had done the most hitting, even though the determined senior citizen had done the most hurting. Big George, with his newfound gift for pinpoint articulation, had summed it up as neatly as a Dave Anderson or Pete Hamill: "He won the points, but I proved the point."

That morning when he showed up at the press conference in Atlantic City's Convention Hall at 1:20 a.m., dressed to play Othello in his red tent of a robe, there was no doubt in any reporter's mind that the real "winner" was not the "Real Deal" but George Foreman, the first heavyweight to take Evander all the way since the champion grew out of the Cruiserweight (or "Jr. Heavyweight") class he had dominated three years ago. Every one of the heavyweights Holyfield had faced were gone by the tenth round or less, including three former champions.

"When I hit them the way I hit George, they went," Evander marveled at his gentlemanly press conference. "But I hit George with everything I had"—in the ninth round we counted twenty in a row—"and he still kept coming. I have to admit that surprised me. I had to fight a technical fight because he was always dangerous, right to the end."

233

What he didn't say was that the crowd was booing him at the end for clinching and trying to coast in while Foreman, a Born-Again-Fighter as well as Preacher, was cheered for his persistence in trying to land that one big right that would take it all.

Even if the fight hadn't celebrated the mystique of age against youth—"The Battle of the Ages"—the middle-aged comeback gourmand against the scientifically trained, undefeated, and undisputed champion, this would have simply been remembered as one hell of a fight, with a ferocious seventh round that brought to mind the almost unbearable intensity of Hagler-Hearns.

Indeed, unlike baseball, football, or basketball, a fight between two determined athletes is such an emotional experience that it seems to affect the senses the moment the men meet in the center of the ring. It is will against will, plan against plan, character against character, creating a chemistry so strong that sometimes I swear it gives off an aroma—you breathe in the fight and its awesome possibilities. You don't know exactly what's going to happen, only in a way you do, or rather you smell: hard fight or easy, long or short, nerve-racking or boring. Only in a bullfight do you get that feeling as the bull charges into the arena—oh God, this is going to be a mess, make it short! Or, this one brings two really good ones together, maybe great ones, this could be an awesome work of art.

One minute into Holyfield-Foreman your senses told you: this is no joke, no fraud, this is not going to be another one of those heavyweight fiascos of the Douglases and the Thomases, the Pages and the Tates, that all but destroyed the luster of the heavyweight championship that had glorified Joe Louis, Rocky Marciano, Muhammad Ali . . . And by the second round, when George lands a mean left hook and follows with a right hand that actually stuns the champion, and the crowd is on its feet screaming "Knock 'em out, George, knock 'em out!," now we know that, whatever happens, Big George is for real, he hasn't come to collect his twelve to fifteen million bucks, he's come to prove that the man who folded in Africa with Ali and ran out of gas in his mess of a fight with Jimmy Young is George Foreman Past and this is George Foreman Present, with a new smile, a new attitude, a new stamina.

Never sitting down through their twelve hard-fought rounds, staggered a few times but always fighting back and moving forward, George begins to take on mythical powers. Holyfield may hit him two to one, but he calmly walks through the hard rain of punches to land his own.

What makes his stand all the more dramatic, of course, and sets him up for folk heroism, is the fact that so many mockers and naysayers wrote him off before the battle as a pugilistic traveling salesman touring the country mugging for TV cameras and selling tickets with a combination of back-country wisdom and back-country jokes featuring his oversized eating habits and waistline.

In the press room before the fight one of the best-informed boxing writers in the business, with whom I've compared pre-fight notes for years, confessed to me that he was really ashamed to be covering this fight. "It's a farce," he said. "It's getting to be more like wrestling all the time. George hasn't fought his way into this fight, he's talked his way into it. I don't see him getting through the second round." And the loquacious Dr. Ferdie Pacheco, who came to fistic fame as Ali's ring doctor and cornerman, worried out loud that a man Foreman's age could suffer a fatal heart attack in there, predicting another black eye for boxing.

There were a few Foreman supporters in the press room, including this one, who remembered how Alex Stewart had shaken Evander in the fifth round before the champion took him out in the eighth. Anyone watching Big George split heavy bags on his ranch in Texas knew the 260-pounder was as strong as the bulls he raised. Sooner or later, we reasoned, even without the speed of the Holyfield footwork and jab, even without the heady tactics of George Benton (which George had given me a demonstration of in the men's room of the Trump Plaza), Big George would get to him with the big punch come Round 7 or 8.

George did land those punches in the second round, the seventh, and even occasionally, as the going slowed, after Round 10. The Holyfield jaw nullified George's power, just as Holyfield's three hundred or more punches beat on Foreman like a drum—giving off a lot of sound and fury, signifying that this time George Foreman had come to prove that he was a better fighter at forty-two than he had been at twenty-two.

I can't remember anything quite like this since Daniel Mendoza, known as "Mendoza the Jew," retired after losing his title to "Gentleman" John Jackson in 1795, and then came back over ten years later to whip young Harry Lee in fifty-three rounds. I missed that one, but I hear that was a hell of a fight, too. Mendoza was forty-two. He retired as a folk hero, lecturing in theaters and giving boxing lessons, his pupils including members of the royal family.

If Big George never fights again, he's given us exactly what we need in these days of cynicism when the underclass, the lower class, and even troubled members of the middle class are groping to find a way.

Into their midst strides Big George Foreman, the Survivor. "If I c'n do it, comin' up from nowhere, you c'n make it," he preaches with that sweet smile that's mysteriously replaced the Sonny Liston scowl we saw in Zaire seventeen long years ago. Just as mysteriously he's taken over Ali's role as Boxing's Philosopher. "What I did means we all got the power to do it," he says, and the pitchman tells us something about what we can do on this Planet Earth. "We don't need no more Chernobyls. We c'n clean up this world. I went into that fight positive. Just the opposite of what I was feeling going in there with Ali in Zaire. I went into this one thinking that nothing he can throw at me will stop me. That's what I feel about life. That's what I tell my people when I talk to 'em in church Sunday mornin'."

236

I look at him and wonder: Is he our Paul Bunyan of the '90s? Our John Henry? On the scorecard it may have been 115-112. But in the game of life, move over Norman and Colin, Big George wins it going away.

[August 1991]

Tyson vs. Tyson

YEARS AGO, writing about quite a different kind of achiever—the novelist F. Scott Fitzgerald—I wrote an epitaph: "In America nothing fails like success." Fitzgerald had said it a little differently: "In America [thinking of success] there are no second acts." Certainly not for Mike Tyson.

It is difficult to think of another young man in America who came from so far down to so far up in so short a time. All the expensive toys of success, some of the things people work all their lives for, can never attain, and only dream about, Bentleys and Rolls, hotel suites à la Donald, thousand-dollar suits, and women, women, women, beautiful women ... it was all there for Mike, the Four Seasons of Success all the famous must endure, squeezed into a few, frenetically short years of Rise and Fall.

Nor did it take a clairvoyant or a know-it-all to predict this fall. Allow me the self-indulgence of quoting myself on the eve of Tyson's defense of his newly won title against artful dodger Michael Spinks. Flash back—four years ago:

"No matter how many different directions Spinks tries to move away from Tyson or toward him, no matter how many distractions, how many public airings of private dirty laundry have interrupted his training, how much he misses the guiding hand of surrogate father [Cus] D'Amato and assistant surrogate, the late Jim Jacobs, no matter if he's only 50 percent of the 100 percent he could have been if he had totally dedicated himself to preparation like the great champions he reveres, no matter.

"So on goes Tyson, on to more astronomical gates and astronomical troubles. One can't help feeling that for this man-child in this gilded world, with his $4.5-million dollhouse, his Bentley, his Rolls, his women, and his business controllers, the worst is yet to come. . . . God help the winner. The biggest fight of all may still be Tyson vs. Tyson."

For make no mistake about it, the fight in the Indianapolis courtroom that ended with the tragic knockout of once-mighty Mike wasn't a mismatch between a comely 108-pound Sunday school teacher and an awesome 250-pound fox in a henhouse of Miss Black America beauty contestants. It was Tyson taking on Tyson, a contest he had been fighting and losing ever since D'Amato got off at his final stop on life's subway seven years ago.

That winter Mike was one of the mourners and speakers in the ring at Cus's 14th Street Gym, where the memorial service was held. Mike spoke slowly and simply and in tears. A very big, little kid, wanting his daddy. Ready to fill in for Cus was Jim Jacobs, the legendary handball champion and a knowledgeable fight fan who had cornered the market on fight films. Jacobs worshiped Cus and thought of the heavyweight prodigy not as an incredible money machine but as a vulnerable human being who needed his devoted support.

I remember suggesting to Jim that I meet him for lunch the day of the Spinks fight. "Budd, I've got to stay close to my fighter!" Jim said like an anxious father. But the tragedy unfolded. Sophocles couldn't have written it better. Jim Jacobs dies, prematurely, of leukemia. His businesslike, very white partner, Bill Cayton, loses the young, rich, wild-blooded, uneducated champion to Don King, he of the electric hair, of wiles and smiles, with all the s's written in $'s.

After the Douglas debacle, Tyson is back winning fights, every one except the Tyson fight. Anyone following boxing

239

knows a great fighter needs a great corner. People not only saying, "Anything you say, Mike—you got it!" but the teachers too, in and out of the ring. D'Amato, and then his assistant, Kevin Rooney, were teaching Mike to jab, move his head, throw combinations. After firing Rooney, his last tie with a meteoric career, Mike was left with only the yes-men. He was slower now, dumb, throwing one ponderous punch at a time. Over the hill at twenty-five!

And out of the ring, blowing every round, street fights, car wrecks, beating on men and women. He wasn't just raping an eighteen-year-old. He confused international celebrity with a license to rape the world. A walking time bomb. In that white stretch limo you could hear the ticking. Now the orphan with the golden chance to fight his way out of juvenile delinquency comes face to face with a woman from Indiana who, ironically, specialized in sex-crime prosecutions before she became a judge.

Cus used to call "Time!" at the end of a three-minute workout. But Cus is long gone, and when Judge Gifford calls "Time!" it's back to the slammer. It's midnight for Cinderella, and Don King is a sorry stand-in for Prince Charming.

And now back to you, Scott Fitzgerald: "Show me a hero, and I'll show you a tragedy."

[February 1992]

The Mystery of the Heavyweight Mystique

WHEN I WAS ASKED to choose "my favorite" for an anthology of "Best Sports Articles," I reviewed in my mind the hundreds of boxing pieces I've written, from my *Sports Illustrated*-Marciano-Liston-Ali days to the more recent Larry Holmes and Holyfield campaign for the *New York Post* and *Boxing Illustrated*. My pick was a piece I did for *Esquire* on "The Mystique of the Heavyweight Championship," how it rose above all sporting events, including the World Series and the Super Bowl, to become a morality play that raised it to a level above mere athleticism.

In the grip of this mystique I flew from L.A. to N.Y. for that first and still unforgettable Joe Louis–Billy Conn thirteen-round epic. When the Supreme Court gave back to Muhammad Ali his right to resume his career and he finally went head-to-head with Joe Frazier, the packed Madison Square Garden was so charged with electricity that it seemed as if we had to hold our breath not to set that historic hall on fire. When Ali was matched with then-champion George Foreman, I knew I had to fly to Zaire to watch "the People's Champion" outthink and dramatically defuse Big George.

My piece on the heavyweight mystique tried to capture that special hush that comes over the crowd, tensing forward in the darkness of the great arena, and the millions plugged into TV around the world as the announcer heralds those magic words, "Ladies and gentlemen . . . for the heavyweight championship of the world . . . !"

Whether he be John L. Sullivan or Jack Johnson, Jack Dempsey or Gene Tunney, Joe Louis, Marciano, Ali, or finally Mike Tyson, the undisputed king of the heavyweights was the undisputed champion of the world, reigning above all other athletes and invariably the most recognizable human being on Planet Earth. When you think of our great ones, Dempsey, Louis, Ali, you think of their championship belts as symbols of magical supremacy. In the court of King Arthur they would have walked with Lancelot and Galahad. The operative word in reaching out and grasping that magical world was *pride*. Yes, money was involved, for after all, these knights are professional fistfighters who make their living by the give-and-take of punishment in the prize ring. But without pride these are warriors going into battle with empty scabbards, who suddenly, as the bell rings for the opening round of their ordeal, reach for their swords and realize in panic that somehow they have left their weapons behind—in their lavish hotel suites, or their white stretch limos, or in the gold-fixtured Roman baths of their new, five-million-dollar, thirty-room palaces complete with indoor swimming pools, bowling alleys, and state-of-the-art projection rooms.

Sitting close to the Evander Holyfield–Riddick Bowe contention for the current heavyweight championship in Las Vegas a few months ago, while doing my job as a boxing reporter, scoring a close, hard-fought twelve-rounder by three points for the recycled Holyfield, other notes involving pride and character and deteriorating patterns of behavior occurred to me.

With the exception of Holyfield, who at least has managed to maintain a work ethic despite his multimillion-dollar, country-gentleman lifestyle, our haunted heavyweight championship has been seriously diminished by a disgraceful parade of what I would designate as a new division: the Overweights. While

Louis and Marciano and Ali liked their good times too, they had too much pride, too much fistic character not to know that their championship comes with a heavy price tag: self-punishment in preparation for their title defenses, so intense that I have often found it almost painful to watch. I think of Rocky Marciano driving himself month after month in the isolation of an old farmhouse above Grossinger's to get ready for Ezzard Charles and Archie Moore. I remember in Angelo Dundee's Miami gym the then Cassius Clay jackknifing fingertips to toes on a rubbing table more than one hundred times and pausing only to groan, "Oh, this is so borin'!" and then resuming with even more intensity. And I watched him up at Deer Lake running mile after mile in heavy boots to make it harder. Was there ever a true champion not willing to pay the price?

A roll call of heavyweight "champions" since the end of the Larry Holmes era suggests that something has gone seriously wrong with our prize-ring morality. When we think (if we must) of interlopers like John Tate, Michael Dokes, Tim Witherspoon, Pinklon Thomas, Greg Page, Tony Tubbs, and Buster Douglas, all of them sadly listed in the record book as "heavyweight champions," we realize what a sea change we've suffered, what a near-mortal blow to the mystique of the heavyweight championship of the world.

I'm thinking of an afternoon when Greg Page, facing Tim Witherspoon for the "heavyweight championship" in Las Vegas that evening, showed up at the bar where I happened to be sitting (I was in training to *write,* not fight) to down a couple of beers. In "fight" after "fight" the champions and challengers removed their robes to reveal a tire of fat or "love-handles" no self-respecting champion would ever dare indulge and expose. And sad to say, these Pages, Thomases, Tubbs, and others weren't your everyday bums, they were big, quick talented men who held the promise of everything—except pride and character. I think of a big, strong fella like David Bey, another might've-been who came to his big nights looking as if he could rent himself out as a nursing mother.

Pride and character, the flags of this hard trade all the way back to Mendoza the Jew two centuries ago, where have you gone? How could you desert a champion on his way to greatness, like Mike Tyson, and abandon him in the sloth and self-indulgence with which he went into the ring to defend this title against Buster Douglas? And Buster, after a hero's welcome back home in a town of winners, Columbus, Ohio, how dare you shuffle into the Holyfield fight looking as if you're ready to go partners with David (Moo-cow) Bey and his fellow Overweights?

Which brings us to the most recent one-year one, Riddick Bowe. A year ago a well-tuned Bowe, at 235, jabbed and out-fought the doughty, smaller Holyfield. Obviously Bowe loved being champion of the world. He world-traveled, tried on an ill-fitting Ali persona, built a garage for his sixteen cars, and ate so high on the hog that he went into training for the Holyfield rematch looking like one, up to 300 pounds. In two months he sweated that off to the official weigh-in figure of 246. He then raced off to his favorite soul-food restaurant to make up for lost time.

My first note at ringside—jotted while the interminable pre-fight celebratory intros drone on—reads: "H. looks in shape 100%. B. jumped through ropes last year. This time climbs through slowly. Trunks pulled high to cover the flab. Soft around the middle."

You could say that was the story of the fight. Bowe stormed out of his corner at the opening bell, scoring so furiously we wondered if Evander would survive the round. Evander did, of course, as he always does, with his notable "bottom," that schoolboy-athlete determination. We also wondered if Riddick had thrown everything into those first three minutes, as if hoping another quick over-and-out would spare him the demands of having to drag those 250-plus pounds through eleven more rounds?

After four rounds the answer was becoming obvious. Holy-field was still there, in shape, composed, and scoring so heavily in the fifth that another ten or fifteen seconds might have chopped big Riddick down.

244

The middle rounds belonged to Holyfield, who was moving in and out this time, rather than standing foolishly and bravely toe-to-toe as he had done in the first one. To his credit, Bowe didn't quit, as we had seen some other overweight "champions" do. He hung in, breathing hard, with "sluggish" turning up in my notes again and again, but coming on to win the ninth, and in the final three minutes trying for a knockout his corner must have told him he needed if he didn't want to blow it, à la Tyson or Douglas.

This is a fight a conditioned Bowe could have won, but the decision went to pride and character over hedonism and self-indulgence. No one will ever call Evander Holyfield a great champion. He neither punches with the conviction of a true heavyweight nor moves with the grace of say, an Ezzard Charles. But at least he's an honest practitioner who takes the championship seriously enough to work for it and not simply assume it's his by right of eminent domain.

In a postfight press conference, an unusually subdued Rock Newman—Bowe's promoter, in an unfamiliar mode of humility—acknowledged that "Riddick was still a growing boy," though it wasn't clear whether the reference was to waistline or emotional maturity. A sad Rock suggested that this loss could be a learning experience motivating Bowe to "reevaluate himself both as a fighter and as a human being." My note on this one: "Good idea, if maybe a little late?"

In this era of overpriced paynights for closed-circuit warriors, when a prizefighter like Bowe can earn $15 million without bothering to show up for the major event of the year even *looking* like a prizefighter, much less the champion of the world, that weird sound you hear emitting from Arlington Cemetery may be Joe Louis rattling around in his grave.

[March 1994]

Epilogue

AS WE GO to press, a most unlikely champion rules the heavyweight division: Big, Lovable George Foreman (once Big, Nasty George Foreman), at age forty-five the oldest man ever to hold the title. He had won it in the fall of '94 from moody Michael Moorer, who had a nifty right jab and won all the early rounds but paid no heed to trainer Teddy Atlas's drumbeat of advice: Keep moving counterclockwise, away from that right hand. That's all old George had left. His jabs were sloppy and his movements slow. If Moorer had listened to his frenetic trainer, he would have won an easy decision, and George would be back shilling for Meineke. But there was Moorer stubbornly in front of Foreman, forgetting all about Atlas and the counterclockwise jazz, and than *boom* Big George saw the opening for the short right-hand chop on the kisser, and down went Moorer, suddenly a glassy-eyed ex-champion (in his first defense after a close win from Holyfield), and there was our born-again preacher, whom all us seasoned boxing experts (or know-it-alls) had written off as over-and-out after Ali destroyed him in Zaire twenty years earlier.

Our theory that heavyweight champions—the real ones, not the Witherspoons, Pages, and Moorers—catch and reflect the spirit of our times, symbols like Dempsey and Louis, Marciano and Ali, seems borne out once again by the second coming of George Foreman. I saw the icon emerging in his stand-up fight with Holyfield. Here is the reformed mugger recycled for the '90s, between fights the humble preacher in Houston, the millionaire huckster for Meineke mufflers on television, one minute the clown prince of jumbo-hamburger consumption, the next moment preaching the prowess of middle age once you bring yourself to believe that all things are possible. He's a blown-up Jimmy Carter with a chopping right hand, a '90s-style faith, and enough Madison Avenue savvy to keep those millions rolling in even if he doesn't hang in there long enough to wait for the springing of Mike Tyson.

If every great fight is a morality play, we have a beauty coming up if forty-six-year-old, gold-plated George can manage to climb through the ropes against Iron Mike, with all the feminists crying, "Rapist!" and "Sexual harasser!" and all the young bloods claiming Tyson was framed or at least unfairly overpunished.

From born-agains to "date-rape" victims to inner-city violence, all the provocative issues of the final decade of the twentieth century will be reflected and hotly debated if we get Old George the Good and Young Mike the Bad into that zillion-dollar ring.

If every major heavyweight title fight holds up a mirror to our society, this mirror would cover the side of the World Trade Center, framed in twenty-two-carat gold. Praise the Lord and hike the prices on those commercials. This is the '90s, when our old new heavyweight champion laughs at us: "In God and Meineke I trust, helping the poor, selling Mr. Nice Guy, getting banged up around the eyes, but never too blind to find my way to the bank."

If it happens, get ready for religious fervor and big-profit redemption versus inner-city anger, pent up after doing five years hard time in presidential-hopeful Dan Quayle's home state, where Family Values seem to have superseded the Bill of Rights.

247

Index

Index

Index

250

253

Budd Schulberg was born in New York City, the son of Hollywood film pioneer B. P. Schulberg, and was educated at Los Angeles High School, Deerfield Academy, and Dartmouth College.

After a brief stint as a screenwriter in Hollywood, he served in the United States Navy during World War II and was in charge of photographic evidence for the Nuremberg Trials. Mr. Schulberg was *Sports Illustrated*'s first boxing editor; he has also covered title fights for *Playboy*, *Esquire*, *Newsday*, and the *New York Post*. He is the only nonfighter to receive the Living Legend of Boxing Award from the World Boxing Association. His writings on the fight game have also won him the Notre Dame Bengal Bouts Award and, recently, the A. J. Liebling Award from the Boxing Writers Association.